HOLD THE LINE

HOLD THE LINE

The Insurrection and One Cop's
Battle for America's Soul

MICHAEL FANONE
AND JOHN SHIFFMAN

ATRIA BOOKS

NEW YORK   LONDON   TORONTO   SYDNEY   NEW DELHI

ATRIA
BOOKS

An Imprint of Simon & Schuster, Inc.
1230 Avenue of the Americas
New York, NY 10020

First Atria Books hardcover edition October 2022

ATRIA BOOKS and colophon are trademarks of Simon & Schuster, Inc.

For information about special discounts for bulk purchases, please contact Simon & Schuster Special Sales at 1-866-506-1949 or business@simonandschuster.com.

The Simon & Schuster Speakers Bureau can bring authors to your live event. For more information or to book an event, contact the Simon & Schuster Speakers Bureau at 1-866-248-3049 or visit our website at www.simonspeakers.com.

Interior design by Kyoko Watanabe

Manufactured in the United States of America

1 3 5 7 9 10 8 6 4 2

Library of Congress Cataloging-in-Publication Data
Names: Fanone, Michael, author. | Shiffman, John, author.
Title: Hold the line : the insurrection and one cop's battle for America's soul / Michael Fanone and John Shiffman.
Description: First Atria Books hardcover edition. | New York : Atria Books, 2022. | Includes bibliographical references and index.
Identifiers: LCCN 2022013608 (print) | LCCN 2022013609 (ebook) | ISBN 9781668007198 (hardcover) | ISBN 9781668007211 (paperback) | ISBN 9781668007235 (ebook)
Subjects: LCSH: Capitol Riot, Washington, D.C., 2021. | Radicalism—United States—History—21st century. | Right-wing extremists—United States—History—21st century. | Trump, Donald, 1946—Influence. | Police—Washington (D.C.)—History—21st century. | Police Psychology—United States. | Racism in law enforcement—United States. Classification: LCC HN90.R3 F36 2022 (print) | LCC HN90.R3 (ebook) | DDC 303.48/40973—dc23/eng/20220324
LC record available at https://lccn.loc.gov/2022013608
LC ebook record available at https://lccn.loc.gov/2022013609

ISBN 978-1-6680-0719-8
ISBN 978-1-6680-0723-5 (ebook)

To the women in my life:
Mom, Caitlin, Piper, Mei-Mei, Hensley, Leslie, and M,
and to Belle

Action is the antidote to despair.

—JOAN BAEZ

CONTENTS

PART III: AFTER

June 2021

When I worked undercover as a vice officer in the projects, I developed certain core survival skills. I learned how to read a room. I learned how to cut through lies and get a suspect to incriminate himself on tape. I learned how to enter a room without a weapon, armed only with my wits, and exit alive.

These skills extended from the streets to the courtroom. There's no substitute for preparation. Whenever I had a case go to trial, I slipped into the courthouse a few days early to scout the judge and defense attorney. Before taking the witness stand, I studied the case file and mastered the facts. When you command the truth, it's hard to lose.

I was a street cop in Washington, D.C., for nearly twenty years, and good habits die hard. So while still on the city force in June 2021, I prepped for a meeting with Kevin McCarthy, the Republican leader of the U.S. House, the same way I would before meeting a meth kingpin in Dupont Circle or a crack dealer on North Capitol Street: I studied the man. In McCarthy's case, that meant days reading speeches, tweets, profiles, and interviews.

It had been six months since January 6, 2021. By then, McCarthy's initial public support of the officers who responded to the Capitol riot had vanished. I was one of the 850 Metropolitan Police Department officers who rushed to help the Capitol Police that day, to defend the seat of our American democracy. Vastly outnumbered, we beat back a mob of crazed and violent Trump supporters engaged in medieval, hand-to-hand combat. During the coup attempt, scores of MPD and Capitol officers were seriously injured. Five died, including four by suicide.

I'm the MPD cop in that famous picture from January 6th, the one with the beard and black helmet with fear etched across my face, surrounded by the Trump mob, about to be tased at the base of my skull and beaten with a Blue Lives Matter flagpole. During the riot, I suffered a traumatic brain injury and a heart attack. As a result of the electric shocks, I have three large scars between my neck and shoulders, scalded flesh that may never heal. I have been diagnosed with PTSD, post-traumatic stress disorder. By June 2021, I felt fucking lucky just to be alive.

Since the insurrection, I'd called out Republicans like McCarthy who'd tried to downplay the severity of the attack. I'd written open letters to Congress, appeared on national TV, and shown riot footage from my body-worn camera to anyone willing to watch. In a month, I would testify before Congress with three of my fellow officers.

But on this day in late June, I was set to meet privately with McCarthy, alongside U.S. Capitol Police Officer Harry Dunn and Gladys Sicknick, the mother of U.S. Capitol Police Officer Brian Sicknick, who died of wounds sustained on January 6th. For weeks, the three of us had made the rounds on the Hill, urging support for a congressional investigation, pushing back against Republicans trying to rewrite history. We also tried to meet with the twenty-one Republicans who voted *against* a bill to award the Congressional Gold Medal to every police officer who defended the Capitol. Several of these Republicans, including Andrew Clyde, refused to even shake my hand.

Now, McCarthy was backing off on a pledge to appoint Republicans to the special January 6th Committee. The only reason McCarthy had agreed to meet with us was because he'd been getting heat for refusing to see me. When I first called to make an appointment, one of his staffers hung up on me. When I told Speaker Nancy Pelosi about this, she issued a press release titled, "Ask McCarthy: Why Won't He Shake Officer Fanone's Hand?" A week later, she issued another statement: "Despite claiming to 'Back the Blue,' McCarthy and his Conference have made a habit of disrespecting the officers who protected them from January's insurrection." The pressure worked. McCarthy agreed to meet with us for an hour.

Our goal was simple: convince the House minority leader to publicly condemn the twenty-one Republicans who voted against the Congressional Gold Medal bill, and commit to a serious insurrection investigation. Before I met McCarthy, I went through the same clear-my-head rituals I did before I went undercover to buy meth, heroin, or crack: I listened to Sturgill Simpson in my truck while doing breathing exercises to lower my blood pressure.

As I entered the Capitol, I did what I always did when I went on a risky op: I hit the record button on my iPhone and stuffed it in my pocket.

"Hello, I'm Kevin," McCarthy said, extending a hand as we entered his Capitol office, a room oddly anchored by impressionist portraits of Lincoln and Reagan. "Sit wherever you like."

I sized up which chair might be McCarthy's favorite and planted myself there. Officer Dunn and Mrs. Sicknick took the couch. McCarthy pulled up a side chair. Dunn is a passionate man and a gentle giant—he played offensive line in the Canadian pro football league.

The Hill was Dunn's turf, so he spoke first. He began diplomatically, noting that McCarthy claimed to be the first to alert Trump about the Capitol riot on the afternoon of January 6th. McCarthy took the cue and took credit for getting Trump to make a late-afternoon public statement urging his seditious supporters to "go home." Mrs. Sicknick scowled and challenged the Republican leader.

"He already knew what was going on," she said of Trump. "People were fighting for hours and hours and hours. This doesn't make any sense to me."

McCarthy was quick to defend Trump, "I'm just telling you from my phone call that he didn't know that."

I'd heard enough. "Not to interrupt you, Mrs. Sicknick," I said, doing exactly that. Turning to McCarthy, I said, "My experience that day was pretty damn horrifying. I'm not sure if you've seen any of my body-worn camera footage."

"Were you here all day or did they call you up?" McCarthy asked.

"I self-deployed," I said, noting that I was working an undercover heroin case that day. "What I heard on the radio was what really inspired me to respond: officers screaming for their lives."

I told McCarthy that I'd been a cop for two decades. I thought I'd experienced everything inner city policing could throw at you: resentment, anger, racism, poverty, violence—and worse, a searing and cruel indifference to the value of a human life. I'd tussled with people so jacked up on PCP that they split my skull. I'd flown through a car windshield in pursuit of a killer and faced the wrong end of a gun held by a fourteen-year-old. I told McCarthy that *none* of that compared to the hatred I saw in the eyes of the people who tried to kill me on January 6th.

McCarthy said, "Did you go report to somebody or, you know, run into the fire?"

I repeated that I responded to radio distress calls from fellow officers. I paused and looked McCarthy in the eye. I saw where this was going. He seemed eager to eat up time and deflect from the point of the meeting. He probably hoped I would launch into a long, blow-by-blow account: how I'd been yanked out of the Capitol's Lower West End Tunnel by Trump rioters; how I'd been punched, dragged, spit on and stomped, electrocuted by taser; how I'd begged for my life, suffered cardiac arrest and a fucking traumatic brain injury, then blacked out . . . Yeah, well, I hadn't come here to recount my story. McCarthy knew the details of my assault.

So I pivoted and said, "Post-January 6th for me and for hundreds of my fellow officers, what I found most distressing—especially as a lifelong Republican, myself—are comments made by Republican lawmakers about January 6th, which were not just shocking but disgraceful. Referring to January 6th as a regular 'tour day' at the Capitol?"

I told McCarthy I felt betrayed by the way some Republicans were twisting a riotous assault on law enforcement officers into a fundraising grift.

"It's crap," I said. "It's disgraceful."

McCarthy offered no response.

I continued, recorder still rolling: "What I've experienced since then has been horrific. It's hell on earth. I am not a political person. I do not enjoy my time here on Capitol Hill. I'd much rather be sitting at home with my daughters drinking a cold beer, but instead I feel an extension of my service on January 6th is to be up here righting this wrong." I asked McCarthy to condemn the twenty-one Republicans who voted against the Gold Medal bill. "A lot of officers almost lost their lives and Mrs. Sicknick lost her son."

Mrs. Sicknick, her face contorting with pain, said, "I just don't understand why people like you won't denounce these people." (Many, many months later it would be revealed that, shortly after January 6th, McCarthy did suggest privately that Trump resign, but then quickly abandoned the idea.)

Squirming in his tiny chair, McCarthy insisted that he was not to blame and made a clumsy attempt at empathy. "My father was a firefighter. It's not an occupation, it's a way of life." We nodded politely. "A calling," I agreed. McCarthy promised to "get to the bottom of this where it never happens again." As he spoke, I caught a glimpse of the spray-on tan line just above his shirt collar. The manicured Republican leader threw up his palms and told us there were "political factors" beyond his control.

"Kevin, I agree with you," I said, using his first name to show I wouldn't be bullied. "It *is* political, because it happened here on Capitol Hill and it involved a political movement. It involved a group of extremist, white nationalist elements of our American society, which were mobilized by politicians. And that's just a fact." I said everyone knows that 99 percent of the nearly 800 rioters arrested were Trump supporters.

"So calling it Antifa or Black Lives Matter or all these other things, it's not disingenuous," I said. "It's a lie."

"I understand the passion everyone has," McCarthy said. "I think we're all headed towards the same place."

I winced. I told him that if he were serious, he would appoint serious people to the January 6th Committee, not obstructionists or fools.

"In law enforcement," I said, "when we get involved in an investigation we don't care about, we assign the biggest humps to participate."

McCarthy feigned insult and said he enjoyed a good reputation on appointments.

I pushed back. "You're an intelligent man, Mr. McCarthy. You know exactly what I'm talking about." Dunn and I described for him the blunt rudeness we encountered when we'd tried to meet with GOP members who'd voted against the Gold Medal bill. Most didn't even return our calls or respond to our visits. I reminded him that others wouldn't even fucking shake our hands.

Here's an idea, I said: "Let's get all the House Republicans together, put me in a room with them, and allow them to watch my body-worn camera footage so that they can experience that. I'm not here to change people's hearts and minds. I just want them to shut the hell up and know the truth. And stop spewing bullshit because I can't even begin to tell you how traumatic that is."

Silence filled the room. I broke it.

"And I'm not going to go away. For whatever reason—God only knows why—I've been afforded a hell of a platform, and I'm going to continue to use it for the sole purpose of making people stop describing January 6th as anything other than what it was: a horrific day in which a lot of police officers almost died. I'm here because you're the leader of the House Republicans."

McCarthy leaned closer, as if to confide a secret. "I'll share something with you. My job is trying to get all the information we can, but also provide it to my members." In other words, *What do you want from me? I can't control my fringe members.*

I struggled to keep a straight face. McCarthy either didn't get it or didn't care. He didn't see how the Big Lie was growing like a weed, slowly strangling truth and democracy.

Until recently, I'd followed politics like the Olympics—I only paid close attention every four years. I thought about telling McCarthy that I'd voted for both Barack Obama and Trump, that I considered myself a moderate conservative. But by this point, I realized that would be a waste of fucking time. McCarthy didn't give a shit about moderates. He only cared about power. So I told him that I'm proud to consider myself a redneck cop, that I'm a walking cliché. On the rear of my truck, I have a hunter's specialty license plate and a Second Amendment bumper sticker. I listen to country music and drink beer from the can.

"It's people like me you're stoking," I told McCarthy.

My people.

I told him about my place in Highland County, Virginia, along the West Virginia border: "I like to refer to it as the land that time forgot. When I go out there to my hunting property and interact with the people that I've known for almost two decades, they have no idea January 6th happened. They source their news from Newsmax and Fox News. They listen to elected leaders who go back to these rural communities and tell them January 6th was a fabrication. So people that I've known and loved—people I still know and love—think I'm full of shit. I show them my body-worn camera footage and they think it was created in a Hollywood studio. There are people on social media that say I'm a paid actor."

McCarthy's response? He asked me if I hunted deer or bear in Highland County.

Dude, I thought, *who fucking cares?*

Thankfully, Mrs. Sicknick jumped in and again asked McCarthy to condemn his twenty-one colleagues. Again, the Republican leader said he couldn't control his fellow Republicans. "People are held accountable by their constituents. I try to lead in certain directions—"

I interrupted, "You've got a platform to call out the BS." I bore my eyes into the career politician's face and let loose. "While you were on the phone with Trump, I was getting the shit kicked out of me!" I asked McCarthy why he would take credit for Trump's pathetic, halfhearted late-afternoon video address to his followers. I said, "Trump says to his people, 'This is what happens when you steal an election. Go home. I love you.' What the fuck is that? That came from the president of the United States."

"How can you defend this man?" Mrs. Sicknick asked. "It's mind boggling."

McCarthy said his members wanted a broader mandate for any January 6th Commission, one that would also study riots that occurred during the Black Lives Matter protests. I'm a white cop, and I guess he assumed I would help him link BLM with January 6th, creating a false equivalency. I didn't take the bait. Instead, I laid a trap of my own.

I told him that my MPD partner, Jeff Leslie, narrowly escaped during a BLM protest after someone placed a Molotov cocktail under his squad car. McCarthy nodded sympathetically and enthusiastically as I explained how the politically charged BLM protests created incredibly difficult and violent challenges for the police.

Then I reminded him that no one from BLM engaged in sedition.

"Trying to overthrow the U.S. Capitol and trying to overthrow a CVS are two very different things," I told McCarthy. "My partner understands that, and most police officers, and most Americans understand that, too."

Incredibly, I told the Republican leader, we were now six months past January 6th and neither the city, the mayor, nor Congress had bothered to do anything to recognize the brave work of law enforcement defending the Capitol.

"These officers feel abandoned," I said. "Law enforcement is in a dire, dire place."

Republicans claim to be the party of law enforcement, I said, except when it's politically inconvenient.

"I may only have a GED," I told McCarthy. "But I know exactly what that is. It's bullshit and it's disrespectful to police officers."

I told the Republican leader that since January 6th, I'd received dozens of calls from fellow officers in absolute despair about attempts to whitewash history and ignore their trauma.

"How we've avoided an epidemic of law enforcement suicides in this city is a miracle," I said. At the MPD, I told him, a dozen officers had voluntarily turned in their weapons, fearful they might take their own lives. I certainly knew that feeling.

McCarthy finally spoke, but he just repeated himself. The Republican leader said he didn't think he could lead his fringe members back to reality—and worse, he didn't think it was even worth trying. "I don't think it's productive," he said. "It might make you feel good but I don't think—"

"No, no," I said, straining not to completely lose my shit. "No, no. Don't address it on an individual level." All we ask, I said, is that he put out a statement affirming the following: "January 6th was horrible. Officers almost lost their lives. I denounce anyone who would utilize language that diminishes that experience for those officers, staff members, and their families."

McCarthy filibustered, throwing out non sequiturs and bullshit platitudes. "Justice is my goal," he said. "The government is made up of individuals, people who make mistakes." And so on.

What the fuck. I couldn't listen to him ramble and interrupted. "I mean, they're raising money off the backs of dead and brutalized police officers!"

McCarthy threw out another false equivalency. "There are people on both sides of the aisle who just want attention." He wasn't wrong. But so what? He was the Republican leader. What are *leaders* for?

I left McCarthy's office in need of a stiff drink. With rare exception, he was just like all the other Republicans I met. In public, McCarthy praised the police. Behind closed doors, he didn't really give a shit.

======

I never expected to write a book. For two decades before January 6, 2021, I was just a street cop, head down, focused on serving the people of my precinct, trying to keep violence at bay, keeping my own ass safe, and training the next generation of officers.

My life changed forever in a single afternoon. I lost my dream job, my anonymity, and my comfort zone—and sadly, many people I considered close friends.

As an undercover and plainclothes officer, I had avoided the limelight. I didn't even tweet or post on Facebook or Instagram. Never in my wildest dreams did I think I would become an advocate for fellow officers who responded to the insurrection. Then again, I never expected the president of the United States to incite a mob to attack the U.S. Capitol as part of a coup to overturn a legitimate election. Nor did I expect that a third of the country would believe him when he said it never happened.

But here we are.

In these pages, I'll share intimate details about January 6th, the rioters who attacked me, and my personal and political traumas in the year that followed. These include my struggles with PTSD, the city, Congress, the MPD, and the police union that was supposed to have my back. Like the exchange with McCarthy, I secretly taped some of those conversations. At the time I recorded the meetings (which is legal in the District of Columbia), I didn't realize I'd be writing a book, so I didn't do it with that intent. Perhaps it was my vice officer's instinct. Either way, I'm glad I did so because I want people to understand what happens behind closed doors.

I'll describe what it felt like to testify before the January 6th Committee in mid-2021, and what went through my mind as I watched the 2022 hearings from the front row. It was one thing to have a gut feeling about Trump's culpability, but quite another to hear the avalanche of evidence in person—for example, to learn that violence by white supremacists was always part of the plan. The indifference to the safety of police officers displayed by Trump and his loyalists made my blood boil.

I'll also draw on my two decades as an undercover street cop to write honestly about the other important issue we face today: how the police do their job. I've always been a bit of a renegade. It's one reason I've never been management material. I made mistakes, all officers do. But I like to think I learned from them, and that I was damn good at my job. I'll trace my evolution from young cop with a warrior mentality to wise, empathetic veteran—a journey I sincerely hope more officers will embrace.

Anyone who knows me understands that I have trouble keeping my mouth shut. I have plenty to say about policing, crime, police brutality, racism, white privilege, the Black Lives Matter movement, Trump, and politics. Coming from a white cop, some of it may surprise you.

As corny as it may sound, I believe that police officers should protect and serve their community. I admit that when I was younger, full of piss and vinegar, this was not always the case. But I matured into a cop who saw himself as a role model, who taught other officers how to protect our citizens while also treating them with dignity. I'm certain that by the time Derek Chauvin choked the life out of George Floyd, he did not view him as a human being.

An important part of my story includes the close bond I developed with one of my sources: a Black transgender sex worker who was HIV-positive. Leslie Perkins taught me more about the streets and human nature than anyone I've ever known. I spoke with Leslie nearly every day, and brought her home to meet my children. Our friendship outlasted my 2010 marriage and several long-term girlfriends.

For most of my life, I viewed racism through Leslie's experience and dozens of others I met on the job. Until Trump became president and Covid hit, I hadn't felt it viscerally. Three of my daughters are Asian American. I've seen through their eyes the racist ways in which Trump labeled Covid-19 the "China virus," "China plague," and "Kung Flu."

With smirks that smack of middle school taunts, Trump's supplicants on right-wing TV and social media repeated the racist tropes, and they've become part of right-wing culture. Cops I worked with regularly used the epithets in front of me. I don't think they thought much about it, until I told them about my daughters. When my youngest, who is still in elementary school, heard the words, she immediately understood the hate was directed against Asian Americans—directed against her. I read somewhere that Trump and his people find community by rejoicing in the suffering of those they hate and fear—that cruelty is the point. This is not easy to explain to a six-year-old.

I'm grateful that a few key elected officials and famous folks have provided unsolicited support, giving me strength to face a storm of threats from Trump sycophants. From time to time, Speaker of the House Nancy Pelosi calls to check in, sometimes via FaceTime at 3 a.m. (I don't think she sleeps.) I've had drinks with Congressman Eric Swalwell, a Democrat, and Adam Kinzinger, a Republican. Liz Cheney and her dad took me out to dinner. So did Sean Penn. When Joan Baez was fêted at the 43rd Annual Kennedy Center Honors, she brought along two guests—me and Anthony Fauci. I say this not to brag, but to explain how surreal my life became in 2021. In a flash, I went from anonymous street cop to instant fame. Longtime friends and family began to worry not only about my physical and psychological wounds from January 6th, but the true motives of some of my new "friends."

Support from the famous and the powerful was of course nice, but what I appreciated the most—and frankly find fucking unbelievable in this era of social media—was the volume of letters and postcards I received from everyday Americans after my congressional testimony. To date, I've received tens of thousands of *handwritten* notes. To all the people who wrote: thank you.

Since the Capitol riot, I've struggled with the physical and emotional aftermath of the attack. On my worst days, the deliberate suppression of my real-life trauma—*it never happened, dude, or if it did, it wasn't that bad*—has triggered very dark thoughts.

People often ask me what it costs to do the right thing. The answer is grim: It cost me nearly everything.

I'm telling my story the only way I know how, from the perspective of a rank-and-file officer who pounded the streets every day. I'm not fucking polished or highly educated. I'm not going to cite a bunch of statistics. I don't think in terms of PowerPoint slides or well-honed talking points. But in two decades on the job, I've learned a thing or two, and have something to contribute.

What happened to me on January 6th is important. But my experiences before and after that day are equally relevant. They represent two of the most pressing issues we have as a nation: what police reform should look like, and how we choose to remember an attempted coup d'état.

We're running out of time to save our country. We need to dig in.

We need to hold the line.

PART I

BEFORE

CHAPTER 1

The Good, the Bad, and the Ugly

My great-grandfather came to America to escape fascism.

Ubaldo Fanone, an illiterate Italian shepherd, grew up in a small village near Monte Cassino, a Benedictine abbey founded in AD 529. Strategically located atop a small mountain, the abbey looks like a fortress. As Mussolini and Hitler solidified their alliance and World War II dawned, my great-grandfather fled Monte Cassino, making his way about sixty-five miles south to the port of Naples, where he caught a ship to New York.

Ubaldo Fanone processed through Ellis Island and joined other Italian immigrants in Sharon, Pennsylvania, a steel town near Youngstown, Ohio. He left behind a wife and two teenage boys: my grandfather Tony and my great uncle John. Ubaldo promised to send money and find a way to bring them all to America, but he couldn't make it happen before the war erupted, and they remained trapped in Italy.

When the Nazis arrived in Monte Cassino, they began conscripting young Italians for duty on the German front lines. Tony and John hid in caves below the mountaintop abbey. They did this for three years, daring to come out only to scrounge for food, moving contraband by donkey and mule. After the war, Tony and John Fanone made their way to Naples, but were so poor it took them a year to earn enough to buy tickets to America. They arrived in western Pennsylvania in 1947, and Ubaldo found them work at a sprawling steel mill.

My grandfather Tony worked at the Sharon mill for forty years. Like Ubaldo, Tony was largely illiterate, but burly and gregarious, and a hard worker. Like me, my grandfather was gruff and spoke without a filter. He drank like a fish and didn't take shit from anyone. His nickname was "The Bull." Tony married another Italian immigrant, Annunziata, and in their later years they opened a small-town restaurant called The Suburban. It was a family enterprise. Every capable Fanone bused tables, tended bar, and washed dishes, including my dad, Joe Fanone. My grandfather pushed my dad hard academically, and my grandmother stressed values of altruism and civic duty. My dad so excelled in his academic and spiritual studies that his parents sent him to an elite boarding school for aspiring priests. Although my dad decided not to become a priest, he became the first Fanone to attend college, enrolling at Georgetown University. Later, he graduated from Georgetown's law school.

My mom's side of the family is Irish. Most arrived in the nineteenth century and a few generations worked as cops in the early and mid-twentieth century for the NYPD and D.C.'s Metropolitan Police Department. My maternal grandfather, Richard Mayer, fought the Japanese at Okinawa, where he was seriously wounded. A Jeep he was driving took mortar fire, and shrapnel from the explosion shredded his passengers. In shock, my grandfather Richard gathered up the body parts, put them back in the Jeep, and drove on.

Like a lot of guys who served in World War II, he didn't like to talk about what happened. It just wasn't done. But it was obvious that the war, especially the searing memory of what happened that day in the Jeep, changed his life forever. He self-treated his undiagnosed PTSD with booze. Later, after serving during the Korean War, my grandfather joined the MPD in Washington, where he was assigned to the Women's Bureau, the precursor to today's Narcotics and Specialized Investigations

Division. My grandfather worked at the MPD until he was injured on the job and retired on disability.

My mom's experiences as a child, as well as her devotion to Catholicism's call to public service, led her to become a social worker who treated traumatized teens.

My parents, Terry and Joe, met shortly after college in the early 1970s. They separated in the late 1980s, when I was eight years old. From that point, they lived in two completely different worlds.

My mom lived a modest, middle-class existence. As a volunteer and a social worker, she exposed my sister, Kathleen, and me to poverty, dragging us along on visits to homeless shelters and the Red Cross. My dad, a workaholic lawyer, was a rising star at a white-shoe law firm, on track to become a millionaire partner. He lived in a ritzy home with a backyard pool and drove a Jaguar. My dad remained supportive while I lived with my mom and sister in Alexandria, Virginia.

Of all my relatives, my mother's brother left the strongest impression. I came to admire the way Uncle Steve approached life: His job did not define him. Work was simply a means to an end, a way to raise a family and enjoy life.

Like most of my mom's relatives, Uncle Steve lived in southern Maryland, among the blue-collar towns on the Chesapeake Bay. Everyone had a working-class job. They were steamfitters, teachers, and electricians. Everyone had a boat and we spent a ton of time out on the Bay. It's where I learned to love the outdoors. It's also where I picked up my southern Maryland, or "Muhr-Lund," accent.

Uncle Steve taught me to fish and catch crabs. We had fun but he also instilled a work ethic. As important, he taught me that it's okay for a guy to be masculine *and* show affection to family members. He showed me that it's okay to get down on your knees and play with little kids or change their diapers. My mom says Uncle Steve and I are a lot alike: Our souls belong outdoors.

When I was a kid, I idolized the cowboy life. My mom bought me a Fisher-Price turntable and I nearly wore it out playing Willie Nelson singles. I still think Willie's "Last Thing I Needed First Thing This Morning" is the greatest fucking country music song of all time. "The last thing I needed / The first thing this morning / Was to have you walk out on me."

I loved westerns. My maternal grandfather, the retired cop, turned me on to John Wayne and I got swept up in the Duke's whole American tough-guy persona. My friends and I played cowboys and Indians. For a while, I rooted for the Dallas Cowboys. My favorite film then remains my favorite today: Clint Eastwood, Eli Wallach, and Lee Van Cleef in the spaghetti western *The Good, the Bad and the Ugly.*

I won't lie. My teen years were rough. Basically, I was a fuckup. Aimless, immature, and scarred by the divorce, it's safe to say that I didn't share my father's fondness for academics or my mother's dedication to service. In middle school at St. Mary's in Alexandria, me and my buddy Danny Sweeney shoplifted cigarettes from Safeway and snatched bottles of wine from the church before the priest blessed them. We'd cut class and sneak to a railroad tunnel near the Safeway to smoke and drink. We thought we were badass. In reality, we were just bored and rebellious.

In ninth grade, with great hopes, my dad sent me to Georgetown Prep, the prestigious Jesuit high school in the ritzy Maryland suburbs. Prep is a training ground for the Washington elite, and alumni include Supreme Court justices and members of Congress. To put it politely, it was a bad fit. Prep's ninety-three-acre manicured campus included a nine-hole golf course and an all-male student body that epitomized an elitist Washington I fucking despised. I was also out of my league, academically and socially. I'd figured my previous Catholic school education had prepared me well, but I found myself drowning from the get-go. A priest who taught Latin took pity and offered a passing grade if I caddied for him. I did so and escaped with a C-minus. I guess they had to let me stay the full freshman year because they'd cashed my dad's tuition check. At the end of the year, I was "not invited back."

After Prep, I spent half a year at an alternative school in Maine. Toward the end of my first semester, when I was about sixteen years old, I dropped out. I didn't tell anyone. I just bought a bus ticket home to D.C. When I showed up unannounced, both parents refused to take me in. I couch-surfed for a while.

I rented a basement room from a guy named Jerry Eubanks, who got me my first construction job at Southern Maryland Installation Group. Jerry and I woke at 4 a.m. every day and for lunch packed a peanut butter sandwich and a fruit cup, about all I could afford. When it was cold, I'd go out a little early and warm up his big Chevy truck, then we'd hit the road, listening to the Greaseman, the shock jock who replaced Howard Stern on rock station DC101.

I was thankful for the work. It felt good to work with my hands all day and shoot the shit with different guys at a work site, the Greaseman riffing in the background as we hung drywall or framed a door. I left work each day with a sense of accomplishment.

The owner of Southern Maryland Installation, Bob Stump, treated his employees like family and I fit in well with his misfit characters, people worlds away from Georgetown Prep. Many of my coworkers had spent time in jail. Most carried drug and/or alcohol addictions. The guys we worked with were white, Black, and brown, and came from around the world. We busted each other's balls, but there was an underlying tone of respect for anyone who worked hard and did their job, no matter their backstory.

One coworker I recall distinctly came from West Virginia and worked with us for six months each year. He brought his lunch to work in a small Igloo cooler. The only thing inside was a six-pack. He didn't drive because he'd racked up too many DUIs. One day he was talking about his wife and described her as a "whore." I asked him why he kept calling her that, and he said flatly, "Because she is. She's a prostitute." He explained that during the six months a year he spent with us, she worked the sex trade. The other six months of the year, they lived together in their cabin on a speck of mountain property in West Virginia.

To my amazement, he spoke about the arrangement without shame or judgment. To him, it was just life, survival.

Another dude Bob hired—I'll call him Bill—was recently released from prison and covered in tattoos. Bill was a good guy but just could not get his shit together. Bob, who had a heart of gold, got Bill a car but the guy couldn't afford to register the vehicle. Bill slapped a "Farm Use" sign on the license-plate holder, figuring he would get away with it. He didn't. I remember driving with Bob to help rescue Bill after a Virginia state trooper pulled him over for misuse of farm tags. Bob pleaded with the trooper to let the man go, reasoning that an arrest would derail his life again. The guy was on the road to rehabilitation, Bob argued. Why mess it up over a relatively harmless administrative violation and fines he couldn't afford? To my surprise, the trooper agreed.

Bob and Jerry rewarded my enthusiasm for work and taught me about money. When I got my first paycheck, I used the money to buy a DeWalt power drill. Bob was so impressed that I'd decided to invest in my occupation that he reimbursed me for the drill. I used that cash to buy a radio to listen to the Greaseman on the job. Most of the guys cashed their paychecks at a liquor store, which took a 15 percent cut. Jerry explained that banks don't take a cut and helped me open my first account.

By age eighteen, I had saved enough to secure an apartment south of Alexandria along U.S. Route 1. The place across the street was littered with drug dealers and sex workers, but I paid my own rent and made my own decisions.

I'm a country boy, but around 1999, when I turned nineteen, I got into the punk scene. I was drawn by the music, the rebellious culture, and the women. I soon met a punk guitarist named Matt Lautar, who worked at a tattoo shop called Rick's in Arlington, Virginia. I got my first tats at Rick's. Matt inked Irish and Italian flags on my right forearm. As I left, I felt elated. I kept stealing glances at my first tattoo. It felt cool.

About a half hour later, while shopping in a grocery store, I reached for a loaf of Italian bread and did a double take at the label. I realized that I'd been admiring the Italian flag on my arm from a reverse angle. Matt had fucked up. He'd reversed the red-white-and-green pattern of the Italian flag. I lost my shit and stormed back to Rick's. I entered so obviously angry that Matt grabbed his gun. I wasn't intimidated and we stood eyeball-to-eyeball for a few seconds.

Matt asked me what I wanted him to do.

"I want you to fix it, motherfucker."

Back in the day, tattoo removal wasn't so easy and it sure as shit wasn't cheap. So Matt came up with a plan to use hydrogen peroxide on my skin, creating a scab that I could repeatedly pick apart, hoping that would remove the wrong colors. It took about twenty painful applications over a few years to create enough scar tissue on my forearm to fix the mistake.

Matt and I became lifelong friends, scraping by together in our early years, sharing apartments from time to time. Matt inked every other tattoo I have. After January 6th, some butt-hurt right-wingers speculated on social media that my tattoos held secret meanings, ones that could blow the lid off the conspiracy to rig the 2020 election.

Yeah, right.

Most of my tattoos are just art. I do have an angel tat for my oldest daughter, Caitlin, and a rendering of my ex-wife in a bikini on our honeymoon. I also have a black rose in honor of James McBride, an MPD partner of mine who died in a training accident. On my back, Matt inked a large tribute to *The Good, the Bad and the Ugly,* complete with Eastwood lighting a cannon.

On the morning of September 11, 2001, I was deep in a muddy hole at a Clark Construction job site in downtown D.C., assisting a journeyman carpenter. At about 9 a.m., while on a smoke break, an electrician came running up cradling one of those old Nextel cell phones that also works like a walkie-talkie. We could hear his girlfriend screaming, saying something about planes hitting a building. We were only three blocks from the White House. A few minutes later, we heard sirens and squad cars converging in that direction. Then the air horn blew and our fore-man announced the job site was closed for the day. I headed over to my dad's law office, a few blocks away. When I arrived, lawyers, secretaries, and paralegals were huddled in a conference room around a small TV. We watched replays of the Twin Towers attack in silence.

One day, while waiting to catch a bus to work, I saw an advertise-ment for the U.S. Capitol Police. It looked cool, though most of what I knew about the police came from my grandfather and watching *Beverly Hills Cop* and *Lethal Weapon*. The way I saw it at the time, movie cops seemed just like modern cowboys—except that instead of riding horses, they drove really expensive sports cars and crashed them into shit. They lived in campers on the beach, carried guns, arrested assholes, and scored hot babes. What was not to like? I was twenty-one, but still just a boy.

In those days, all you needed to get hired by the Capitol Police was a clean record and a high school degree. The District of Columbia had a special program for older teens who wanted to finish their high school degree in person. It was located at a nearly all-Black school called Ballou in one of the city's most dangerous neighborhoods. I was the only white boy in my class.

The Capitol Police hired me in 2002. They sent me to the Federal Law Enforcement Training Center in Georgia, where just about every government agency except the FBI and DEA sends recruits to learn the law, investigative techniques, driving tactics, and firearm use. At FLETC, I trained alongside men and women headed to the Amtrak Po-lice, the Border Patrol, the Park Police, the Marshals Service, the Bureau of Prisons, and agencies as obscure as the Federal Reserve Police. Our class was filled with people inspired by 9/11 to serve their country. One of my fellow Capitol Police trainees had quit a high-paying Wall Street gig to sign up.

At that point in my life, I was hardly what you'd call a fan of authority, and I almost derailed my law enforcement career on the first day at FLETC. An instructor who styled himself as a drill sergeant instantly took offense at my tattoos, which by this point included a spiderweb creeping up my neck. This was 2002 and most people over thirty still associated tattoos with outlaws and lowlifes. When the instructor made a crack about my tats in front of other recruits, I snapped back, giving him an earful. The instructor tried to make an example of me and have me tossed from FLETC for insubordination. Luckily, a new friend squared things. Mike Schmidt, a sergeant in the Capitol Police, was close to my tattoo buddy Matt, and we'd met before I left for the academy. I'm not very good at apologies or begging for forgiveness, but I sucked it up and called Mike. I couldn't blow my chance to become a cop. Mike called the stuck-up instructor and learned that guy was ready to expel my ass.

"That dude is gone," the instructor said. "I'm fucking sending him back."

Mike vouched for me and explained that we got our tattoos from the same guy. "Listen, man, I know Fanone and he's a good dude," Schmidt told the instructor. "Leave him the fuck alone."

He did and I didn't waste my second chance. For the first time in my life, I excelled in the classroom. I learned police law and procedure. I learned how to subdue an arrestee and how to protect myself. I learned the basics about illicit drugs and how to make a narcotics case. Each day, I looked forward to the punishing physical training. I loved it all. I couldn't wait to become a police officer. I was ready to kick ass.

I didn't realize it at the time, of course, but my experiences at Prep and Ballou, and especially in construction, would serve me well as a police officer as I matured over two decades. Given my background, I could communicate with almost anyone and moved easily between different worlds—white, Black, rich, poor, blue-collar, white-collar.

As a cop, I would become as comfortable buying crack from an addict in an alley as I would be presenting evidence to professionals in a courtroom. I could empathize with fuckups just struggling to get by, and also call bullshit on those trying to game the system. Though I was called to duty as a cowboy, I would develop a greater calling: serving and protecting law-abiding D.C. residents living amid poverty, discrimination, addiction, and violence. But that career would come a few years later.

Meantime, I reported for duty at the U.S. Capitol.

CHAPTER 2

Capitol Cop

In 1998, a mentally deranged gunman burst into the Capitol and shot Officer Jacob "J.J." Chestnut at a security checkpoint on the House side. The crazed man then entered the offices of House Majority Whip Tom DeLay, where Capitol Police Special Agent John M. Gibson was posted, and shot the agent dead. Chestnut and Gibson became the first Capitol Police officers killed inside the Capitol.

In fact, until the 2021 insurrection, only three other Capitol Police officers had died in the line of duty. In 1952, Private Fred J. Crenshaw succumbed to a gunshot wound suffered while apprehending a robbery suspect on the Capitol grounds. In 1984, Sergeant Christopher S. Eney was accidently killed by a fellow officer during a training exercise. In 2014, Sergeant Clinton J. Holtz died of a heart attack shortly after confronting an uncooperative witness to an assault a few blocks from the Capitol.

In 2017, a pair of Capitol Police protection agents—officers assigned as bodyguards to senior congressional leaders—saved countless lives after a gunman opened fire on a group of Republicans practicing for an annual congressional baseball game at a park in Virginia. Representative Steve Scalise, the same man who went out of his way to avoid shaking my hand after January 6th, was seriously wounded in the 2017 attack, along with two officers, a congressional aide, and a lobbyist. The Capitol Police officers, Crystal Griner and David Bailey, had been assigned to protect Scalise, then the third-ranking House official. They held their ground, returning fire even after they were wounded, and killed the gunman. For their heroism, Griner and Bailey were awarded the Law Enforcement Congressional Badge of Bravery at a bipartisan congressional ceremony in 2019.

I arrived at the Capitol Police in 2002. Early in my tenure the Washington, D.C., area was rocked by the so-called Beltway sniper attacks. In the space of three weeks, ten people in the region were randomly murdered from long-range as they went about their everyday lives. They were shot while mowing the lawn, pumping gas, and shopping. An FBI intelligence analyst was killed as she and her husband walked to their car after leaving a home improvement store. No one knew who was behind it. Everyone was freaked out. People were afraid to shop for groceries or get gas. The dash from the car to any store became stressful. Most outdoor events were canceled. Every weekday during that crazy month, I wore my new Capitol Police uniform to my daughter's school and helped escort the kids from their cars to the entrance. At work, we were told to be on the lookout for Middle Eastern terrorists driving a white van. So we stopped and searched almost every white van we saw at gunpoint. When the killers were caught, I learned one of my first on-the-job lessons: In a panic situation, don't rely on initial reports or racist assumptions. They're usually flawed and can steer you in the wrong direction, prolonging the manhunt. It turned out that the killers were Americans and they drove a blue Chevy Caprice.

Once things settled down, and I eased into the routine of the job, I hit an unexpected wall. I'd arrived at the Capitol Police full of piss and vinegar, adrenaline and ambition, ready and eager to fight crime. It didn't take long for me to realize I was in the wrong job. At FLETC, we studied real-world police techniques. We were taught the rules of probable cause, search and seizure, investigative techniques, and the best ways to secure evidence to prove a criminal case. In Washington, the Capitol Police taught me how to use a magnetometer and a hand wand to screen visitors for weapons. I soon realized that I would be no more than a glorified security guard, a concierge with a gun. Worse, most of the people we'd pledged to protect—members of Congress and their staff—treated us like crap. We were "the help."

Members were supposed to wear a special lapel pin or flash an ID to enter the Capitol complex without passing through the magnetometers. Sometimes members forgot their pin or left their ID in the car. I learned that one of the easiest ways to insult a member of Congress is not to recognize one on sight. To say that members of Congress have egos is like saying that I like cold beer. When I challenged members without ID, few understood that I was simply doing my job, protecting them. Most became pissed, expecting that a good police officer ought to be able to memorize the faces of all 100 senators and 435 representatives. We'd been issued a picture book with all their faces, and they'd steam whenever I'd pause to look 'em up. If I found a member especially rude, I'd take my time turning the pages. "Uh, sir," I'd say, offering an even bigger insult, "could you please repeat your name?"

Many of the members' young staffers were worse. Arrogant Ivy League twentysomethings berated me for forcing them to submit to the most basic security protocols. It was as if running a metal detector over the Starbucks cup they carried might curdle the soy milk in their grande vanilla latte, or delay them from A VERY IMPORTANT meeting. The job was demeaning. The first six months sucked.

It did not take long for me to develop the most dangerous attitude in law enforcement: indifference.

As my first year wore on, and the verbal abuse and boredom rose, I started to care less and less about protecting the staff at entry points. *You might have a bomb in your bag? A gun hidden in your coffee? Whatever. I don't give a fuck. I just don't want to hear your shit.*

About a half year into my Hill stint, I got lucky. A congresswoman who objected to my tattoos, which now covered my arms and part of my neck, demanded that I be removed from checkpoint duty. She thought my tats would spook the tourists. My bosses complied, and made me less visible. I did not hide my glee. I was thrilled to get to work outside, away from self-absorbed people.

At the start of the Iraq war in 2003, they posted me in a squad car at the base of the Hill, as a lookout for potential truck bomb attacks. The car they assigned had been in mothballs for years and had to be towed to my post. Like a lot of security theater around the Capitol, the car and I were merely props.

I worked the three-to-eleven shift, basically watching traffic crawl by for eight hours. To kill time, I listened to the police radio. Our frequencies were dull as shit, so I tuned to the channel for the Metropolitan Police Department's First District, which included the Hill. I listened to hours and hours of First District MPD radio calls, drawing an adrenaline rush from reports of drug dealing, shootings, and random mayhem.

The radio crackled with action, and I got to know names, call signs, and key addresses in the First District, eavesdropping as actual policemen did their jobs. I tuned in each shift, like a kid listening to episodes of *Gunsmoke* on an old-time radio. I recognized some First District officers by name because they were former Capitol cops. As I listened to broadcast snippets of their work, I thought it sounded like the most exciting thing in the world.

Bored beyond belief and posted in an immobile car, I started finding ways to drift toward the action in the First District, on foot or in squad cars that actually rolled. Sometimes, my buddy Ramey Kyle joined me, and we got other officers to cover for us at the stationary posts. As sworn federal officers, we had the power to arrest anyone within the city limits, though we weren't really supposed to go hunting for crime that far away from Capitol Hill. Ray and I got our hands dirty and made a few arrests, pulling guns and dope off the street.

Ray shared my passion for real police work. He was about a year older, and we'd known each other since the late 1990s, long before we became police officers. Today, Ray is a respected commander in the D.C. Metropolitan Police Department. And a certified hero: As it turns out, Ray is the MPD supervisor who directed officers inside the Lower West Terrace Tunnel on January 6, 2021. Like many of us, Ray self-deployed, supplying badly needed leadership to an emergency situation. His bravery, wearing no more than a policeman's hat, supervisor's uniform, and trench coat, inspired an exhausted crew of fifty officers for more than three hours, preventing the Trump mob from taking the tunnel and completely overwhelming the U.S. Capitol. Ray is the supervisor you can see on my body-worn camera footage in the tunnel coughing and convulsing from tear gas, then whirling back into the fray, like a modern-day General George Patton, shouting "Hold the line!"

Ray and I met during our punk years. He played in a hardcore band that I liked and we ran in the same social circles. A few months after I started on the Hill, I bumped into Ray in the police locker room, and from that moment we became pretty tight. Our friendship survived two decades. At one point, we even dated two women who were close friends. On the Capitol Police force, we were both assigned to protect the Longworth House Office Building, across the street from the U.S. Capitol. We spent many lunch hours exploring surrounding neighborhoods, on the hunt for actual criminals. One time, Ray and I returned to the Hill an hour late from a foray into a housing project riddled with drug dealers. The officer I was supposed to relieve was pissed.

"What the fuck is wrong with you?" he said of my off-campus adventure. "That's not our job."

The officer and I exchanged a few words, then came to blows. We wrestled to the ground, two Capitol cops in uniform brawling in broad daylight on Independence Avenue, in full view of tourists.

A short while later, Ray and I both quit and joined the MPD.

CHAPTER 3

The First District

A be Lincoln created the Metropolitan Police Department in 1861, three months after the start of the Civil War.

At the time, the city had only an "auxiliary watch," consisting of sixteen men. The war brought thousands of soldiers and new government employees to D.C., and put the city near the front lines in Northern Virginia. As described in an official MPD history, "hordes of unsavory elements descended upon the District's few square miles," and President Lincoln recognized the need for a professional force to preserve law and order in the nation's capital.

When I joined the MPD in 2004, I was so eager to get to work that I graduated at the top of my academy class.

It wasn't hard. As at many police departments in the early 2000s, training was seen as a chore, a check-the-boxes school. Most days, we'd show up in the morning for a few hours of class, and watch an instructional video. This included—I shit you not—*Lethal Weapon, Die Hard*, and *Beverly Hills Cop*. Around 11 a.m., the instructor would break for lunch, and then tell us to study on our own until 3 p.m. So basically, we were done for the day at 11 a.m. I didn't care because I'd already learned the basics of police work at FLETC.

That first week, our recruit class met with Dr. Beverly Anderson, an expert in police trauma and psychology. She didn't speak like any doctor I'd ever met.

"You're going to see some fucked-up shit over the next twenty years," she told us. "It's okay to get upset. It's okay to cry. It's okay to say you need help."

I liked her style, but I felt pretty confident I'd never see her again. No cop I knew needed a shrink.

The best training we received at the MPD academy came during the two weeks we spent with prosecutors. They focused on the city laws we were most likely to enforce and cool tips on how local judges expected officers to act when making an arrest, especially what was permissible and what wasn't.

We also spent two weeks on firearms instruction. Much of it was pretty worthless in the real world, because we practiced on static paper targets at a sterile range, without any stress. That's the way most cops train with their weapons today. They fire monotonously at targets that don't move and pose no risk. Poor training can't account for all the mistakes even well-meaning cops make—officers are human. But with the stakes so high, I always thought it was crazy that we spent so few resources on the practical and appropriate application of deadly force. At MPD, we were only required to qualify at the range once every six months.

Military vets who joined the MPD told me they were stunned by the almost casual approach to guns, in terms of both officer and citizen safety. The vets were accustomed to training under fire, repeatedly. They understood that in stressful situations, with lives on the line, things happen so fast you have to rely on your training. This remains a glaring police problem with a simple solution: Officers should train with their weapon at least every ninety days in stressful simulations. You can't completely replicate the tension an officer feels as he or she approaches someone suspected of carrying a weapon, but enhanced firearm training under duress would go a long way to help reduce our national epidemic of officer-involved shootings.

At the MPD academy, I met some cool people and heard some good stories. But almost everything smart I learned about policing—how to deal with people, how to treat them with respect and serve them as law enforcement officers—I learned from mentors on the street. One of them, a tough as nails sergeant named Barnes, relentlessly quizzed us about our beats. If you ran into Barnes, you better know the name of the pastor at the church on your beat, and have his phone number handy. You better know the names of all the bodegas and mini-marts on the beat, and who owned them. Barnes understood this shit mattered and he demanded old-school accountability.

As a top academy graduate, I got my pick of postings. I chose the First District, which includes the most significant landmarks in Washington—among them, the White House, the National Mall, the Supreme Court, and the Capitol. The city's commercial center, a canyon of office buildings that reaches from Dupont Circle to Union Station, is part of the First District, too. So are the city's indoor hockey and basketball arena, located in the Chinatown restaurant district, as well as the three other outdoor sports venues, Nationals Park, Audi Field, and RFK Stadium. While there are pockets of wealth and gentrification along the First District's commercial corridors, the majority of its 100,000 residents live beyond the city seen by tourists, commuters, and suburbanites who venture downtown for a ball game or a meal.

Most First District residents live in a very different Washington, D.C. Poverty, drugs, and violence are part of everyday life. I mostly patrolled those neighborhoods, and specialized in a ten-square block near the Capitol, known as "Public Service Area 101." PSA 101 included the Sursum Corda public housing project, a depressing collection of brick and beige low-rises built in 1968.

Sursum Corda is Latin for "Lift up your hearts." In two decades, I never met a Sursum Corda resident who believed the place lived up to that promise.

I arrived in 2004, shortly after the shocking execution-style murder of a seventh-grade girl inside Sursum Corda. The fourteen-year-old, Jahkema

"Princess" Hansen, had been "dating" Marquette Ward, a twenty-eight-year-old drug dealer who went by the street name "Corleone," an ode to the Mafia family in *The Godfather*. One evening, Princess witnessed Ward shoot and kill another man during a botched drug buy. Later, MPD detectives summoned her to a police station for questioning, and a suspicious Ward secretly followed her there. When Princess returned to Sursum Corda, Ward warned her, "Little sis, you best not be snitching." Princess told Ward the truth: She had refused to help the police. Ward didn't believe her and hired a hit man for $8,000. A few days later, as Princess and Ward ate dinner in a Sursum Corda apartment, the hit man burst in and opened fire. He put two bullets in the back of the middle schooler's head.

I would have been hard-pressed to find a more dangerous place to work. PSA 101 felt like a choice assignment. In my early, less-mature years, I sometimes felt like a deputy patrolling the Wild West. I could not fucking wait to get to work each day. I arrived early and left late. I rarely took vacation or sick days. I was too worried I'd miss out on the action.

Like a lot of cops, I spent my first years going balls out, drawn to the adrenaline and ego rush of pursuing and subduing suspects. My street name was "Spiderman"—in part because of the webbed neck tattoo, but mostly because I used my rock-climbing skills to scale buildings on stakeouts. Once, I leaped from a second-story window, like some kind of caped crusader, to tackle a fleeing suspect.

On surveillance, I hid in trees and trash cans. After the deadly anthrax attacks in 2001, the city issued MPD officers disposable Tyvek hazmat suits. They were awesome. I wore them whenever I hid in a dumpster, so I wouldn't ruin my uniform.

Unlike Spiderman, I didn't always catch the villain. Sometimes the villain got me. Once, we were targeting a group of dealers near a strip club called Rouge, which also had private peep-show booths. People in the neighborhood would buy crack, then slip into a booth to smoke and catch a quick show. I used a ladder to climb up on a nearby roof to set up an observation post. The plan called for me to witness drug buys, creating probable cause for arrests, then radio fellow officers on the street.

Things didn't go according to plan. While I had binoculars trained on a suspect, a crackhead stole my ladder, stranding me on the roof.

Losing a ladder cost me little more than pride, at least compared to the injuries I received over the years trying to make arrests. I got punched or kicked too many times to recall. It's likely, in some way, that those beatings helped me survive on January 6th. I knew how to take a punch. If I had still been a Capitol Police officer at that point, I'm not so sure that would have been the case.

One of my first violent encounters was with Christopher Barry, the son of our infamous former mayor, Marion Barry, then a city councilman. One cold February night in 2005, my partner Jeff Sipes and I responded to a call for a domestic-assault-in-progress near the 700 block of Fourth Street, just a few blocks from MPD headquarters. Outside the apartment, we heard loud music and smelled pot, which was then illegal. The door was open.

Christopher Barry met us with wild eyes, dressed only in his underwear, and tried to slam the door closed. Jeff and I pushed harder, and tumbled into the apartment. Barry squared up and started throwing haymakers. Before we could get him in cuffs, he landed a strong crack to my head, one that left me with a concussion and blood spattered on the floor. On a coffee table, we found a half-ounce vial of PCP, a drug that fries your brain but also gives you superhuman strength.

Anyone familiar with Marion Barry's political power—elected four terms as mayor, including once after serving six months in prison for crack possession—will not be surprised to learn that his son got away with assaulting a police officer. Chris Barry was released before he even saw a judge. The felony charges for cracking my skull were reduced to a misdemeanor, and he served no jail time.

═══

The first time I truly got my ass kicked on patrol came on a cold December afternoon, near the railroad tracks that lead to Union Station.

I was already in a lousy mood, passing time on a temporary shit assignment, the consequence of what I'll politely call a "strong philosophi-cal disagreement" with my supervisor. I was in the unit block of H Street, Northeast, when I witnessed a hand-to-hand drug transaction. The dealer lingered on the street and I pulled my cruiser toward him.

In those days, dealers commonly stashed drugs in their mouths. They found it more convenient than hiding it up their ass or lodging it under their balls. Some dealers who stored dope in their mouths were super slick. They would accept the money, then spit the drugs on the sidewalk. The buyer would scoop up the dope and walk away. The dealers thought this made it harder for the police to see or record drug transactions, and they weren't wrong. With this guy, though, I saw him actually hand something to his buyer.

As I rolled up to the dealer, it hit me that this dude was big, really big—at least six foot three and probably 300 pounds. He was smart enough not to run when I got out of the cruiser.

I tried to outsmart him. As casually as possible, I asked for his ID.

"Just need to check for warrants, man," I said, keeping things calm and steady.

The guy handed me a D.C. license and mumbled a few unintelligi-ble words. I soon realized he had something hidden in his mouth, but I didn't let on. I made up a story—accusing him of a crime I was sure he couldn't have committed—just to make him think he had nothing to fear.

"Hey, don't you have a warrant for child molestation out of San Francisco?"

"Nah," he mumbled. "Never been to San Francisco."

"Alright, probably someone else," I said. "I'll just run your name and DOB. Sorry, I've got to cuff you while I do that. Procedure."

The man turned as if to comply, figuring I'd make a radio call, realize I had the wrong guy, and let him go. I got the first cuff on, but when it clicked, he freaked out.

He whirled and slammed a fist into my chest. Then he took off, racing toward North Capitol Street, a handcuff dangling from his left wrist. I was faster and caught him after about half a block. I leapt, going for a flying tackle, wrapping my arms around his torso, but the dude was so fucking big, so superior in size and strength, that he just kept running with me attached to his back. Thinking back now, it was kind of comical. But at the time, I held on for dear life.

Just before he hit North Capitol Street, he stopped suddenly and kneeled, and I fell off. He squared up on me, ready for a fight. I was not prepared to go toe-to-toe with a guy who could eat me for breakfast and shit me out before lunch. Most criminals just try to escape arrest. They rarely turn on you.

This one started swinging and I swung back.

We grabbed at each other and wound up on the pavement. My training kicked in and I reached for my radio, hoping to push the big orange distress button, which alerts dispatch that an officer is down and needs assistance. But the radio was gone. I scanned the ground and saw it in the gutter, a few feet out of reach. In the tussle, the radio must have been knocked from my utility belt. I was fucked. The big guy slammed my head into the sidewalk.

Then I got lucky. A homeless man I recognized, someone I'd spoken with many, many times, appeared out of nowhere. He picked up my radio and said, "Spiderman, what do I do?"

"Push the orange button! Push the orange fucking button!"

He did, and the orange button activated an automatic distress call. In those days, it did not activate any kind of GPS, so it took a while for help to arrive.

While I awaited help from colleagues, I distinctly remember cars slowing to watch me struggle—a police officer in full uniform rolling on the ground with a large man—and then the cars moving on. Except for the Black homeless man who made the distress call from my radio, the only person who approached us until the police arrived was a young white guy on a scooter. I was flailing, pinned and screaming, when Scooter Boy stopped.

I reached out my hand for help.

Scooter Boy leaned into my face and spit. "Fuck you," he said, and sped off.

I was stunned. A citizen passing an officer in distress intervenes not to help, but to make a hostile political statement? Today, this is far more common, but this was the mid-2000s and it was the first time I'd felt such vitriol. Sure, I expected shit from people we arrested, but not from people who seemed to "oppose" the police on principle.

Afterward, I told my supervisor about Scooter Boy and he dismissed it. He didn't believe me. No one, he said, especially a white guy on a scooter, would have the stones to do such a thing. This occurred long before we wore body cameras, so it was my word against his—at least for a few days.

When detectives checked surveillance cameras from a nearby building, the tape confirmed my account. Detectives also found an old lady who had been across the street at the time and she verified the whole thing. When she testified before the grand jury, she said, the memory she found most appalling was of a uniformed cop trying to keep her streets safe, fighting for his life, wrestling a violent criminal, reaching out for help, and seeing a guy take the time to stop, remove his helmet, spit in the cop's face, and ride on.

I received the first of my six concussions that day. I have trouble remembering them all, but I vividly recall two others. One came on January 6, 2021. The other came early in my career, while I was patrolling a public housing project called Potomac Gardens, about thirteen blocks from the Capitol.

My partner Rob Elliot and I spotted a man holding two guns, one in each hand. Rob and I hopped out and took off after him. Two veteran plainclothes officers, Jody Shegan and Mark Nassar, guys I admired and hoped to work with someday, heard the radio call and joined pursuit in their unmarked car.

Racing on foot, I caught up to the suspect just as he rounded a corner and as Mark roared in with his car to block any escape. It was a perfectly legitimate tactic and a smart move, but the police car narrowly missed the guy and clipped me instead. I flipped into the air, bounced off the hood, and crashed headfirst through the windshield. The hospital sent a helicopter to medevac me but there were too many power lines in the area for the bird to land, so an ambulance drove me to the ER.

At the hospital, I felt woozy as hell, but I played down my bruises. I wasn't afraid I'd hurt myself. I worried that if my injuries were deemed too severe it might keep me off the job for a few days, and I might miss something important or interesting.

I always returned to duty the next day. Always.

Was I reckless at times?

Yes.

But a halfhearted approach never appealed to me, and I guess I had to learn the hard way. One time we were patrolling a housing project notorious for violence, responding to a complaint about heroin dealers selling on a street corner. We arrived in tactical gear, and after witnessing three street buys, a few officers went for the bust. To my surprise, they arrested only the buyers, and did not pursue the sellers as they scurried back into an apartment building. I was confused and furious at the other officers. I couldn't tell if they were being lazy or cowards.

"What the fuck?" I fumed. "Did we lose our balls? Do we not go after sellers anymore?"

I stripped off the tactical gear that hid my plainclothes. I pulled a black Adidas hoodie over my head and shuffled over to the building, doing my best to look like an addict. I stepped inside, hid beneath a stairway, and waited. Soon, I realized I'd forgotten my radio. But before I could leave to retrieve it, the seller emerged from an apartment, not ten feet away, cradling a package.

I rose from beneath the stairwell and we locked eyes. He darted back into the apartment and I pursued him, catching him from behind as he entered a bathroom, hoping to flush the evidence. I beat him to the toilet and had my arms wrapped around him, when his enormous roommate, who did not realize I was a policeman and thought I was a robber, began whaling on the back of my head. He pounded me until fellow officer Richmond Phillips, who had had the wherewithal to shadow my movements, burst in and saved my ass.

We recovered the dealer's package, and it turned out to be the largest heroin bust of my career.

After I left the ER, I learned that the dealer I jumped was also wanted for murder. I'd been lucky. If armed, the guy could have easily killed me.

It hit me then that if I planned to have a long career in law enforcement, I needed to work smarter, not harder. It wasn't worth risking my life, or a suspect's life, to get into a brawl if I could de-escalate a situation. I needed to change my warrior mentality.

One trick I learned: If a guy you've arrested and cuffed refuses to get into the back of the squad car, don't force him. If you use force, odds are excellent one or both of you will get hurt. My strategy was to just sit with him on the curb, handcuffed by the open door, and say, "Look, man, I have three hours left on my shift and we can just sit here until you get in the car on your own. And if you can last three hours, there's an officer who will come relieve me." Usually, the guy would sit there defiant for ten or fifteen minutes, then realize his neighbors were watching and that the wait was futile. Eventually, he'd get in the car.

Here's another rule of thumb: Never chase anyone you can't catch on foot—know when to hold them and when to fold 'em. That way you keep your reputation as a cop you don't want to fuck with.

Some nights on the proactive prowl for guns, we set up roadblocks about twenty blocks east of the Capitol, where a well-traveled bridge crossed the Anacostia River, connecting two of the city's most violent neighborhoods. Two of my mentors, G.G. Neil and Kurt Sloane, who helped create a gun recovery unit in the mid-1990s, ran the checkpoints. We lined up in the hours after midnight and, following rules set by the Supreme Court, we stopped every car and asked to see everyone's driver's license. Guns were so prevalent in that area that sometimes we failed to bring enough cops to handle the volume, creating a traffic jam. One night we recovered twelve guns in the first twenty minutes.

Most nights, we'd finish around 4 a.m., grab a six-pack, and report back for duty when court opened in the morning. We showed up hung-over and wearing the same dirty clothes, still jazzed from a solid night's work, ready to give brief testimony about the weapons we'd recovered. I thought it was the coolest thing in the world. We were confiscating guns and removing violent offenders from the streets.

CHAPTER 4

Vice

Two years into the job, at age twenty-six, I was promoted to a dream assignment: Vice.

No more patrol. No more days spent responding to 911 calls. No more uniform.

I dressed for comfort and camouflage, ready to make an undercover drug buy one hour and take up an observation post the next. Most days, I dressed like a construction worker just off work from a downtown project, a redneck in scuffed boots, job-site vest, and paint-splattered jeans. Sometimes I carried a hard hat.

More experienced partners, including Jeff Leslie, taught me three important skills: patience, persistence, and paperwork. They helped me pivot from the go-go-go mentality of my early, cowboy days. They taught me how to make complex cases, investigations that led to real results.

Jeff and other mentors taught me why street-level drug suppression is one of the best ways to reduce violent crime. Ninety percent of the people we detained for drugs walked away without charges or served little (if any) jail time. That was by design.

My philosophy on drugs was simple: As a police officer, I didn't make moral judgments. I didn't harass addicts. I didn't see the point of sending someone to prison for moving a few zips of crack.

Instead, the goal was to use street-level drug arrests and prosecutions as a means to an end. It's pretty hard to catch someone red-handed committing a violent assault or murder, or moving wholesale amounts of heroin or crack. But in certain neighborhoods the odds were excellent that such violent criminals would know or hang out with street-level drug dealers and their addict customers. So we'd pop a guy for buying or selling a tiny amount of meth, heroin, or crack, then question him about bulk suppliers, and unsolved murders and rapes in their neighborhood. We took what we learned, busted an associate, learned more, and kept digging until we found a witness to a major crime or found a way to disrupt a violent drug crew.

In late 2013, for example, two homicide detectives approached me for help identifying witnesses who might cooperate on open murder cases in Sursum Corda. The killings were believed to be related to the Borda Boyz/Y-Squad, a violent gang that trafficked crack. Jeff and I, along with Officers Randy Done and Phil McHugh, worked with FBI agents at a grueling pace, racking up eighty undercover crack buys in two months. We called it Operation Broken Heart, and we indicted fifteen people on serious drug and gun charges. The homicide detectives took it from there. The goal was to take the worst of the worst off the streets, and maybe catch a killer.

My philosophy on traffic stops was similar.

If I pulled someone over for a minor traffic infraction and found no drugs or weapons in the car, I let the driver go with a warning. I never wrote tickets because I'd lived below the poverty line myself.

As a paycheck-to-paycheck kind of guy, I know how shitty a $150 fine can be when you can barely pay the rent and have maxed your credit cards, or when you realize that you have enough money to buy dinner for your family or gas for your car, but not both. The last thing I wanted to do was saddle someone with a fine they couldn't pay. In fact, most people I stopped preferred to be arrested, rather than receive an expensive ticket. They knew that if they went to jail, their time inside would be brief, and at least the city would pay for their lawyer.

I was lucky to get to partner with Jeff in Vice for nearly a decade, from 2009 to 2019. We spent a lot of time together off-duty, too, drinking. We also covered for each other—him for me, if I had a hot date, and me for him, if he had an emergency Bible study. Jeff is from Montana and the son of a pastor. A lean and laid-back evangelical, Jeff rarely cursed and liked to size things up before speaking. He was tough and wise, courageous and kind. He taught me the value of slowing down, thinking things through.

Jeff also served as my translator.

Once, later in my career than I'd like to admit, I charged into First District commander Morgan Kane's office without knocking, ripshit about some lazy bureaucrat or some new asinine rule preventing us from fighting crime. It's very, very likely that I presented said remarks at extremely high volume, and laced them with profanity and an air of insubordination.

The commander kept a straight face. "Please ask Jeff to step in here," she said.

When Jeff entered, the commander said, "I need a translator. What's Fanone trying to say?"

Jeff explained, calmly and diplomatically. And I got what I wanted. Soon, it became a routine. Whenever I needed to see the commander, she demanded that I bring Jeff to translate. Jeff said the commander actually liked me, but couldn't admit it publicly, given my rants. And she liked to bust my chops. I hope that's true. I certainly liked and respected her.

Jeff and I were both city dwellers, but we witnessed so much mayhem at work, we fled to the country as often as possible to try to clear our minds and cleanse our souls. Usually, we headed west to wide-open spaces in western Virginia, between the Blue Ridge and the Appalachian. We fished, we hunted, we hiked, and we rock climbed. We craved quiet spaces off the grid where we could shake the stain of the city. It wasn't easy. On one trip, I spotted specks of blood on the heels of Jeff's new hiking boots. It took me a moment to realize it wasn't dried animal blood from an old hunting trip. It was a teenage boy's blood, residue from a homicide scene. A few days earlier, we had been among the first to respond to a murder. On a blood-spattered city street, Jeff had stood guard over the body as we waited for the coroner to arrive.

I can't emphasize enough how dangerous it was to work in Sursum Corda. A few days after Christmas in 2007, an undercover officer, King Watts, was viciously beaten about the head by two men in masks and robbed of $80. After the robbers took his money, the officer managed to stand and, as one of his assailants came at him again, the undercover shot him. Later, after we rescued the officer and arrested his assailants, we watched the video from the undercover's hidden camera. The violence was chilling.

In Vice, we worked complex neighborhood drug investigations, focusing on one block at a time. We set up observation posts, ran undercover operations, and proactively sought to disrupt the most violent drug crews in the city. Sometimes, the MPD loaned me to the FBI, DEA, and ATF as a task-force officer, a program in which the feds deputize seasoned local cops to work side by side with their drug agents. I learned plenty from the feds, but it was Jeff, a meticulous investigator himself, who schooled me on the importance of paperwork and court prep.

Paperwork sucks. But anyone who has watched *Law & Order* knows that there are two equally important parts to any case: the police investigation and the court prosecution. A cop's job doesn't end with an arrest. If an officer hasn't prepared for trial, he'll trip on his dick. The first few times I got on the witness stand, I tried to wing it and paid dearly. Like most young cops, I focused too much on the rush of the collar and too little on documenting my work. It took me a while to realize how much easier I could make it for myself (and the prosecutors) if I kept my paperwork tight.

The trial system in the District of Columbia is unlike any other in the nation. Here, every case is handled by federal prosecutors, in both city and federal court. Assistant U.S. attorneys prosecute everything from misdemeanors to murder, and they are bound by Department of Justice rules. They are an elite group and they don't fuck around. They don't waste time on cases with mediocre cops. There's just too much to do. I was proud of my reputation with the assistant U.S. attorneys and worked hard to keep it.

So the paperwork matters. Details matter. You write a sloppy arrest report or a flimsy search warrant affidavit and a good defense attorney will shred you on the stand. They'll exploit any discrepancy. The District of Columbia has one of the highest acquittal rates in the nation. I came to understand that if you're going to take the time and trouble to arrest someone on serious charges, you've got an obligation to get the paperwork right.

I put as much effort into being a good court witness as I did being a good investigator. I recognized early on that certain aspects of trial are theater. Judges and juries pay close attention to the way officers act in the courtroom, not just on the stand but while interacting with lawyers, bailiffs, and spectators. On the stand, I was never one to play fast and loose with the facts, but I understood that the way they were delivered could make all the difference. I learned to be detail-oriented and to present evidence in a clear and concise method without manipulating the truth.

I also came to believe that as a police officer you have to take the facts as they come. There's no such fucking thing as two sets of facts, or alternative facts. If you make a mistake during a traffic stop or omit a key detail in a search warrant, you have to live and learn. You have to accept your fuckup and move on. It's human nature to minimize one's mistakes, but if you try to rewrite the facts, or assemble them in a way that reflects better on you, things rarely end well.

If we lost a case, whether at trial or because of a judge's ruling, I tried not to take it personally, unless my mistake set the suspect free. I didn't like losing—no one does—but as a professional I realized that if the police automatically prevailed in every case we wouldn't have much of a justice system. Some officers approach trials like a contest. They decide they can justify just about anything, including exaggerating on the witness stand, to secure a "win." I saw too many officers focused solely on "winning," whatever the fuck that is, instead of justice. I don't subscribe to that Neanderthal approach to policing. Nobody "wins" when a suspect is arrested or convicted. Families on all sides of a crime suffer. An adversarial attitude only inflames existing tensions between police officers and the community. It fuels an unhealthy *us vs. them* mentality.

Again, you can trace this problem back to training. Police departments spend a lot of time teaching recruits about the law and the mechanics of firing a weapon, but they rarely take the time to *show* young officers how to engage with the community. New officers should be taught they can catch more flies with honey than vinegar. They should be taught that the police aren't deployed as some kind of occupying force. They should be taught that when they are out on the streets, they should treat everyone they meet as a peer, a fellow American.

You never know. The next person you meet could change your life.

One evening on a Vice detail early in my career, I met such a woman.

CHAPTER 5

Leslie

On the surface, Leslie Perkins and I could not have been less alike. I was a healthy, fit white cop in his midtwenties from the suburbs. She was a Black transgender sex worker, a fifty-year-old woman raised in extreme poverty and addicted to crack cocaine.

Leslie stood nearly six feet tall, with brown eyes, a black wig, and the build of a linebacker. She favored floral print dresses and heels, but felt as comfortable in sweats and sneakers or a miniskirt and knee-high boots. Leslie was the first person I knew who had full-blown AIDS, and she was also my first transgender friend. She carried pretty much every illness that comes with street life, including hepatitis C and diabetes. Given her line of work, her sagging health, and her crack addiction, it was a miracle that Leslie lived into her sixties.

Fellow sex workers called her "Grandma," but I usually called her Leslie or Les. Sometimes, I called her Klinger. Like the Jamie Farr character in the TV series *M*A*S*H*, Leslie had used her cross-dressing ways to try to get out of the U.S. Army.

I met Leslie early in my career because we worked the same streets. Heterosexual sex workers frequented the Fourteenth Street and Logan Circle area, near K Street and the central business corridor. The transgender sex workers gathered about ten blocks to the east, closer to the Capitol and in my patrol area, not far from Sursum Corda.

In our early encounters, I followed the simple philosophy ingrained by my mentors: Let the other person set the tone. I wanted to develop information and nail violent criminals as much as anyone, but as I said earlier, you catch more flies with honey.

Leslie and I bonded, in part because we were both outgoing and un-filtered, a pair of Jokers in the deck. One day, she casually told me about someone with a drug stash, and it led to an arrest. Much later, when I asked her why she began to help me, Leslie said, "Because you treat me like a normal human being, not a fucking freak show."

That's true, but I also paid her for her work as a confidential informant. Leslie worked harder and longer hours than some cops I knew.

Leslie taught me the economics, logistics, and lingo of the drug trade. She helped me break preconceived biases and phobias about race, gender, and AIDS. When I went undercover, I trusted her with my life. Leslie helped me with hundreds of arrests. In her own way, she was an unsung community activist, improving her neighborhood.

She also risked her life.

One warm May afternoon in 2011, I arranged for Leslie to buy crack in Sursum Corda with another undercover MPD officer. The first buy went fine, no problem. But the next day, when Leslie and the officer returned to the same spot to buy more crack, the seller didn't show. Instead, he called Leslie and let her know that a buddy recognized the undercover guy as a cop. He was certain he'd once seen the officer make a bust in a nightclub. Leslie told the guy he was nuts, abandoned the deal, and we dropped her off near her home.

Moments later, a gray Honda Accord pulled up on the sidewalk where she stood. A window peeled down and one of the targets of our investigation called out to Leslie. The guy claimed he not only recognized the undercover as a cop, he recognized the blue sedan he drove as an unmarked police vehicle.

The guy said, "You need to stop bringing the police around here. You tryin' to set my man up, bitch, you gonna get fucked up. We see you even when you don't see us."

I was worried enough that I started the paperwork to get Leslie into the federal witness protection program. We ended up hiding her in a suburban motel for a few weeks, until Leslie realized that entering witness protection meant she'd never be able to return to D.C. or see her friends ever again. She decided that returning was worth the risk.

Leslie and I spoke almost every day, and became so close that we sometimes blurred the lines between professional and personal. I never paid her a dime more than she earned as an informant, but we became like family. Several times, Jeff and I talked her out of suicide. Whenever Leslie filled out a form, she listed me as her emergency contact. If she got arrested in Baltimore, I'd get a call and drive up in the middle of the night to fetch her. If she landed in the hospital after a scuffle with a john, I'd come to her bedside and hold her hand.

If Leslie Perkins were still alive, she'd tell you that she was my mama bear and I was her cub.

"Oh, honey, I raised Mike," she'd say in her falsetto voice. "I taught him how to be an officer. You should have seen him when we first met. He was jumping out of trees and hiding in dumpsters. Motherfuckers be dealing, and I'd say, 'Why'd you keep looking up in trees?' They'd say, 'Because Spiderman might be up there.'"

———

Before I joined the MPD, I had only a passing familiarity with cocaine, crack, meth, or heroin. I'd only seen or heard about hard drugs at the academy. I knew nothing about drug culture—the lure of fast cash, the clandestine sales rituals, the desperation that comes with addiction, and the violence the business breeds. Leslie took me inside that world. She's the one who taught me the trick about dealers hiding crack under their tongue.

We'd roll up on a corner and from the back seat Leslie would gesture at a man about a block away. "See that dude? He's selling."

All I saw was a guy standing on the corner. I did see someone pass by, give a quick fist bump, move along for a few steps, then stumble briefly, steady himself with a hand to the sidewalk, then walk on. "See, there!" Leslie said, excitedly.

"Leslie, what the fuck are you talking about?"

The money was exchanged during the fist bump, she said. The dealer spit a zip of crack from his mouth to the sidewalk and the buyer scooped it up. Most cops could go an entire career without picking up those furtive details. Leslie's tutorials were a revelation. Too many street cops spend too much time relying on data, license-plate checks, and responding to 911 calls. I learned more by scanning the streets with my eyes than I ever did staring at a computer.

One time a data-obsessed rookie and I rolled up to the entrance of a housing project. Instead of downloading data about the block, or worrying about checking IDs for outstanding warrants, I told him to keep his eyes up. We got out of the scout car about twenty feet from where a crowd of about thirty men had gathered. As we approached, a few residents stepped forward to greet us. I walked past them, pointed to a guy standing by the door, and told the rookie to put him in cuffs. The rookie asked why.

"Look behind the door and you'll see his gun," I said. Sure enough, the rookie found a gun on the floor just inside the doorway. The rookie looked confused. I explained, "This is the only guy who took off, walking away from the crowd." The rest of it, the dudes coming to talk to us, was just noise, a distraction to protect the man with the gun. A lesson from Leslie to me to the rookie.

Leslie was a talker, but for years she avoided discussing her childhood. Eventually, Jeff and I learned that she was born in Gary, Indiana, in 1957, and that while growing up near Chicago, a family friend abused her repeatedly. At the time, Leslie was a seven-year-old boy.

When she told us about the rapes, Jeff and I became visibly angry, the way anyone would upon learning that a loved one had been violated. We wanted to do something. We vowed to track the rapist down and make a case, or at least make his life miserable.

Leslie said it was too late. He was dead. Hiding pain behind laughter, she said, "Besides, he made me the queen that I am today."

I laughed. Jeff remained stone-faced. "I still want to know his name," he said, "so I can find his grave and piss on it."

Though neither of us condoned Leslie's lifestyle, we tried to empathize. We might argue with her fiercely, almost like siblings over little shit, but we always reconciled within days. Sometimes, we became frustrated when she'd call or visit, claiming some minor or imagined emergency—we were busy with our own lives and knew she was probably just lonely. But what can I say? We loved her. Les became family.

It's sad but safe to say that in Leslie's world, love was a rare commodity.

In her world, everyone manipulated everyone else. Nearly every act, nearly every conversation was transactional, a hustle. She trusted almost no one and expected everyone to lie. Many men who paid her for sex were conflicted about their own sexuality and often took it out on her, sometimes horrifically. In Leslie's world, acts of kindness were rare. Quid pro quos were expected. Nothing came for free.

Leslie was forced to become a master manipulator herself. It took us a long time to understand how her mind worked. One day, I pulled her aside and said, "Hey listen, you don't have to hustle me. If you want something, just ask."

"Okay," she said. "I want a Wild Cherry Pepsi and a Ding Dong."

Leslie may have tried to manipulate me on the margins but she never lied about anything that mattered, certainly never about a case. And she was honest. Once, I mistakenly gave her six $100 bills instead of five—the fresh bills must have stuck together as I counted them out. Leslie called me a few hours later to let me know I'd overpaid her. What kind of person does that? Someone you can trust and grow to love.

To kill time while we sat in an undercover car on surveillance, Leslie would tell crazy fucking stories—about drugs, sex, jail, violence, porn, corruption, and bizarro clients, men with means who sought blow jobs on the street from a transsexual. It took Jeff and me some years to realize that almost all the wild stories Leslie told us proved to be true, even the crazy-ass ones. Sometimes, during our early years working together, Leslie would return from a controlled crack buy with some insane tale about how the deal went down, and I just didn't fucking believe her. But inevitably, I'd come across a piece of hard evidence confirming her account—from another informant, an arrestee, a court record, or a surveillance tape.

That's why I believe her story about a late-night encounter with Marion Barry, then D.C. mayor and self-described "Night Owl." The two met at Club 55, a strip club seven blocks from the Capitol. They hit it off so well, Leslie said, that at one point she lowered her blouse, lay across a table, and the mayor snorted a line of coke from one of her fake double-D breasts.

Selling dope is more stressful than it looks, and Leslie helped us understand why, and why that matters. Because the job is per se illegal, you can't rely on normal societal and economic safeguards. Every customer is a presumed addict and a potential threat, looking to hustle or jack you. It's an all-cash business, so you're in constant fear of getting ripped off. If you're a crack dealer and you get robbed or scammed, you can't call the police for help. Successful drug dealers work long days. There's no such thing as an eight-hour shift. You've got to find ways to be available to customers nearly 24/7/365. Customer loyalty is key. If you're a heroin dealer, you can't afford to take a day off or a vacation. If you do, your customers will go elsewhere. They won't wait for their fix until you get back. They need their medicine *now*. You have to hustle *every day*.

Leslie also helped me understand that most addicts have one drug of choice. They rarely mix and match. Leslie smoked crack. One day, I asked Leslie to buy heroin and she refused, telling me, "I don't know how to do that."

"What the hell are you talking about?" I said. "You've been buying drugs your whole life."

She shook her head. "Are you trying to get me killed?" Everybody in the 'hood, she said, knows that she smokes crack, not heroin.

I pressed. She resisted.

"Okay," I said. "What if you're buying it for a friend? That work?" She slumped in the back seat of my plainclothes car and said nothing. We rolled on and I caught a glimpse of her glancing out the side window. After a minute or two, she said, "Yeah, we can do that."

I had a lot of sources on the street, and their workload varied. Some worked for me on one or two major cases, then disappeared. Some provided tips two or three times a year, floating in and out of my life on an unpredictable schedule. Leslie was a workhorse, ready to roll almost every day, one of the most effective crime fighters in the city. Some afternoons she'd just show up in the lobby of the First District and I'd get a call from the front desk, "Hey, Fanone, your girlfriend's here." I'd head down to meet her and she'd say, "I got something for you. Let's go to work."

Most days Leslie earned $50 to $100 working for us. In larger or longer-term cases, Leslie could earn $250 or $500, but she didn't trust herself to carry that much cash. She worried she'd buy too much crack, or get robbed. So I became The Bank. If she earned $250, she'd say, "Okay, give me $100 now and hold the rest for me."

I got in the habit of asking other sources what they planned to do with their money. Most knew what I meant, and saw it as a discreet way of asking if they wanted it all at once. If a source wanted his full pay, I gave it to him or her. But most liked the idea of banking the cash, so they wouldn't blow it all at once or get ripped off. We kept meticulous records, and sometimes it became a hassle. Sources would call or text us at all hours to make small withdrawals.

Did I violate MPD police-source guidelines by holding cash for sources?

Abso-fucking-lutely.

It took a tragedy for me to confirm that it was the right thing to do. We lent a good source of ours, an addict who often banked his payments, to the FBI. I really liked the guy and thought both he and the FBI would benefit from working together. The FBI made a major case and paid the source several thousand dollars for his services, far more than the MPD ever paid anyone. It was too much money for the source to handle. He went straight out, bought an exorbitant amount of heroin, and died of an overdose. Jeff and I were crushed.

Sometimes I used Leslie to vet new informants in preparation for search warrant affidavits, the sworn statements an officer and a prosecutor present to a judge for permission to execute a drug raid. I put my credibility on the line each time I signed a search warrant affidavit. An officer who uses a shaky or untested source is playing with fire. You don't want to kick in someone's door based on bad information, nor do you want to develop a reputation as someone who plays fast and loose with a defendant's constitutional rights. So whenever I used a new source, I'd send them in first to make a buy, then a few days later, I'd send Leslie in to confirm the new source's information.

A lot of cops treated their sources like shit, as if they were disposable. Some cops treated them worse than the people they arrested. I might have done the same had I not learned better from veteran narcotics officers Joe Abdalla, King Watts, Alvin Cardinal, Mike Ianichionne, Dale Sutherland, and J. J. Brennan, as well as FBI agent John Bevington. They were incredibly dedicated cops, and they were good to me. When I was younger and on patrol, they would send me out to help identify suspects for longer-term investigations. In between routine radio assignments, I'd cruise around and keep my eyes up, mugshots of the suspects handy. When I'd spot one on the street, I'd drive on, cool as I could be, until I could radio J.J. or Joe. I was thrilled out of my fucking mind to be working with these legends.

Joe treated his sources like friends. He got to know them, learned about their families and what they loved and feared. He treated them with dignity and they rewarded him. He taught me that you don't have to like your sources, but you need to treat them with respect and compassion. You have an obligation to care about their personal safety.

The source-handler relationship is tricky. You're dealing with people addicted to drugs, desperate for cash for the next fix, or people who just enjoy the rush of providing information to the police. The latter kind of source truly terrified me. Like a small-town gossip, they enjoyed their role too much. They cared less about money or civic duty, and more about the rush of power that comes with being part of a police investigation. In their excitement to insert themselves, they could be reckless, exposing others, including police officers, to unnecessary risks. People could get hurt.

As a source, Leslie always played it straight.

=====

Leslie spent a lot of time in the back seat as Jeff and I rolled through the First District, a lot of it catching up on sleep and making a mess with junk food. I'm a neat freak and once a week I'd take our car to a city-owned site to wash it down and clean it out. One evening, a few years into our relationship, I reached under the seat and pulled out a slimy condom. I went nuts, assuming I might have just exposed myself to AIDS and hepatitis. At a minimum, I assumed Leslie had used a police car to turn a trick. When I finally reached her, she laughed and told me to relax. She was so broke, she said, that she took condoms she got from the free clinic, tore off the rubber bands at one end and used them as hair ties.

When I first met Leslie, I'll admit I was afraid to even touch her. But as I matured and learned more about AIDS, I moved from handshakes to hugs. By the mid-2010s, we regularly asked Leslie to massage our shoulders. From the back seat of our plainclothes vehicle, she'd reach her large hands into the front seat to expertly rub our necks and shoulders. The stress-reducing massages became as much a part of our routine as trips to 7-Eleven for a Wild Cherry Pepsi, or to the projects to buy a zip of crack.

A lot of cops were repulsed by Leslie. They expressed shock that I would hug an HIV-positive transgender woman, or kiss her on the cheek. They couldn't believe that I'd bring this woman home to meet my daughters. I guess they couldn't see her as I did: a human like any other,

seeking only survival and love. I used to take her to meet younger officers after hours, to drink and play Ping-Pong, to help them understand
and get to know the kind of people they'd sworn to protect.

For fifteen years, I spoke with Leslie more than anyone else in my
life; that includes my ex-wife. To me, she served as a constant reminder
of the city residents I was proud to serve, resilient men and women,
trapped in poverty, just looking to survive.

CHAPTER 6

White Privilege

Until January 6th, the most arrogant son of a bitch I'd ever confronted was a white Georgetown Law student named Marc Gersen.

Gersen looked like a dork. He had thin lips, a scrawny build, and matted black hair. A scholar since high school in Florida, he earned an undergraduate degree from Georgetown's prestigious Foreign Service program in 2004. He majored in international economics, earned summa cum laude honors, and his professors awarded him a medal as best economics student in his class. He won a scholarship to pursue a master's degree at the University of California, Berkeley, and enrolled at Georgetown Law in 2010. In fall 2011, his second-year coursework included criminal law and a field seminar that took him inside D.C.'s prisons.

Gersen also had a secret and deadly side gig: He sold methamphetamine wholesale. He'd fly out to California to buy bulk quantities of meth and then have them shipped to D.C., where he sold them to street dealers and other wholesalers. Gersen moved meth in quantities as small as an ounce and as large as a half pound. At the time, the wholesale price for a half pound was about $12,000. So he was into some serious shit.

Crystal meth is mostly known for the devastation it's wrought throughout rural America. But on D.C. streets in the late 2000s and early 2010s, the highly addictive drug became popular in our city's large gay community. The hub of the District's gay district is historic Dupont Circle, at the intersections of Massachusetts and Connecticut Avenues, and the MPD placed a special LGBTQ+ substation there.

The Gersen case began with a phone call about a domestic dispute.

A gay couple living in an apartment complex on M Street in North-east, not far from Union Station, got into a fight and one of the men wound up in the hospital. An officer called me from the ER and said, "Hey, listen, this guy says he's got a bunch of information about drugs. He wants to talk to somebody."

I was at the First District station and it was close to the end of our shift. I asked for a volunteer to join me and Officer Brian Daniel raised his hand. We threw on MPD raid jackets and grabbed a cruiser. At the hospital, the victim told me that his boyfriend was a meth dealer and kept large quantities of meth and cash in the apartment. Hustling, I dialed a prosecutor and he helped me work up an emergency search warrant. We got it approved by a magistrate, hit the apartment, and recovered about a quarter pound of crystal meth and cash. Then the guy we arrested started talking. He told us about a bigger fish, and within a few days, we got a search warrant and hit that guy's house. When we busted that dude, he told us about Gersen. Everything happened within days. In each case, the people we arrested turned so quickly on their dealer we felt lucky.

Over Thanksgiving weekend 2011, we searched Gersen's apartment. No one was home—Gersen was visiting family in Florida—and we seized a small amount of meth, $3,500 in cash, and a couple of bottles of gamma-hydroxybutyric acid, or GHB, a clear and colorless liquid that the DEA commonly calls the date rape drug. We also sealed the apartment, so Gersen and his roommate would know we were closing in on them. A Gersen associate rented a room in a boutique hotel near Dupont Circle, and they started trying to unload as much meth as possible. Staking out Gersen's apartment, we came across one of their associates trying to access it. Like the others, he crumbled in seconds.

He told us where to find Gersen and his roommate. It wasn't lost on us that the members of this meth gang turned on each other faster than most heroin or crack dealers. As the prosecutors later put it in a court filing, "The participants in the ring have a strange and not often encountered proclivity to inform on each other without hesitation and fear of consequence."

I used the new information to obtain another search warrant affidavit and on the morning of December 1, we drove to the hotel. The evidence we found inside was overwhelming: 614 grams of meth, packaging materials, pipes, digital scales, $4,680 in cash, and bottles of GHB. We also found a handwritten ledger filled with customer names and amounts sold. Helpfully, the notebook's cover page included a typewritten header that said, "If Lost Return To:" One of the defendants in the case, Lee Hylton, had written his own name there. Brilliant guy.

While we were still searching the room, the hotel phone rang. Another officer picked it up. Gersen was on the line and didn't realize he was talking to a cop. "Is it safe to come up?" he asked.

"Sure, man," the cop replied.

An officer stationed on the street arrested Gersen as he approached the building. The gang's audacity and contempt for law enforcement surprised even the veteran magistrate who considered whether to grant them bail. "I find it thoroughly remarkable that even after the search has occurred and it is quite clear to the conspirators that they are the focus of police activity, they once again seem ready to resume their activity."

This was not Gersen's first arrest. In 2009, while a graduate student at Berkeley, police executing a search warrant at his home arrested him for possession of MDMA, the club drug ecstasy. Gersen was caught with 1,979 MDMA pills. While out and awaiting sentencing on that charge, the San Francisco police arrested Gersen in a hotel room with dealer-sized quantities of meth, two scales, razor blades, ziplock baggies, and handwritten notes filled with references to ounces, grams, and dollars. He never served any time on the California charges, and I never figured out why.

After we arrested Gersen in 2011, his lawyers filed a ballsy request for bail. He proposed that while he awaited trial, instead of jail, he could live with a local elected city official, the neighborhood commissioner for Dupont Circle, who would take responsibility for making sure he didn't get into trouble. The judge denied the request, but as someone who patrolled predominantly Black neighborhoods, I thought it reeked of arrogance and white privilege.

At first, Gersen lawyered up. I can't say I blamed him. The economics and legal scholar faced serious prison time. We'd seized 614 grams of meth, well above the 500-gram threshold that triggers a sentence of ten years to life. For a year following his arrest, Gersen paid his lawyers a shit ton of money to contest the charges by challenging the validity of our police work and other routine defense tactics.

Meantime, we continued to go through everything we'd seized using the search warrants. I don't think the public has any idea how tedious this can be, or realizes that this is a major reason police investigations can take months. Poor Jeff, the evangelical, had to scan through every image on Gersen's computer and cell phone. Much of it was adult porn, irrelevant to the case, but the protocols called for us to view every image. Of far greater value, we found audio recordings of drug deals on Gersen's laptop. Apparently, he taped himself. On the phone, Gersen bragged about the size of his operation and the brilliant ways in which he eluded the police. Looking back, I guess you could say Gersen was the first stable genius I encountered.

After Gersen's expensive pretrial motions failed—and he realized the scope of the evidence we had against him—he reached a deal with prosecutors, pleading guilty to a single count of conspiracy to distribute and possess with intent to distribute methamphetamine. He also agreed to forfeit $120,000. The lesser charge—conspiracy to distribute *less than* 500 grams—meant he would likely face about four years in prison.

As part of his guilty plea, Gersen was required to sit down with me and disclose all of his illicit business. He loved every minute of our conversation. He told me he thought all cops were dumb, and boasted about working with the Hells Angels and moving $2.5 million worth of meth.

At sentencing, Gersen's lawyer portrayed him as a brilliant young man who struggled with addiction, citing his self-enrollment in treatment centers before his arrest. In a letter to the judge, Gersen's constitutional law professor wrote, "His law school performance—remarkable under any circumstances—is truly incredible given the other things going on in his life." The Georgetown Law dean wrote a similar letter. He said he'd found his visit with Gersen in the D.C. jail "inspiring," and was impressed by Gersen's work tutoring other inmates.

Wow, I thought. If only the professor and the dean could have witnessed my debrief with Gersen, and heard him boast about moving mass quantities of crystal meth.

At the hearing, the prosecutors pushed back on the defense lawyer's narrative. Gersen may well be a scholar who deeply cares about the law and may struggle with addiction. However, they told the judge, "We have some difficulty reconciling that image with that of the defendant who was trafficking in wholesale quantities of methamphetamine, while knowing full well the devastation of methamphetamine use on the lives of those addicted to it. The defendant was not someone who sold drugs only to the extent he needed to do so to support his own addiction. He trafficked in wholesale quantities of drugs and bragged of his success in doing so. What emerges from accounts of his fellow drug dealers, his customers, and his own words, is of a drug dealer who believed that because of his intellectual ability, he was able to outwit law enforcement and avoid detection in conducting his drug trafficking operation."

Amen.

In private, many judges will tell you that sentencing people to prison is one of the hardest parts of the job. But they do it often enough that they usually have a good sense of what sentence a person deserves. The judge in this case, Reggie B. Walton, had been on the bench for more than a decade, and was among the most prominent Black judges in the nation. He had handled several high-profile cases, including the perjury trial of Vice President Dick Cheney's aide, Scooter Libby. Walton also served a seven-year term on the prestigious and mysterious Foreign Intelligence Surveillance Court. Perhaps most relevant to the Gersen case: Walton served as an associate drug czar during the George H. W. Bush administration, so he knew a lot about meth and the destruction it can cause. In my line of work, Walton had a reputation for being tough on drug dealers.

So I was surprised to see him so enamored by Gersen at the sentencing hearing. The judge wanted to know how and why someone with such a promising future would take such risks. He engaged Gersen in an unusual back-and-forth, a philosophical conversation that seemed better suited for a classroom than a courtroom.

"Somebody as intelligent as you are had to have known," Judge Walton said as Gersen stood before him in an orange jumpsuit. "It's just perplexing."

Gersen told the judge he used meth to relax and have fun, but that his use became increasingly destructive, addictive, and anxious. Walton asked Gersen, "How can you or I be sure things won't change in the future?"

"I can't tell you that temptations won't come," Gersen replied. "But when they do, I will do what I need to do to make sure I stay on the right path."

The judge sentenced Gersen to four years and the case made international headlines. Every story cited Gersen's impressive résumé, his meth addiction, and support from family and professors who struggled to reconcile the scholar with the criminal.

I saw the case quite differently.

What I saw was a perfect example of white privilege.

A Black defendant in this situation would have been sentenced to much more time in prison. Sure, Gersen struggled with addiction, but so do most street buyers and sellers. Gersen's bulk sales of meth spread poison through my city, ruining countless lives. And this wasn't his first bust. I felt enraged.

Many of the Black defendants I arrested did not possess this white man's academic credentials and employment skills. The Black defendants broke the law, too, but at least most of them dealt drugs to survive, to feed their families. In my career, I'd sat through dozens of sentencings for Black defendants, and rarely heard a judge speak the way Walton did to Gersen, focused on a promising future ruined by drug addiction. With Black defendants, judges usually focused on the bad behavior.

As I sat in court, I recalled that I'd had a hell of a time trying to help a Black informant land a job as a janitor at a federal health agency, after he helped with a big case. To secure the job, I'd had to swear on my firstborn that the guy wasn't dangerous.

But Gersen? He got every break. At sentencing hearings, it is common for a defense lawyer to ask a judge to recommend that a defendant be allowed to serve time in a prison near relatives, so they can visit. Judges typically do so, but with the caveat that the Bureau of Prisons gets to make the final decision. In my experience, Black defendants convicted in Washington, D.C., were shipped all over the country. Gersen was assigned to a prison in Florida, near his parents.

The breaks continued even after Gersen's release from federal prison in late 2014. He was permitted to finish law school and then—I still cannot believe this actually happened—a fucking federal judge hired him as a law clerk. Then he landed a similar job with the public defender in Oakland, California.

Gersen's case is a classic example of how we have one criminal justice system for white privileged kids who go to Georgetown, and another for Black kids raised in the First District. A federal felony drug conviction for a Black law student would have been devastating, certainly foreclosing any chance of a federal clerkship.

And what did this educated white man do with his third chance?

Yeah, you guessed it, he returned to crime.

Less than two years after taking the public defender job, the San Francisco Police Department arrested Gersen on drug charges. The SFPD posted a picture online of all the dope they seized: nearly 7 kilos of meth, 5.4 grams of cocaine, 10.5 grams of ecstasy, a gallon of GBL, 30 grams of the club drug ketamine, assorted morphine and Adderall pills, and $22,710 in cash.

A repeat offender arrested with 7 kilos! And yet, Gersen was sentenced to probation, no jail time.

What a joke.

CHAPTER 7

Black Lives Matter

One of the most dangerous parts of a cop's job is the traffic stop.

To an officer approaching a car, the interior of the vehicle represents the unknown. Are there guns? Knives? Contraband? Is anyone inside the vehicle dumb, desperate, or high enough to kill me to try to get away?

In my head, I knew that 99 percent of the time, it was going to be fine. But there was always that lingering 1 percent. Every officer brings his or her years of knowledge and experience to every stop. The tension is always there.

I can't recall the first time someone pulled a weapon on me, but I clearly remember an early close call during an overnight shift on patrol with Rob Elliot. We were in a marked patrol car, just off Benning Road, about twenty-five blocks northeast of the Capitol, when we rolled up behind a gray Nissan Altima. The Nissan was idling on a narrow street in a housing project, a spot where only one car could get through at a time. The car's emergency lights were blinking, as if the driver was waiting for someone to join him. We had no intention of pulling the car over. We just wanted to get through. Rob hit the air horn a few times but the guy didn't budge. I figured he was either high, wearing heavy headphones, or just didn't give a shit. Rob sighed, flipped on the emergency lights, and we got out to take a look.

Rob approached from the driver's side and I took the passenger door. The driver was the sole occupant. I kept my eyes locked on his hands while Rob questioned him. The driver seemed oblivious to my presence. I couldn't hear what he was saying to Rob, but as he spoke I saw his left hand go for something in the car door.

It happened so fast I didn't have time to yell "Gun!" I yanked open the passenger door, jumped into the Nissan, and went for the guy's forearms. The man was large and so was the weapon he grabbed, a .44-caliber Magnum—the one Clint Eastwood carried in *Dirty Harry*, "the most powerful handgun in the world."

Rob reached in from his side and we wrestled awkwardly for what felt like a minute, but was probably just seconds. The .44 fell to the floor and we struggled to get the guy in cuffs. Inside the trunk, we found wholesale quantities of dope. The guy with the .44 was no mastermind criminal. The ones we caught rarely were.

Legally, I could have shot the man dead. He pulled a deadly weapon on a police officer and therefore I was authorized to use deadly force. I made a split-second decision, and, fortunately, things turned out okay.

It was never lost on me that as a police officer I carried a gun, with the trust and authority to take another human's life.

I thought about that every day. Each morning before work, I looked myself in the mirror and repeated the same mantra: *See the humanity in the people you will meet today.* Because once you no longer see the humanity in people, you cease to see them as people at all. They become the enemy and therefore disposable. I'm certain that by the time Derek Chauvin choked the life out of George Floyd, he did not view him as a human being.

There's a long history of racism in this country. Unfortunately, law enforcement played a significant part in that—and I'd like to be part of that conversation going forward. I don't believe that police officers are above reproach, but I also don't believe that all police officers are evil. In fact, I think it's one of society's most honorable, selfless professions.

Some of the "Defund the Police!" rhetoric on the left is moronic. At the same time, I see people on the right saying "We love the police, we just don't love the police who responded on January 6th." That kind of pandering makes me want to fucking vomit. If we truly want police reform, we need to have sincere conversations that include everyone affected.

That includes police officers. In the years between Michael Brown's death in Ferguson in 2014 and George Floyd's murder in Minneapolis in 2020, cops in Texas, Louisiana, and New York were killed for no other reason than that they wore the uniform. In 2014, NYPD officers Rafael Ramos and Wenjian Liu were assassinated while sitting in their patrol car. In 2016, five Dallas police officers—Lorne Ahrens, Michael Krol, Michael Smith, Brent Thompson, and Patrick Zamarripa—were killed sniper-style, near the end of an otherwise peaceful social justice march. The same year, two officers from Baton Rouge and one from East Baton Rouge—Matthew Gerald, Montrell Jackson, and Brad Garafola—were killed by a mentally ill man who became so enraged by the police shooting of a Black man in Louisiana, Alton Sterling, that he drove all the way from Kansas City to target officers from the same force.

The cop killings spread fear through our ranks. At MPD, we changed the way we deployed: We halted regular single-officer patrols and doubled up in each car. This reduced our response time and visibility. It made the streets less safe.

The changes didn't affect me as much because I rarely wore a uniform in public, but I saw the toll it took on fellow officers. They'd walk into the same restaurant where I was having lunch with other plainclothes officers—no one there knew we were cops—and the vibe would change instantly. Customers, usually white ones, would start berating the uniformed officers.

"How many Black people you gonna kill today?"

"I hope you choke on that burger, pig."

"Fuck you, bitch cop!"

You can tell officers to compartmentalize, that these idiots are just attacking the uniform, not individuals. But cops are human, too. Insults based on the uniform alone wear them down.

All of this occurred, of course, as Black Lives Matter emerged as a national movement. The police rightfully became subject to increased scrutiny, particularly for the way some officers mistreated Black Americans, in too many cases lethally.

My daughter Caitlin, who was eighteen years old at the time, went to a few BLM protests in the summer of 2020 in Washington. We talked about it before she went. She had a lot of misconceptions about the way most officers treat Black people. Some of the misinformation she spouted felt as factually inaccurate as anything a Trump diehard might say. But I knew better than to argue with her. I focused on safety.

"Go," I told her. "Do whatever you want. Shout, chant, kneel, dance, whatever. But the moment the protests turn violent, specifically against cops, you have an obligation to leave immediately. Number one, by remaining there, you're making it harder and more dangerous for the cops already trying to keep order. Number two, you're lending your support, intentional or not, to people breaking the law. You're emboldening them to turn a lawful protest into a riot."

I was not assigned to work the BLM protests, though I followed them closely. My former partner Jeff Leslie, who spent the summer in the thick of it, kept me posted. People spit and yelled at him nearly every day—and remember, this occurred during the first months of Covid. One evening, while sitting in a cruiser during a BLM protest, Jeff caught a glimpse in the side mirror of someone placing a Molotov cocktail under his left rear tire. He escaped just before the bottle exploded.

As someone who rarely kept my opinions in check, I supported the protesters' First Amendment right to peacefully assemble. As a cop, I applauded much-needed calls for police reform. But I also worried deeply about officer safety, and attempts by certain groups to hijack the BLM protests to serve their own agendas.

Here's what I believe:

I believe that Black lives matter and that criminals like Derek Chauvin deserve to go to prison for a very, very long time. I believe that crime and police brutality have roots in systemic poverty and racism. I believe the police need to be more transparent and release body-cam footage as soon as possible after an officer-involved shooting.

But the answer to these problems is not to "defund the police." That's about the dumbest fucking thing we can do. The reality is that when you reduce a police department's budget, the pencil pushers cut training because it's among the easiest things to cut. It's what happened in my department.

It's like cutting off your nose to spite your face. You can draw a direct line from poor training to unjustified police killings. We need more training, not less. I think some departments have just decided that it's easier politically to deal with these singular catastrophic situations one at a time, rather than change how we operate.

Speaking of stupid, politically motivated moves, in response to some of the earliest protests, MPD eliminated the Vice units in 2015. Jeff and I were transferred to "crime suppression" in the First District.

Under the new system, drug crime would no longer be fought at the street, PSA, and District level. All cases would be funneled through headquarters, and the stats would be counted that way.

On paper, this brilliant plan worked. Following orders, we made far fewer drug arrests, and the statistics reflected this downward "trend." Absurd as this sounds, MPD brass then cited the lower arrest numbers to claim a drop in crime.

Unfortunately, you can't measure a city's drug problem by the number of arrests in the same way that you can gauge violent crime by data on assaults and murders. Residents don't call 911 to report the dealer on a street corner, the way they report an assault or murder. The only way to combat drug trafficking is with proactive policing. Following the chief's logic, if we stopped arresting people for homicide, then I guess the murder rate would fall, too.

The chief, Cathy Lanier, also eliminated district-level plainclothes drug operations and ordered everyone back into uniform.

I refused to wear one.

My supervisors in the First District didn't seem to care. They let me continue to do my thing and mentor younger officers. I think they just figured that as long as I continued to remove violent criminals from the streets, they didn't give a shit how I dressed.

I'm also sure they saw the irony in the situation: Plainclothes and vice officers were removed as part of a knee-jerk political reaction to repeated citizen complaints about reckless cops hassling too many non-criminals, sweeping into neighborhoods like some occupying force. It's true that too many commanding officers misused the plainclothes units as "jump-out" squads, a brute-force tactic in which groups of officers roll up on suspected dealers and leap out of their cars to make arrests. Commanders loved jump-out squads because they drove up arrest stats. Now the brass wanted fewer drug arrests, so they could declare victory and keep community activists content.

Street cops began to question the chief's loyalties. The way we saw it: Given a choice between the needs of the officers and the demands of the activists, the chief usually chose the louder, politically powerful voices.

I understood the chief's political reasons for eliminating plainclothes operations. But to anyone interested in fighting crime, the switch to uniforms made no sense.

The whole purpose of putting officers in plainclothes was to allow them to blend into the community, conduct surveillance, and develop sources, things a uniformed cop can't do. It was naive to think that residents would meet with uniformed police officers in broad daylight to discuss violent crimes committed by people they knew—snitches get stitches. The new policy was as ridiculous as it was dangerous.

Worse, the chief publicly announced the new policy. At first, savvy street drug dealers were very, very skeptical that police had been ordered to stand down. They thought it was a ruse. At first, informants told me, the dealers laid low and sent out the youngest and most expendable hustlers to work the streets. Then, when the dealers realized that the chief was serious, and that no one was getting locked up, they returned with gusto.

In fact, brazen open-air drug markets resurfaced in D.C. for the first time since the late 1990s. In my career, the gutting of Vice was the dumbest fucking thing the MPD ever did. I don't think there's any doubt that the elimination of the Vice squads in 2015 coincided with a staggering increase in property and violent crime. I attribute a big chunk of that to the decrease in proactive policing.

Unfortunately, every police department is a bureaucracy. Bureaucracies are dependent on budgets, and those budgets are driven by statistics. In government, success is measured by the stats. When a city council member or a neighborhood advisory commissioner forwards a citizen complaint about crime to the police, the police brass want to have a stat handy to show they're doing something about it.

That's why policing today is driven by quantity (how many arrests did you make? how many tickets did you write?), rather than quality (which violent criminals did you take off the street?).

The reliance on stats triggered inane quotas for street cops like me. We got weird mandates, like "Make five arrests a shift" or "Engage with eight people on the streets, take down their names and location, and file them on index cards for future reference."

Some guys would go out, arrest five guys in an hour for carrying a couple of zips of crack, and call it a night. They'd go back to the precinct and drink beer and play poker the rest of the shift. I'm no St. Michael, and I admit that I joined them at times. But it pissed me off. You go and arrest five people for carrying a little crack every night, without any other goal than to pad the stats by locking people up, and pretty soon people in the neighborhood fear and hate you. You start stopping eight people on the street for no fucking reason other than to gather information on index cards and you get the same result: resentment.

A few of us found a way to dodge the eight-names-a-day index-card mandate. At the start of each shift, we drove to a cemetery near RFK Stadium, found eight tombstones, and jotted down the names of former city residents. We stored the cards in the car's glove box, ready to turn in at the end of the day.

Then we devoted the rest of the shift to real police work.

When Jeff transferred to Harbor Patrol in 2018, I was partnered with someone I knew well, Jimmy Albright. Jimmy and I had worked together in the First District for years, and off-duty we hunted and crabbed together. He lived in southern Maryland, near some of my relatives. Jimmy was six years younger, and he reminded me a lot of me in my earlier days. We made a good team. He offered me safety and security. I offered a cooler head and twenty years' experience. I tried to keep him from making the same mistakes I did.

Jimmy was one of the go-getters in the office, a former army sergeant who earned a Purple Heart in Iraq for wounds sustained during a roadside bomb attack. As a combat vet, Jimmy understood what it meant to lead people into harm's way. He knew how to take a punch and how to treat a wounded comrade, training that would prove invaluable on January 6th.

In 2019, I got very, very lucky. Phil McHugh, a young homicide detective, transferred to the First District and became my supervisor. Phil and I first met when he was assigned to the First District back in 2009. To be blunt, I was an asshole and hazed him in his first months. Phil, with his boyish, eager face, had arrived with a master's degree in public affairs from American University. Not only did he have a couple of degrees, he had worked as a civilian in the chief's office. A college boy with connections! Phil also liked to talk about shit like empathy and compassion, something we really didn't do in the police locker room. Later, Phil would say that the grief we gave him only inspired him to try harder. Maybe that's true.

But let me fucking tell you, Phil worked his ass off.

He was also smart enough to ask for help. Despite all his schooling, no one had bothered to teach Phil the basics of investigations and search warrants. Phil asked me to show him and so I did. I not only explained how to write a search warrant, I explained why it was so important to get it right: You're asking a judge to authorize armed government officials to forcibly enter a person's home. You best not fuck up.

Phil's dedication impressed the shit out of me. Over beers, I came to appreciate and adopt his mantra—*See the human element of what we do; never take arrests lightly, as they will forever alter a person's life.* I developed a ton of respect for Phil as he pursued violent criminals in D.C.'s most dangerous neighborhoods, including Sursum Corda. He made great cases and developed his own street sources. He talked a thirteen-year-old boy out of jumping off a bridge. He became an advocate for the kind of smart, proactive policing I craved. In 2011, he was named Officer of the Year.

So I was fucking elated years later when he returned to the First District as my supervisor. By that point, Jimmy and I were de facto leaders in our crime suppression unit. I'll be honest: As a leader, I was not the easiest fucking dude to work with. I did not suffer fools. I held no respect for indifferent or lazy officers, and I let them know it. As Phil told me many years later, he tried to set the other guys in the unit straight. He told them I actually knew what I was fucking doing, and that if they were willing to look past what he called my "rough exterior," I could help them.

For nearly two years, we made a damn good team.

We did so despite all the external noise—the scrutiny, the BLM protests, the police assassinations, the politics, and the calls for reform.

Jimmy, Phil, and I tried hard to just focus on our jobs.

But it was tough to ignore the new guy in the White House.

CHAPTER 8

Bunker Mentality

The greatest trick in American history was Donald Trump convincing rednecks and cops that he somehow speaks for us.

This redneck cop certainly fell for it. Like most cops, I voted for Trump with enthusiasm in 2016.

Law and order! Back the Blue! Drain the Swamp! As a veteran city employee, I certainly supported anyone who pledged to hold lazy and corrupt bureaucrats accountable.

I recall a twinge of doubt when Trump said he could shoot someone on Fifth Avenue and get away with it. Polls showed he wasn't wrong. At the time, I recall thinking, *Whoa, hold on. Elected officials shouldn't be above the law.* But I shrugged it off. That's just the way Trump talks, right?

For whatever reason, I couldn't see Trump's corruption or racism until years later. I realize now that when he said we need to be "tough on crime," what he really meant is that we need to be "tough on minorities."

I don't think Trump bears sole responsibility for creating racially tinged divisiveness in this country, or for stoking the outrage that led to January 6th. But he did an amazing job of exploiting it for his own personal gain.

He also had great timing: He launched his presidential bid in 2015, about the same time that the racial justice protests grew into a national movement. Most cops, reeling from the new dynamic, including demonizing and degrading rhetoric leveled against police, turned to the comfort food offered by Donald Trump and Fox News.

Like a lot of Republicans, I figured Trump would change once he entered the White House. Or at least that his advisors—the "adults in the room"—would provide guardrails to stop him from harming the country. My confidence first slipped when Trump fired FBI director James Comey for refusing to make a Mafia-like loyalty pledge. Trump lost me for good when Secretary of Defense James "Mad Dog" Mattis resigned in protest over Trump's weak decision to abandon Syrian freedom fighters. I respected Mattis because, like me, he had dedicated his life to serving his country. Donald Trump, with his five Vietnam War draft deferments, had spent his entire life serving no one but himself.

I couldn't understand why so many cops and military vets fawned over a coward and draft dodger. I guess they ignored Trump's hypocrisy because he showered them with sweet nothings. They let him use law enforcement and the military as a prop, often literally.

A good example—one that turned my stomach when I saw it—was Trump's speech to Long Island cops in July 2017. Channeling his best Archie Bunker, the president of the United States stood in front of a group of police officers in dress uniforms, complete with white gloves, and told them to violate citizens' rights.

"We have your backs, one hundred percent," Trump said. "Not like the old days."

Linking crime and immigration in a familiar dog whistle, Trump introduced his new Immigration and Customs Enforcement (ICE) director, Thomas Homan, who'd flown up with him on Air Force One. "He's a tough cookie," the president said of his appointee. "Somebody said the other day they saw him on television . . . and said he looks very nasty. He looks very mean. I said, 'That's what I'm looking for.'"

The cops staged behind Trump roared with laughter and broke into applause.

Trump blamed weak borders and a lax immigration policy that he said brought drugs and violence to cities and towns across America. "They're there right now because of weak political leadership, weak leadership, weak policing, and in many cases because the police weren't allowed to do their job. But hopefully—certainly in this country, those days are over. We're going to support you like you've never been supported before."

Like trained monkeys, the cops behind Trump beamed and clapped again.

"One by one, we're liberating our American towns—can you believe that I'm saying that?" Trump said, acting amazed by his own wit. "I'm talking about liberating our towns. This is like I'd see in a movie: They're liberating the town, like in the old Wild West, right? We're liberating our towns."

Liberating our towns? The Wild West? What the fuck?

As an officer committed to protecting communities hit hardest by drug violence, I was gobsmacked. Soaking in the applause, Trump told the law enforcement crowd to stop worrying about treating citizens with respect. Go ahead, the president of the United States said. Feel free to abuse people you've arrested.

"Please don't be too nice," Trump said. "Like when you guys put somebody in the car, and you're protecting their head—you know, the way you put your hand over [their head so that they] don't hit their head. I say, 'You can take your hand away,' okay?"

His comments felt egregious, patronizing, and manipulative. Trump didn't really care about cops. He just wanted votes.

One day in 2019, while killing time in the surveillance van, I told Jimmy that I was done with Trump.

"Aren't you tired of being pissed off all the time?" I said. "I know I'm tired of getting texts that say if I don't give $5 right now, the radical Democrats will take away my guns and take away my country, that there won't be any whiteys in America anymore."

Suffice to say, Jimmy did not agree. Soon, we stopped talking politics, fearing it might end our friendship.

All that said, Trump's bullshit and racism didn't hit me personally until the pandemic began and he started calling Covid-19 the "China virus," an obvious dog whistle that drove a spike in hate against Asian Americans. As I've mentioned, three of my daughters and my ex-wife are Asian American. Even my youngest, age six, was old enough to let me know she was pissed off. It hurt me deeply, in ways I'd not previously imagined, when she told me classmates taunted her about Covid.

Some cops I worked with were as bad as the first graders. They threw out terms like "Kung Flu" with snide smirks, not realizing I have Asian American daughters. I rarely let that shit pass. I'd whip out my phone and show 'em pictures of my beautiful girls.

In November 2020, I voted for Joe Biden. It was an easy call. Like millions of Americans, I would have voted for Donald Duck over Donald Trump.

Afterward, I didn't pay much attention to Trump's bullshit about a rigged election. I was more focused on the deteriorating situation at work.

Though I remained dedicated to the job, I began to realize that the job was not necessarily as dedicated to me. This realization came slowly, as I watched living legends retire from the MPD, mentors who I credited with making me a good cop and the District of Columbia a safer city. One by one, veteran officers retired to great fanfare one day, and then the next day, it was as if they'd never even worked there. Life, and the MPD, moved on without them.

A sad memory from a few years back kept popping into my head: A detective I respected was wounded and wound up in the hospital, shot in the face while pursuing a fugitive down a dark alley. This detective had dedicated his entire life to the job. He had no wife or kids. I'll never forget the scene when my partner and I visited him in the hospital. A bunch of brass, including the chief, came in cradling their phones. They spoke with the detective briefly, but didn't really engage. They didn't even use his name. They just stood around staring, eyes down, tapping their phones, and finally drifted off into the hospital hallway.

My partner and I caught the detective's eyes, all three of us thinking the same thing: *Wow, you spend thirty years in fucking public service, make it to within a couple of months of retirement, nearly die in the line of duty, and this is the thanks you get.*

We were just cogs in the machine.

I began to develop an unfamiliar, queasy, and dangerous feeling. I wasn't angry anymore. After wave after wave of bullshit policy changes and nasty politics, I feared I was well on my way to becoming the kind of cop I'd always hated: an indifferent one.

I had a ton of personal leave stored, so I took off the back end of November and most of December. I hunted, I drank, and I hibernated. I caught up with friends and family I'd ignored for too long.

Just after New Year's Day, I returned to work.

On the first Tuesday evening in January, Jimmy and I grabbed a piece-of-shit undercover van and headed out to set up a surveillance post. On the way from the First District station to the Sursum Corda neighborhood, we rumbled past Capitol Hill. I can't recall if we noticed anything unusual. I guess we were focused on the job at hand.

The next day, January 6, 2021, we planned to meet Leslie and send her out to buy some dope.

PART II

DURING

CHAPTER 9

"Let's Hope Things Stay Calm"

On January 6, 2021, as is my habit, I woke at 6 a.m.

It figured to be a routine Wednesday: Lazy morning. Hit the gym. Head into work around 2 p.m. Buy heroin with Leslie. Maybe make an arrest, maybe not. Clock out around 10 p.m. Hit a bar with Jimmy.

But first: coffee.

I sat with my seventy-two-year-old mom in her kitchen, just shooting the shit. By now, she'd retired as a therapist, but still lived in the same brick, four-bedroom home where I'd spent some of my teen years during the 1990s. It was a middle-class neighborhood well south of Old Town in Alexandria, close to good public schools. The laundry room and garage were filled with toys for weekend visits with my girls. An American flag flew on the front lawn.

I'd been temporarily living at her place for a few months, and our morning talks had become a routine. A good daily grounding and mental reset.

It was still dark, an hour and a half before sunrise. The forecast was unremarkable: cloudy skies and temperatures in the forties. Headwinds were expected to sweep across the city in the afternoon, dropping the windchill to the high thirties. Just another gray and chilly day in early January. Hoodie weather.

Mom had CNN on in the living room, adjacent to the kitchen, and the television played in the background at low volume as we spoke. She rarely watched cable news but today I guess she felt the need. There was a lot going on.

The CNN headlines at that hour: Overnight, two special runoff elections in Georgia were tipping control of the U.S. Senate to the Democrats. That afternoon, Congress was set to certify Joe Biden's election. While Trump supporters vowed to mount a challenge, a CNN anchor predicted this would amount to no more than political theater. Vice President Mike Pence, who would preside over the vote, told reporters that he had concluded that he did not have the authority to block Biden's election. Still, things felt unsettled. A large crowd of Trump diehards were streaming toward the Ellipse, a park between the White House and the Washington Monument, for the president's last-ditch "Stop the Steal" rally.

"An enormous line at the Washington Monument, gathering since before three a.m., and waves of supporters for the president are still arriving now," a CNN reporter on the scene said. "We should note: There is an enormous law enforcement presence all across this city. There are street closures all around the city. A lot of vigilance over what is happening. The president is expected to speak here at eleven a.m. And then shortly after that, at around noon, these marchers are expected to walk all the way down to the Capitol, hoping to essentially overturn the results of the 2020 election."

I rolled my eyes and moved into the kitchen to grab another cup of coffee and something to eat. I pulled a carton of eggs from the fridge and tossed two in a frying pan. I filled the kettle with water, put it on the stove, and grabbed a plastic tub of oatmeal.

At 7 a.m., my mom dialed into a weekly Catholic prayer call with longtime friends from across the country. From the kitchen, I overheard the conversation turn to politics.

"Trump's not gonna go out easy," she said into the phone. I heard her lead a prayer for me and other officers.

I wasn't really concerned about my own safety because I never worked protests. The Secret Service and Park Police would be responsible for security at the Ellipse and the Capitol Police guarded their own grounds. MPD would assist on surrounding streets. Our specialized Civil Disturbance Units, known as CDUs, trained and deployed to handle demonstrations. During large protests, MPD also deployed dozens of CDU officers to protect property in the ritziest shopping districts, Georgetown and CityCenterDC.

In Washington, demonstrations, motorcades, and brief road closures are part of daily life. Most D.C. demonstrations are peaceful. The greatest risk is to property, not people. Most protests just create traffic hassles, and I assumed that would be the worst of it. The demonstration near the White House was more than a mile away from the First District station.

Jimmy and I had other plans for January 6th. A couple of younger uniformed officers, including Dan Kelly (with whom I'd worked on a number of recent cases), had received a complaint about heroin sales from a house near a public housing project. To get enough evidence for a search warrant, Kelly needed someone to make at least one undercover buy. Though we hadn't hashed out all the details, I expected that either Leslie or I, or each of us in separate trips, would enter the building around nightfall and buy a few zips.

Just another day at the office.

Around 8:40 a.m., I heard a reporter on the TV describe an overnight confrontation between Trump supporters and police on the other side of the White House, between Black Lives Matter Plaza and Lafayette Square.

"Remember," the reporter said, "that was the site of so much drama in the summertime, when social justice protesters confronted law enforcement. We heard President Trump demand law and order. We're not really hearing that from the president this time around. He seems fixated on trying to undo the 2020 election. We'll wait and see what he has to say at eleven, when he's set to speak. After that, all these supporters are expected to march over to the U.S. Capitol as proceedings start to get underway there."

"Let's hope things stay calm," the anchor replied.

No shit. I thought about my former partner Jeff, who I knew would be working crowd control. Jeff was probably already on the job. It sounded like he was going to have a long, long day.

Around 9 a.m., I headed to the gym to lift for an hour or so. I planned to grab some lunch, make a quick stop at my mom's to shower, and then head out around 2 p.m. to join Jimmy at the First District station.

I usually rotate my workouts daily. January 6th was a Wednesday, so I focused on cardio and leg lifts with free weights.

The TVs at the gym were tuned to cable news stations. I was cranking tunes through earbuds as I lifted, but caught glimpses of the TVs on the wall, which showed crowds massing near the Ellipse. I couldn't hear the TV, but I could follow the closed captioning.

A reporter near the White House said, "A number of things stand out to me about the event the president is holding this morning. First, the enormity of the crowd. It is massive. I don't think you can really appreciate it from what you're seeing behind me. It goes out towards the sides, beyond behind our cameras and the Washington Monument and there's a sea of people. The event organizers got a permit for about thirty thousand. I believe they're going to have to stop letting people in soon and from what I can tell on the sidewalks, throngs of people are still showing up. That's one.

"The second is the mood, the temperament. I have been to a number of Trump rallies, more than two dozen, and the animosity and the anger in the air are palpable and are being pushed forward by the rhetoric that's coming from the stage. A lot of them are not only peddling false-hoods but also ratcheting up the idea that these folks have to fight—in their eyes—to keep President Donald Trump in the White House to save the Republic. You pair that with what we saw last night, violence in the streets, some of the president's own supporters going toe-to-toe with police officers, not far from the very doorstep of the White House. It is a toxic mix."

Back at my mom's house, I found her on the living room couch, glued to the TV, flipping through cable news channels:

"In about two hours, Congress will begin counting the Electoral College votes . . ."

". . . Rudy Giuliani, who just spoke a few moments ago, saying they want trial by combat . . ."

". . . You can see the crowd forming behind me there on the National Mall, where the president is going to speak at any moment now . . ."

I went upstairs to shower. When I returned, my mom was watching Trump speak. He was bundled in a winter coat and gloves, red tie, white shirt, pumping his fist behind bulletproof glass, the White House in the background. He was talking about one of his favorite topics: crowd size.

"We have hundreds of thousands of people here and I just want them to be recognized by the fake news media," Trump said. "We will never give up, we will never concede. You don't concede when there's theft involved. Our country has had enough. We will not take it anymore and that's what this is all about. And to use a favorite term that all of you people really came up with: We will stop the steal. Today I will lay out just some of the evidence proving that we won this election and we won it by a landslide. This was not a close election."

From the kitchen, I laughed out loud. It sounded like standard Trump bullshit. My mom was not amused.

Trump went on: "We're gathered together in the heart of our nation's capital for one very, very basic and simple reason: To save our democracy . . . Republicans are constantly fighting like a boxer with his hands tied behind his back. And we want to be so nice. We want to be so respectful of everybody, including bad people. And we're going to have to fight much harder . . ."

Trump basked in applause, then said, "Now, it is up to Congress to confront this egregious assault on our democracy. And after this, we're going to walk down, and I'll be there with you, we're going to walk down. Because you'll never take back our country with weakness. You have to show strength and you have to be strong. We have come to demand that Congress do the right thing and only count the electors who have been lawfully slated. I know that everyone here will soon be marching over to the Capitol building to peacefully and patriotically make your voices heard."

═══

Trump was still speaking around 1 p.m. when I started receiving text messages from MPD cops already on the job. They warned that the crowd near the White House was massive—much larger than expected.

I flipped on my handheld MPD radio. I also carried an FBI radio because I worked so closely with the bureau on violent crime in Washington. The law enforcement radio frequencies were strong enough to reach my mom's house in Alexandria, and on the main MPD channel, I heard a call sign I recognized, "Cruiser 50." It was Commander Robert Glover, the head of our Special Operations Division, which includes the CDU crowd control units. I have a lot of respect for Glover. He's smart, dedicated, resourceful, and all about the job. He's also a savant—I've teased him that he's like Rain Man when it comes to the tactical deployment of officers.

"Has the Mall cleared up?" a dispatcher asked.

"Negative," Glover responded. "The crowd is shifting to the Capitol. We're supporting Capitol [police] on the west front."

The Capitol's West Terrace faces the Mall and Washington Monument. Every four years, a stage and scaffolding are erected on the West Terrace for the presidential inauguration. By January 6, 2021, much of it was already set up. From that side of the Capitol, the central entrance is the Lower West Terrace Tunnel. It's where the new president emerges on Inauguration Day to take the oath.

I was not alarmed by Glover's initial broadcasts. At that point, all I knew was that Trump protesters had shifted to the Capitol and that the

MPD's Civil Disturbance Units had been deployed to help. On CNN, talking heads droned on about the debate inside the Capitol, cutting in and out of boring speeches on the House and Senate floors.

Glover's next two transmissions jolted me.

"Cruiser 50. Authorizing hard gear. Hard gear at the Capitol."

"Hard gear" was an order to don riot equipment—helmets, gloves, batons, gas masks. Until that moment, most Civil Disturbance Unit officers had been defending the Capitol in regular uniforms. Every CDU officer arrived in a bulletproof vest and a few wore bicycle helmets. But as part of the city's de-escalation strategy, designed to prevent provoking protesters, most officers had stored riot gear out of sight.

The call for riot equipment was a turning point. It meant protesters had turned violent against the police.

Glover's tone surprised me. On the radio, he sounded rushed and out of breath. He also struggled to be heard over the roar of the crowd—also a bad sign.

About a minute later, I heard Glover call for munitions, including tear gas, rubber bullets, and flash bang grenades—another major escalation. Glover ordered another CDU unit to the West Terrace, and described the scene, growing more chaotic by the moment. He said the crowd had breached the mobile metal blockades, which look a lot like bike racks.

"They're throwing bike racks!" he said over the radio. "They're throwing bike racks!"

My mom was sitting on the couch, a few steps away, and could hear the radio reports, too. She stared at me. I tried not to betray my own concern.

Then we heard Glover say: "Multiple Capitol injuries. Multiple Capitol injuries." I understood that meant that officers, not protesters, were hurt. The shit was getting out of hand.

"Be advised," a dispatcher said, "you have a group of fifty charging up the hill on the left."

Charging up the hill? What the fuck? It sounded like a coordinated attack, not a protest.

At 1:16 p.m., Glover repeated his call for munitions.

"Multiple law enforcement injuries!" he said, voice now frantic. "Get up here!"

On the TV in my mom's living room, I saw the first images of people and flags converging on the West Terrace. Even from the initial pictures, you could tell that a shitload of Trump people came ready to fight, dressed in camo and battle rattle. On the radio, I heard something go boom, and an officer said, "We just had an explosion go off. I don't know if it's fireworks or what."

My phone lit up with Jimmy's name.

"Dude, are you watching this?" Jimmy said.

"Yeah. About to head in now."

"What are you hearing?"

Jimmy lived out in rural Maryland, too far from the city to catch the MPD frequency on his police radio. I told Jimmy what I'd heard, and said I'd meet him at the First District station. I grabbed my gear and loaded my truck.

My mom came out to the driveway and insisted that I wait while she said one more prayer. It was the same one she always said when I headed out to work, though she rarely spoke it to me out loud. The prayer includes a reference to St. Michael, the patron saint of police officers.

In the driveway, we bowed our heads.

"Holy Spirit," she said. "Protect my Michael. Be in his eyes in his seeing, in his ears in his hearing, his lips in his speaking, his heart in his thinking. St. Michael, surround him. Amen."

My mom dipped her finger into a cup of holy water, and made a cross on my forehead. I'm not very religious. But I'm smart enough to take whatever help I can get. I gave her a quick hug and told her not to worry.

I climbed into the truck and hit the road, weaving through neighborhoods toward the George Washington Parkway.

CHAPTER 10

"10-33"

On the parkway, I raced past National Airport, doing 70 mph in a 35 mph zone.

The FBI radio, mostly silent, came to life with a chilling call to deploy two units of the Hostage Rescue Team to the Capitol.

Holy shit. Had rioters kidnapped members of Congress?

I floored it up the parkway, weaving in and out of traffic, which slowed to a crawl as I approached the 14th Street Bridge, my route into the city. Where I could, I roared off-road onto the grass between the parkway and the river, holding my badge out the window. At the ramp to the bridge, I hit a wall of standstill traffic. There are no shoulders on the bridge. I was trapped.

On the MPD channel, I heard Glover give another urgent update. "They're scaling the scaffold. They are scaling the scaffold to the Capitol!"

What the absolute fuck?

I knew the Capitol well enough to know that the protesters were now yards away from breaching several key entrances and congressional offices. I leaned on the horn and tried to power across the river.

Dispatchers and officers are trained to keep their emotions in check on the radio. Everyone understands the broadcasts are recorded and that officers in stressful situations perform better when everyone stays calm and professional. But it was hard to miss a growing sense of panic on the radio.

At 1:49 p.m., while still on the bridge, I heard another insane exchange over the MPD channel:

"This is now effectively a riot."

"Dispatch, 1349 hours. Declaring it a riot."

I hit the horn again and called Jimmy. The decision to change plans was an easy one. It went something like this:

Over the phone, I said, "What the fuck, dude?"

"Yup," Jimmy said. "Better call Leslie."

"Yeah. Look, grab your uniform. I'm about five minutes out. Get us a car?"

"Yup."

I dialed Leslie and explained that Jimmy and I had to help out with the trouble at the Capitol, and so we'd have to meet another time.

"Well," she replied, "maybe later tonight."

"Yeah, we'll see." I told her I had to jump, and promised to call back later.

Back on the radio, I heard Glover report that his officers were overrun. "They're behind our lines!"

"If you need to, pull back," someone responded. "If they're getting behind you, you don't have enough resources."

Glover rejected that. "If I give this up, they're going to have direct access," he said, his voice straining against crowd noise. "We gotta hold what we have."

A minute later, Glover returned, desperate. "We cannot hold this without more munitions and manpower . . ."

As I finally made it over the bridge, I heard more units deployed.

At 2:28 p.m., Glover said grimly, "We've lost the line. We've lost the line!"

Then he ordered a retreat. "All MPD, up to the upper deck! ASAP!"

I pulled into the First District station, five blocks south of the Capitol, on the other side of the freeway. At about that moment, Glover sent out a 10-33 distress call, the code for "officer down," requesting an all-hands response. In this case, he made the 10-33 call on behalf of his entire unit, not just one or two officers.

In my twenty years as a police officer, I'd never heard such a call.

"We're flanked, 10-33!" Glover said. "I repeat: 10-33, west end of the Capitol. We've been flanked and we've lost the line."

A dispatcher's voice broke in, her voice cracking: "All units respond to assist him! Do what you're trained to do!"

I bounded up the stairs to our second-floor office. I found Jimmy near his cubicle pulling on his uniform and black riot gear.

"What's the plan?" he said.

"I'll suit up and grab the BWCs," I said, referring to the rechargeable body-worn cameras MPD officers wear on their chests. "You get us a car?"

I bolted to my locker, which I visited about once a year. My uniform and pants were still wrapped inside the original plastic bag. As a plain-clothes officer, I rarely wore a bulletproof vest and so I had to assemble that, too.

I grabbed my gas mask and the black riot helmet with the letters "MPDC" stenciled across the back. I swung by a docking station and grabbed two body-worn cameras, which are about half the size of a cell phone.

I met Jimmy in the hallway and tossed him a camera. He held up a pair of keys. Usually, it took time and a bit of bureaucracy to snag a car. I asked how he got one so fast.

He said, "There's a sergeant giving them to anyone willing to help."

Willing to help? By now, anyone watching TV or listening to the MPD radio knew that fellow officers were in fear for their lives, counting on a rescue. Our district station was the closest to the Capitol. But as Jimmy and I headed to the cruiser, we saw a few officers just standing around, watching the TV. I don't know what the fuck they were doing or what the fuck they were thinking. It's possible they were simply awaiting orders, or were just indifferent. We didn't stop to ask.

Jimmy drove. Siren wailing, lights flashing, we reached the Capitol in three minutes. We found MPD and Capitol Police cruisers stacked parallel along Independence Avenue, but one lane was open. I pointed to an entrance and Jimmy sped onto the Capitol grounds on the House side.

A barrier at a checkpoint blocked our path, and two Capitol cops calmly strolled toward our car, as if it were just any other day. The cops said we needed a pass to park on the grounds.

Jimmy went ballistic. We were in uniform in a marked police car. We'd come to help rescue officers in distress during a riot and we needed . . . a parking pass?

"You've gotta be fucking kidding me," Jimmy said, and floored it in reverse.

We both understood what these cops were thinking. In times of stress, officers fall back on training. These guys were trained to deny entrance to anyone without a pass. It's all they knew. Ninety minutes into the Capitol riot, they were too shell-shocked to improvise.

We wasted another two minutes looking for a spot to dump the car. Jimmy found some sidewalk space near a congressional office building, and I put on a thin blue Covid mask. I didn't always wear one on the job, but here I was headed into the unknown, into a confrontation with screaming, mostly maskless Trump protesters—not exactly the kind of crowd you'd expect to be closely following Covid protocols. At this point in early 2021, vaccines were not yet available to police officers or the elderly, just frontline health care workers. I wasn't worried about what might happen to me if I caught Covid, but the last thing I wanted to do was pass it on to my seventy-two-year-old mom.

As I got out of the squad car, I struggled to loop my tear-gas mask onto my belt. After a half minute of messing with it, I thought, *Screw this*, and dumped the thing in the front seat.

CHAPTER 11

Patriots

It took us about two minutes to hike uphill to the Capitol grounds.

We crossed Independence Avenue and hopped over a bicycle rack barrier. Approaching from the southeastern entrance, things seemed fairly calm. Eerily quiet. We saw small bands of protesters drifting around aimlessly. From our vantage point on the eastern side of the Capitol, we couldn't see the chaos on the other side.

Over the radio, I heard Glover call out another 10-33. "MPD platoon inside the Capitol. You've got to send resources!"

Jimmy and I were moving quickly, about a hundred feet from the Capitol's southeastern entrance, when we passed through the first stream of Trump supporters. It was not a large group, maybe a few dozen. They screamed like maniacs into the brisk January air.

"Every fucking door! Every fucking window! Whoooo!"

"USA! USA! USA!"

"Here we go, patriots!"

They heckled us as we marched past.

"1776!"

"You're on the wrong team!"

"Fuck you, you traitors!"

The insults didn't faze me. It did piss me off to hear them call Jimmy a traitor. The man had earned a Purple Heart for wounds sustained in Afghanistan while serving his country. He'd returned for multiple tours of duty. He was already a certified American patriot, a hero.

Jimmy brushed off the taunts with sarcasm. "That's hurtful." My body-worn camera caught him smiling as he said it.

It was the last time either of us would smile for a really fucking long time.

A radio call came out that the CDU units had run out of riot-control munitions. Not just at the Capitol. The entire department was dry, and the CDU units were being overrun. As I began to grasp what this meant—*those guys were fucked*—an MPD cop asked me where they were holding prisoners. I told him I had no clue.

Jimmy and I were now about thirty steps from the Capitol. Over the MPD radio, we heard someone say: "Capitol [police] has requested our assistance clearing the Rotunda."

So we headed inside. On the elevated ramp to the southern Capitol entrance, Jimmy turned to point out pools of blood. A few Trumpers with flags strode past us, headed outside. Entering the Capitol on the first floor, we passed members of the FBI SWAT team toting automatic rifles and about a dozen MPD and Capitol officers. They stood at the entrance to a hundred-foot hallway called the Hall of Columns, which led to the Capitol Crypt, directly below the Rotunda.

In the Hall of Columns, we passed statues of real-life patriots. Heroes like Roger Williams, seventeenth-century advocate for religious freedom; Francis Preston Blair, abolitionist and Civil War general; and Esther Hobart Morris, nineteenth-century women's rights pioneer.

As Jimmy and I moved through the Hall of Columns, the roar of the crowd outside grew louder.

The scene inside the Crypt was much more chaotic. The Crypt is a round, vaulted space at the center of the Capitol, and has thirteen statues representing the original thirteen colonies. There are also a bunch of historical exhibits, including a replica of the Magna Carta.

When we arrived in the Crypt, there were about thirty or forty MAGA rioters, and about a dozen police officers. There was a lot of yelling going on, but we didn't see any physical confrontations, just Trump morons marching around in circles, screaming, prancing, and waving flags. A few tried to provoke the officers with verbal taunts. Others just stood there, gawking at the scene, recording it with their phones. In the distance, we could hear muffled chants of "USA! USA!" But it was hard to know where they were coming from.

Across the Crypt, the voice of a protester with a bullhorn echoed off the stone floor. A man in a gas mask held a DON'T TREAD ON ME flag, with his other hand casually in his pocket, oddly fixated on one of the historical exhibits. A man with a MAGA hat climbed up on a statue and let out an insane primeval wail. A Capitol cop rushed over and pushed him away.

A clean-cut, thirtysomething dude in a red hat approached Jimmy and mumbled something. The man wore a T-shirt that said, THERE WILL BE A WILD PROTEST, WASHINGTON, D.C., JANUARY 6, 2021, 12:00 P.M. (Later, that shirt would come back to haunt his ass. In pictures the FBI posted online, it made it that much easier to identify and arrest him.) At that moment, though, Jimmy just shrugged at the guy and we kept walking.

A fat, middle-aged man dressed mostly in black passed us as he circled the Crypt, jabbing the air with his finger as he shouted at police. "You are traitors to your own house! This is the United States of America! And you're on the wrong fucking side!"

Maskless, the fat guy approached a masked Capitol officer, still raging, flailing his finger, spewing spit and hate. The masked officer pushed back, but the guy kept yelling. His face was beet red. I thought he was going to have an aneurysm.

Slumped along a wall, I saw a few Capitol officers who looked like they'd gotten the shit kicked out of them.

I grew impatient and thought, *What the fuck are we doing here? How can we help?* So far, the protesters didn't seem too violent, just really, really fucking obnoxious. Maybe we'd missed the worst of it. Maybe things were settling down.

Jimmy and I paused in the Crypt to catch our bearings. We stood beside a marble statue of another actual patriot, John Peter Gabriel Muhlenberg, a general for the Continental Army during the Revolutionary War.

With all the yelling, it was hard to hear the radio. We heard snippets of other departments responding from Maryland and Virginia. Then I heard a voice I'd recognize anywhere.

It was Ramey Kyle, my buddy since my punk rock days. At MPD, Ray had risen swiftly through the ranks—from patrol to detective to sergeant to lieutenant to captain to commander. Apparently, Ray had self-deployed, too.

Over the radio, I heard him say, "10-33 Lower West Tunnel."

Ray repeated the 10-33 call a couple of times.

Hearing no response, Jimmy and I scrambled. We had no idea where the fuck the Lower West Terrace Tunnel was. We asked a Capitol cop and he pointed down a set of stairs, just off the Crypt.

We passed a sign for a restricted area for members of Congress, just below the House chamber. We scurried down three dozen marble steps toward the tunnel. The chants grew louder.

"USA! USA! USA!"

At the first set of double doors to the tunnel, everything changed.

The floor was stained with blood and vomit. In a makeshift triage area, exhausted officers sat against a wall, dry heaving. A few lay on their backs, while other officers tended to them. They looked beat to hell.

I saw abandoned gear scattered everywhere: MPD mountain bikes, Capitol Police riot shields, Covid masks, water bottles, and batons. The floor was littered with shit the rioters had thrown at the officers: poles, sticks, shoes, *fucking sledgehammers*, ladders, rocks, bricks, batteries, and spent cans of bear spray. A yellow DON'T TREAD ON ME flag lay crumpled in a corner.

A large officer in shoulder pads burst through the doors, helmet in hand, spinning in agony, trying to flush his eyes with a bottle of water.

Ahead, I saw hazy white smoke floating above a crowd of maybe forty officers, plugging the tunnel with their bodies. They were crammed so tight you couldn't fit a credit card between them.

Another step and I could taste and smell the smoke.

Tear gas.

Instinctively, I fumbled at my belt for the gas mask I'd left in the car. *Shit*, I thought. *This is gonna suck.*

We went in.

CHAPTER 12

"Hold the Line"

At 3:13 p.m., precisely the minute I entered the Lower West Terrace Tunnel, Donald Trump sent out a tweet.

"I am asking for everyone at the U.S. Capitol to remain peaceful. No violence! Remember, WE are the Party of Law & Order—respect the Law and our great men and women in Blue. Thank you!"

Too little, too late, asshole.

Of course, no one on the front lines saw the tweet at the time. The police were too busy defending the Capitol. The rioters were too busy rioting.

Inside the tunnel, the forty officers, almost all MPD, jammed the narrow space, wall to wall, and about thirty feet deep. Picture a rugby team pushing in a scrum, body pressed against body, dodging flying debris. It was a barbaric scene.

The West Terrace Tunnel is the carotid artery of the Capitol, its veins leading toward the House and Senate chambers. Although a handful of rioters had already breached those chambers through other entrances and by crawling through broken windows, the officers in the West Terrace Tunnel did not know this. At the time, all they knew was that the size of the crowd pushing to enter the tunnel numbered in the thousands. If the West Terrace Tunnel fell, the Capitol would be overrun.

As Jimmy and I approached the tunnel, MPD Sergeant Bill Bogner, someone I knew well, emerged. Bogner worked at the MPD academy, and had also self-deployed. At that moment, he was trying to flush his smoke-filled eyes with a bottle of water.

"You okay, Sarge?" I said.

"Yeah, just got a face full of bear mace," he said. It was obvious he didn't recognize me.

"It's Fanone," I said. "You good?"

He reached out his hand, awkwardly, to shake mine, as if we were meeting for the first time. At that moment, things began to turn surreal. Time slowed.

Bogner told us that the cops at the other end of the tunnel had been fighting the rioters for thirty minutes. It was a little after 3 p.m., so in reality that meant these guys had been defending the tunnel for nearly ninety minutes. I didn't see the point in correcting Bogner.

Then I saw someone in a commander's outfit emerge from the tunnel scrum—no helmet, no vest, no protection, just a trench coat and a policeman's hat adorned with silver eagles. It was Ray, coughing and rubbing his eyes. I felt weirdly comforted to be surrounded by friends. With his command presence, Ray looked like General George Patton. I was prepared to follow him anywhere.

I tightened the chinstrap on my riot helmet.

Ahead, I could hear officers coughing and choking, and I could hear the roar of the crowd outside. Jimmy and I joined Ray by pushing on the backs of officers in the tunnel, using the weight of our bodies to hold off the angry mob.

"Hold it!" Ray screamed.

Three exhausted officers in gas masks peeled out, hacking from gas, and the rest of the police line surged forward to fill the space. Jimmy and I kept pushing from behind.

"Hold the line!" Ray shouted. "Do not give up that door! We are not going to lose that door! Hold the line!"

Jimmy and I looked at each other. We hadn't come to help hold the line from the back. This is where we would make our stand. We pushed forward, pulling dazed colleagues to safety, some still standing only because there was no place to fall.

"Let's get some fresh guys up front!" I said, gagging as the gas hit my nose, my Covid mask worthless.

"Alright," Jimmy said. "Let's go."

"Let's get some fresh faces up front!" I said. "Fresh faces up front!"

I clawed my way forward, past exhausted men and women, blood and chemical irritants smeared across their faces and hands.

"C'mon," I said. "Who needs a break?"

Jimmy called out, "Back up if you need a break."

No one volunteered.

Jimmy and I started extracting officers anyway. "Get 'em to the back!" I said as I pushed two fatigued colleagues toward the rear. Later I learned that one of the injured was MPD Officer Daniel Hodges, who'd been crushed between doors at the entrance just one minute before I arrived. A close-up video of the officer pinned helplessly and wailing in horror would soon go viral and become one of the more visceral scenes from January 6th.

I reached the front line at a set of brass double doors, about twenty feet inside the tunnel, and came face-to-face with the rioters. I got my first sense of the sheer scope of what we were up against—*thousands* of crazed, violent Trump supporters, facing off against a couple dozen police officers for control of the tunnel.

Officers tried to beat them back with batons, but the rioters blocked the blows with stolen Capitol Police riot shields. The mob threw whatever they could find—ladders, fire extinguishers, and bricks. I pushed against a man wearing a MAKE AMERICA GREAT AGAIN hoodie, military-grade gas mask, and a motorcycle helmet with a go-pro camera on top. I battled a guy dressed head-to-toe in olive militia gear, pushing one of the stolen police shields against us.

"Get out of our house!" a male rioter screamed. "This is our fucking house!"

"Why are you doing this to us?" a female Trumpster yelled.

In my best deep-bass police voice I bellowed, "Back it up! Back it up!"

I don't know why, but I tried to reason with them.

"C'mon, we've got injured officers," I said. "We've got to get these doors closed. Help us out."

Big fucking mistake. That only enraged the mob, triggering a "heave-ho!" call-and-response, and they started ramming us again, swaying rhythmically, synchronizing leverage, like a human battering ram, inching us backward.

"Heave, ho! Heave, ho! Heave, ho! Heave, ho!"

Then, "Push! Push!"

The mob charged forward with more riot shields. A rioter shouted, "You're attacking the wrong people!"

We pushed back.

"MPD dig in!" I grunted. My bare hands were pushing the door back against the rioters. "What the fuck! MPD, dig in! C'mon, push!"

It was brutal hand-to-hand combat, a meat grinder. We were packed together so tightly, I didn't even have enough space to cock a fist and punch back. My only weapon was my body weight, and the strength of the officers pushing behind me.

A rioter smashed me in the head with a stolen police shield. Separated by the four-by-two-foot plexiglass barrier, we were inches apart and I could read the white supremacist patch on his T-shirt.

I felt someone grip my left shoulder, and Jimmy said, "I got you, Mike. That's my hand."

"Push 'em back!" I yelled. I took a poke to the eye, but kept shoving forward, toward the threshold of the tunnel.

"That's it, MPD!" I shouted, choking on tear gas. "Push them the fuck out!"

We were doing just that. We were pushing them the fuck out of the Capitol. Jimmy was right behind me. "Keep pushing!" he yelled.

We were nearly outside, gaining momentum, when someone yelled, "Knife!"

I turned toward the warning, and as I did a rioter pulled me into a bear hug, wrapping his forearms around my neck. We tumbled sideways and he yelled, "I got one!"

My boots left the ground and in a flash, I was outside.

CHAPTER 13

"Kill Him with His Own Gun"

I **was** sucked into the crowd, yanked face-first down the marble steps.

It felt like I'd been smacked by a wave at the beach and dragged by the undertow. I took a blow to the upper back, probably from a pipe or a police baton, in the unprotected space between my helmet and vest. Punches came from all directions. Rioters pounded my arms, stomped my back, kicked my legs, and scratched at my face. When I managed to look up, I saw eyes lit with fury and hate.

Surrounded, I was lifted to my feet and violently frog-marched into a raging mob.

I caught my first wide-angle glimpse of the crowd and was stunned by the scene, which we couldn't see from inside the Capitol. A chaotic sea of terrorists, thousands of them, stretched to the horizon. Rioters in red hats, camo, helmets, goggles, Trump gear, and American flags. Everyone seemed to be converging toward this one choke point, toward me.

A bearded man with a skull on his shirt took a swing at my head. The pole of a Blue Lives Matter flag crashed into my shoulder. It hurt like a motherfucker. A guy in a gray DON'T TREAD ON ME sweatshirt lunged at me, wild-eyed, arms flailing.

My first fear was that I'd be trampled to death. I took more punches from every angle to my head and biceps. My forearms pinned, I was pulled and shoved and kicked.

My next thought was that I would be torn limb from limb. A scene from *Black Hawk Down* flashed through my mind: the downed U.S. helicopter pilot in Mogadishu, getting dragged, dead and half-naked, through a mob of celebrating Somalis.

I felt hands grabbing at my gear. Rioters ripped off my badge and took my radio. They tugged at my spare ammunition clip. I caught a glimpse of a hand on the butt of my gun and pushed it away. I tried to fling my elbows to create some space, but there were too many hands holding me back.

A man with a head wound came at me, teeth bared, blood streaming down his face. I recognized that lethal look in his eyes; he was jacked up, probably on testosterone, steroids, or some other ball-shrinking drug.

I managed to right myself, and realized I was now about fifty feet from the tunnel entrance. *Fuck*, I was being pushed in the wrong direction.

My path was blocked by a very large dude, maybe six foot five. He wore dark sunglasses, a black helmet, and an olive military vest with a patch for the Three Percenters, an anti-government militia whose philosophy includes the belief that a small armed force can overthrow a tyrannical government. On his left upper arm, he had a QAnon patch.

I tried to push past a gray-bearded man in a TEAM TRUMP cowboy hat, but someone held me back. A white-bearded man grabbed my right hand with both of his hands and tried to yank my fingers apart.

It was then that I felt an insane fucking jolt of pain on my neck, near the base of my skull. My limbs shuddered and I howled in agony.

Someone had a fucking taser. They were electrocuting me.

I felt another hot poke on my neck and another debilitating surge through my body. My legs buckled, but I didn't fall. I shrieked like a wounded animal.

I whirled and came face-to-face with a disheveled maniac with long, red stringy hair and an overgrown goatee. Someone bellowed, "Kill him with his own gun!"

Fuck. Fuck. Fuck. Getting shot with your own weapon is every cop's nightmare.

Decades of training, street experience, and undercover improvisation kicked in. Amid the chaos, it's amazing how time slowed even further.

I forced myself not to panic. I began thinking slowly, deliberately: *I've been threatened enough to use deadly force. I have a gun—a Glock 19 with fifteen shots. But can I even get the gun out of my holster? And if I pull my weapon, what will happen next? These people are all already fucking outraged. No doubt, more than a few of them are armed. Why pull my gun and give them a reason to kill me?*

I moved to Plan B, psychology. I thought, *What's the best way to de-escalate the situation?* I appealed to the crowd's humanity.

"I've got kids!" I screamed. "I've got kids!"

I said this consciously and deliberately. I would have said it even if I didn't have kids. In truth, I wasn't thinking about my daughters. At that moment, I was only thinking about survival.

It worked.

=====

I have no memory of what followed, but various videos, including my body-worn camera, recorded the next few minutes:

A small group of rioters pushed their way toward me, and someone shouted, "Don't hurt him!"

Another screamed, "We're better than this!"

The mob started shoving me back toward the tunnel. Disoriented and in shock, I struggled to put one foot in front of the other.

I slipped and someone gripped me under the arms. "Hold on," the guy said. "I got you!"

He was met with anger. "What the fuck are you doing?" "You can't let him through!"

Saner voices prevailed. "Let him through! Let him through!"

"Make way! Make way!"

They pushed my limp body up the stairs.

"Bring him up!"

"I got ya."

"Don't hurt him."

A voice said, "You're safe," and asked me which way I wanted to go.

"Back inside," I said.

Thankfully, the rioters did not take my body-worn camera, and it continued to record.

At the tunnel entrance, I collapsed and lost consciousness.

"Officer down!"

I lay sprawled among debris from the riot, the rocks, poles, and police shields. One cop grabbed my feet and another lifted me under the arms. They carried me back through the tunnel, through the phalanx of officers guarding the Capitol. "Make way!"

They laid me flat on my back.

"We need a medic! We need EMT now!"

"Take his helmet off."

"Need a medic!"

Someone put in a radio call for help. "Need an ambulance, code blue."

A cop leaned over me, presumably to begin CPR, but Jimmy appeared and pushed him away.

"I got it," Jimmy said. "It's my partner."

Four guys lifted me up by my limbs and carried me deeper inside the Capitol.

"Mike, stay in there, buddy," my partner said. "Mike, it's Jimmy, I'm here."

After a few steps, Jimmy said, "Hey, take his fucking vest off. He's having trouble breathing. Hold on."

They laid me on a carpeted floor.

"Mike?" Jimmy said. "Mike, I'm here for you, buddy. C'mon dude."

Other officers joined in, trying to bring me back to consciousness.

"Fanone? Fanone?"

"Fanone, what's up, brother?"

I stirred. I was on my back, looking straight into a harsh ceiling light in one of the Capitol's labyrinth passageways. Officers in helmets and gas masks hovered, studying my face. They looked like aliens in some kind of sci-fi movie. Hazy smoke lingered. My eyes stung.

Jimmy returned into view, maskless. "C'mon, Mike. C'mon, buddy. We're going duck hunting soon."

I snapped back to full consciousness. "Did we take that door back?"

"Yes, we did," Jimmy said. "We took that fucking door back and they're all outside. I've got your gun, buddy."

I rolled onto my left side and let out a roar.

CHAPTER 14

"My Neck Hurts So Bad"

In the makeshift triage area about fifty feet inside the tunnel, Jimmy pulled me up to a sitting position.

"Alright, Mike," Jimmy said. "We're about to go for a ride. C'mon, man."

On the body-cam footage, you can hear me huffing and puffing, breathing like Darth Vader.

Someone rolled up a cart, a metal dolly for moving heavy shit.

Fuck no, I thought. "I'll walk," I said, foolishly. "Help me up."

Officers helped me stand and I immediately realized I was in bad shape. I didn't feel physical pain, as the adrenaline was still flooding through my body. But when I tried to walk, my equilibrium felt off, and once more I struggled to put one foot in front of the other. Jimmy and another guy helped me shuffle forward as we followed a Capitol officer who led us to an elevator. He pushed the buttons and nothing happened.

"Hmm," he said. "It's not working." *No shit*, I thought to myself. *We're in the middle of a fucking riot in the Capitol. Shutting off the elevators is probably part of the security protocol.*

Jimmy and I moved on, arms around each other's shoulders, weaving through smoke and debris, making our own way through the maze of tiny corridors, fumbling for any safe exit.

The journey out was excruciating. In total, it probably took about five minutes but it felt like much longer than that.

With blurred vision, I walked through smoke, fighting for air, past injured cops and terrorists. When we finally emerged into daylight, I told Jimmy I had to rest for a sec.

"Dude," I said to Jimmy, "my neck hurts so bad."

Jimmy took a look. I could tell from his face it wasn't good.

"Dude, what happened?" he said.

"They were tasing me."

Jimmy took a picture with his cell phone and showed me. My neck was red, scalded with burns.

Jimmy spotted an FBI SWAT team and knew that many of the guys on those units cross-trained as medics. His instincts were correct. An FBI medic checked me for wounds and other visible signs of trauma. He told me I needed to get to a hospital.

Before we could ask questions, he took off with his team, headed into the Capitol. Jimmy decided our best bet was to walk back to our squad car. In the chaos, we both knew it would be pointless to wait for an ambulance.

We headed toward our makeshift parking spot near South Capitol Street, about three city blocks away. Staggering down Capitol Hill, we passed a group of badass-looking Virginia State Police troopers in riot gear, marching into the mayhem. Once we crossed Independence Avenue, we stopped again to catch our breath on a stoop outside a congressional office building. A Capitol officer still standing a post outside the entrance approached us. He looked fresh-faced and uninjured, as if he'd spent the entire riot right there, pretty much guarding nothing.

He said, "You guys good? Everything okay?"

I started to respond, but, as if on cue, Jimmy projectile vomited.

When we reached the car, Jimmy tried to raise a supervisor on the radio, but the channels were jammed with chatter. He decided to swing by the First District station, which was only a few blocks away, check in, and then head to MedStar Washington Hospital Center. (MedStar is about three miles north of the Capitol and it's the city's best trauma center.) I don't remember much about the drive. Jimmy says I drifted in and out of consciousness.

I do vividly recall that when we pulled up to the ER entrance—one cop in uniform dragging a fellow uniformed officer, clearly injured, from a marked police car—that a security guard blocked our way.

"Are you guys coming inside?" the guard said.

"Yeah," Jimmy said. "He's really hurt."

"Alright, well you have to wear masks."

I thought Jimmy was going to fucking kill the guy. Jimmy picked me up and carried me past the guard and through the front doors to the intake station. The woman at the desk asked me for my driver's license and insurance card.

It was at that moment I fucking collapsed.

The next thing I recall is rolling through a hallway in a wheelchair, passing a dozen battered cops on chairs and the floor, and nurses tending to them in full Covid protection gear. They wheeled me into a curtained-off area in the ER, laid me on a gurney, and stripped off my clothes. As a precaution, they put me in a neck brace.

I spent the next few hours enduring tests, including an ear-splitting MRI and a seemingly endless CT scan. Back at the ER, while waiting on my test results, a nurse asked me how I was doing.

"I don't know," I replied. "How *am* I doing?"

"Everything's great," she lied. "You're doing fine."

"No, no," I said, pointing to my crotch. "How am I doing?"

She laughed. "I'm sure that'll be fine."

I closed my eyes for a while.

I woke to screams from the other side of the curtain in my ER room. "Who shot me in the face?" a man fumed. "Who shot me in the face?"

It soon became pretty obvious the guy was a Trump supporter and had stormed the Capitol. I realized that if he'd been shot in the face, he'd made it pretty far inside the building. He was a terrorist—not a protester—and we lay only a few feet apart, separated by a thin blue curtain.

"They shot me in the face!" he whined again and again. "They shot me in the face!"

He just kept hollering and my head pounded. I started screaming, too. "Shut the fuck up! Somebody shut that guy the fuck up!"

I don't know what they did to him, but he fell silent.

I lay in the bed for a long time, locked in a neck brace, hooked to monitors, and surrounded by the privacy curtain, but still close to the hustle and chatter in the overwhelmed ER.

Someone helped me call my mom. Jimmy had already briefed her on my condition.

"Mom?"

"Wink, are you okay?"

As a child, I liked to sleep a lot and my mom used to call me Rip Van Winkle, or "Wink" for short. She hadn't used that nickname in decades.

It was tough to talk with the neck brace. "Mom, they tried to kill me."

"Oh, Wink."

"Mom, they tried to kill me."

"I'm sorry, I'm sorry. Any broken bones?"

"You should have seen their faces, Mom. They tried to kill me."

"I love you, Wink."

"Love you, Mom."

At some point, a doctor emerged from behind the curtain and gave me the bad news: I'd suffered a heart attack and brain trauma severe enough to require close supervision. But because Covid and the Capitol riot had overwhelmed MedStar and most other local hospitals, there were no beds for me anywhere in the city. A nurse said they planned to fly me by helicopter to Mercy Medical Center in Baltimore.

"You've got to be fucking kidding me," I said.

I spent the next hour dreading the transfer. At this point, the last thing I needed was a loud, bumpy helicopter ride to Baltimore. I was already nauseous and my head still fucking pounded. It was so intense my brain rattled with every high-pitched bleep from the heart monitor. I don't know how it happened, but thankfully MedStar ultimately found a bed for me there, and I was allowed to stay.

No one could visit, of course, because of Covid, and frankly I didn't want to see anyone anyway. I was a mess. I don't like narcotics and refused most of the pain meds they offered. Still jacked up on adrenaline, I couldn't sleep.

Sometime after 2 a.m., I flipped on the TV and CNN appeared.

At the time, I hated CNN. I wasn't a big Fox News guy, but before January 6th, I was an aggressive CNN hater. It was more about style than substance—too many talking heads screaming at each other. If I was out getting my tires rotated and I saw CNN playing in the waiting room, I'd walk over and shut that shit off. But now, for some reason I can't explain, I became transfixed as I watched Don Lemon and Chris Cuomo host the resumption of the presidential election certification at the Capitol.

I'm sure the meds I did accept made me woozy. I couldn't make out much of what they said, but I do recall thinking: *Those guys look drunk.* I don't remember specifics, except that I have a clear memory of Mike Pence standing in the well of the House of Representatives, next to Speaker Nancy Pelosi, as they resumed the Joint Session of Congress.

Reading from cue cards, Pence spoke in a weird, flat voice. To me, his administrative tone failed to match the tension or significance of the moment. I'm not sure what I expected, but Pence presided over the proceedings with all the excitement of a county clerk at a Board of Supervisors meeting.

"The whole number of electors appointed to vote for president of the United States is five-hundred and thirty-eight," Pence said. "Within that whole number, a majority is two-hundred and seventy. The votes for president of the United States are as follows: Joseph R. Biden Jr. of the State of Delaware has received three hundred and six votes. Donald J. Trump of the State of Florida has received two hundred and thirty-two votes."

As part of the formalities, Pence repeated the same tally for Kamala Harris and himself, then added a sentence or two of legalese. Finally, he paused, looked up from his cue cards, and said, "The chair declares the Joint Session dissolved."

It was over. The man who received the most votes won.

I felt a sudden urge to take a shower.

Gingerly, I sat up, swung my legs to the floor, and steadied myself on the bedrail. Dragging a pole on wheels that held my IV bag, I shuffled toward the bathroom. I felt sore as hell and exhausted. I hadn't eaten anything in nearly twenty-four hours. I stepped into the shower stall, cranked up the hot water, and exhaled.

In the first few seconds, the shower felt amazing, soothing both body and soul. But as the water mixed with residue from all the crap I'd been sprayed with during the attack—tear gas, pepper spray, mace, whatever—my skin erupted with a stinging sensation. My body felt like it was on fire. I remember looking down at the drain as the different chemicals hit the shower tiles and congealed, and I realized they formed a river of orange.

I laughed, and through the pain I thought to myself, *This is what it looks like whenever Donald Trump takes a shower.*

PART III

AFTER

CHAPTER 15

Recovery

At my bedside on January 7th, the doctor said, "Can I get you anything?"

I said, "A cold beer?"

The doc laughed and left. A little while later, he poked his head back in the room and said, "Actually, I think there is something we can prescribe beer for."

I said, "Whatever that is, I've got it."

The next thing I knew, a nurse entered with a chilled Miller Lite.

A few hours later, Jimmy texted and asked if I was hungry. I asked him to pick up my regular order from Cava—romaine lettuce, white rice, extra chicken, corn, cucumber, tomato, onion, feta cheese, and dill yogurt dressing. Comfort food.

It's good that you have an appetite, Jimmy texted back.

Jimmy swung by the hospital and talked his way into my room. With dinner, Jimmy smuggled in a six-pack of Dogfish Head SeaQuench Ale. I scarfed down the Cava and sipped the ice-cold beer.

Jimmy looked exhausted, sleepless and bruised from body blows he took during the riot. He said he still felt like he'd been hit by a truck. He couldn't raise his left arm above his shoulder.

After Jimmy left, I started scrolling through my phone and for the first time saw the pictures from the riot—me in the middle of the mob, eyes locked in terror, that pole from a Blue Lives Matter flag about to smack me on the shoulder. I looked so frightened, my first reaction was embarrassment. I put the phone down.

The next day, I was discharged and Jimmy picked me up. Before I left, a doctor prescribed an antidepressant and the equivalent of extra-strength Advil for pain. As I had when admitted to the hospital, I declined an offer for stronger pain narcotics, like opioids, because I was terrified of addiction. The doc also gave me a drug called montelukast, used to prevent asthma attacks, because the scans had revealed a potential lung injury from all the chemical sprays I had inhaled during the riot. Given the mild heart attack and traumatic brain injuries, the doctor said I should schedule follow-up visits. He also warned me that my recovery would take time.

"Weeks?"

"More like months," the doctor said.

I had no civilian clothes with me, so I was presented with a choice of leaving the hospital in a gown or the still-stained uniform I wore during the riot. I wore the uniform.

Jimmy drove me directly to the First District, where I was met in the hallway outside my office by Chief Robert J. Contee III and my First District commander at the time, Morgan Kane. Sergeant Phil McHugh, the man who helped me become a more compassionate police officer, was there, too. As it happened, Phil now served as a liaison between the department and the union as part of its employee assistance program. A big part of that program is mental health, and Phil had been busy meeting with as many officers as possible.

After a minute of small talk, someone asked if I wanted to see my body-worn camera footage from the riot. The battery-operated recorder works like a GoPro, with a wide-angle lens attached to an officer's breast. The device records audio, video, the precise time of day, and approximate location via GPS.

So far, only a handful of people had seen my body-worn camera footage, and it would not be made public for many months. To lighten the grim mood, Phil joked that given my preference for plainclothes, he was surprised to discover that I'd actually remembered to grab a camera before heading to the riot.

Phil warned that the video was pretty chilling. He said I didn't have to watch, at least not yet.

I said I did.

Someone opened a laptop and people gathered around me in a cubicle. No one said a word. The video begins as Jimmy and I approach and enter the Capitol. It shows our entry into the Hall of Columns, past the statues, and into the Crypt. For such a chaotic scene, the audio is pretty clear, and shows us responding to Ray's 10-33, heading toward the smoke-filled Lower West Terrace Tunnel.

At that point—before the video turned violent—Phil stood up and left the squad room. Later, he told me that he just couldn't watch the footage again. As a patrolman and a homicide detective, Phil remained haunted by many memories, the kind that never go away—like removing the body of a twelve-year-old boy who'd hanged himself with a wire coat hanger. But this was different, the first act of violence he'd witnessed against a friend. Phil said that hearing me beg for my life on camera by citing my kids—kids he knew—just broke him.

Back on the video, Ray came into view, looking like Patton, and then Jimmy and me, following Ray's command to hold the line. The camera catches my bare hands reaching out for injured officers and straining to stop rioters from entering the tunnel. At times, rioters push so close that they block the camera lens, and the video turns black for a moment or two. Then in an instant, there's a burst of bright sky, and I'm outside and in the middle of the mob. For a hectic minute, flashes of hands, menacing faces, and flagpoles rush in and out of the frame. The picture goes dark and then I'm back inside the Capitol on my back, with officers calling out my name to try to revive me.

After watching the video, I didn't know what to say. It was too soon to process the trauma. I thought, *That couldn't be me*. The doctors at Washington Hospital Center had warned that I'd remain jacked up on adrenaline for days, if not a week. Viewing my body-worn camera footage on January 8th, I understood for the first time what people meant when they said they had an out-of-body experience.

I coped by making a lame joke. "Oh man, that poor bastard is getting the shit kicked out of him."

I stepped out into the hallway and saw Phil staring at the floor.

He asked me what I thought.

"It's just too much," I said.

"Well," he said, wrapping me in a hug. "I'm just glad you're still here."

Jimmy drove me to my mom's home in Alexandria.

I had no idea how weird things were about to get. While I had seen two news photographs of me getting my ass kicked, I had no clue they'd gone viral. Both were shot at nearly the same moment, capturing the chilling seconds after I'd been tased but before I was beaten with the Blue Lives Matter flagpole. One picture was in color and the other in black-and-white. The black-and-white photo was shot by Mel D. Cole, a photographer who published a book of images from the Black Lives Matter protests. The color picture was made by Shannon Stapleton, a Reuters photographer who had been covering wars and disasters since 9/11. His picture was published by media outlets around the world. The black-and-white image got splashed across social media, and my eldest daughter, Caitlin, saw it. No child should see their father about to be ripped limb from limb.

Although the MPD had not yet publicly identified me, the ruthless right-wing conspiracy mill, with help from Rudy Giuliani, was already at work. Their echo chamber created a disorienting alternate reality:

The cop in the picture was part of an Antifa false-flag operation.

He wasn't really hurt.

He just slipped and was rescued by law-abiding protesters.

He was a professional crisis actor.

He was the same guy seen carrying a Confederate flag inside the Capitol.

You get the idea . . .

Shortly after I left the hospital, my ex-wife, Hsin-Yi, stepped up and tried to set the record straight. Hsin-Yi and I had met in 2009 and were married a year later. Over the next five years, we were blessed with three daughters—Piper, Mei-Mei, and Hensley. I loved growing a family with my little girls, but I worked too many late nights, straining my marriage to the breaking point. We divorced in late 2016. We shared custody of the girls but they lived with their mom, close to their school and friends.

Next to the black-and-white image of me in the midst of the riot, Hsin-Yi wrote on Instagram: "This is Michael Fanone. The girls' father and my ex-husband. While a lot of times he's not my favorite person but yet he is."

Hsin-Yi was the first to tell my story publicly. "This past week, he was a father, a fighter, an MPD, a son and a hero. The news won't report this story. Michael went to the front lines to help his fellow peers when the distress call came out regarding the situation at the Capitol. He was dragged into the mob, his badge ripped off, beaten, tased, and pepper sprayed . . . I can't imagine the fear and distraught he felt, not knowing if he was going to make it out alive . . . Thank you, Michael, for standing your ground and doing what is right. We are so proud of you."

I was grateful and laughed my ass off at her description of me, thinking, *Well, she's not always my favorite person either, but yet she is . . .*

My ex's words of support drew an insane amount of attention, triggering media requests for interviews.

The week after the Capitol riot, I was among a handful of officers whom Chief Contee authorized to speak with Peter Hermann, the D.C. crime reporter for the *Washington Post.* Jimmy and I spoke with Peter, as did Ray, the chief, and Robert Glover. Daniel Hodges, the officer pinned at the West Terrace Tunnel door just before Jimmy and I arrived there, also spoke with the reporter. We all posed for portraits by *Post* photographer Sarah Voisin. The story, which appeared online on January 14th, ran on the front page the following day. The article opened with my experience inside the mob, but it quoted each of us at length, and the newspaper posted pictures of everyone.

The next day, other media flooded MPD with interview requests, and the chief's spokesman reached out to ask if I'd be willing to appear with other officers at a press conference. This time TV cameras would be rolling. It was an unusual request. The *Post* article mostly quoted supervisors and the chief because rank-and-file officers were rarely authorized to speak to the press. We certainly didn't have any media training, and I'd never been interviewed on television before. But these were unusual circumstances, so I said sure.

Dan Hodges and I were joined by another MPD officer, Christina Laury, on the roof of a building overlooking the Capitol. Christina was a seven-year MPD veteran who worked in the gun recovery unit. On January 6th, she'd been detailed to work crowd control. She, too, wound up in the Lower West Terrace Tunnel scrum.

"They wanted to get in by any means possible," she told the reporters. "I can't say enough about the officers who were on the front line, and when I say that, I mean literally officers at the front of the line, where people were beating them with metal poles and spraying them with bear mace. This went on for hours. I witnessed officers going down, leaving for a moment to decontaminate and coming back. I don't know if you've ever been sprayed with this stuff, but it's not only painful, you literally cannot open your eyes. When you cannot open your eyes in the middle of a fight, that's scary. The bravery and the heroism that I saw in these officers, the moment they could open their eyes, they went back up front."

Dan and I told the reporters essentially the same things we told the *Post*, but this time, I added an offhand comment on the handful of rioters who steered me back to the tunnel and safety.

On camera I said, "A lot of people have asked me about my thoughts on the people that helped me. And now that I have kind of processed it all, I will say, 'Thank you, but fuck you for being there.'"

Yes, I said the words "fuck you" on television.

I didn't plan to cuss. I wasn't trying to be cute or trying to attract attention. That's just the way I talked, and the way I felt. The words just fell right out of my mouth. I assumed the media would censor it or bleep it out. I was as surprised as anyone that most didn't.

The "thank-you-but-fuck-you" sound bite went viral. Initially, MPD was thrilled by the positive publicity. A raw street cop, offering specific details and expressing emotion, including fear, stood in sharp contrast to the standard police press conference—chiefs, their spokespeople, and mayors standing in a semicircle, taking turns at the microphone making grave but sanitized statements.

The good vibes from the brass didn't last long. From what I heard, political operatives in the mayor's office stepped in with a different take. The mayor's image-obsessed aides, who'd spent years navigating the politically charged BLM/police protests, were not accustomed to patrol-level cops speaking their mind, much less cussing on television. The word came down: no more interviews.

I figured my fifteen seconds of fame was over. I was fine with that. I turned most of my energy toward my mental and physical recovery, as well as the criminal case against my attackers.

For that investigation, the MPD assigned a detective named Yari Babich. We already had a bit of history. I'd last seen him in fall 2020, when he showed up at the First District seeking help from our crime suppression team with an arrest warrant. During the pre-arrest briefing, Yari told us that the suspect was accused of throwing a concrete block at an MPD sergeant during the summer Black Lives Matter protests. The assault had shattered the sergeant's leg. The op plan called for Jimmy and me to set up an observation post to maintain officer safety, while the others moved in to arrest the suspect.

Yari's briefing seemed routine and his op plan made sense, but I did a double take when he began talking about the suspect.

"He's not a bad guy," Yari said of the man who intentionally hurled a chunk of concrete at a police officer. "He just got caught up in the moment, and so, you know guys, let's go easy on this one."

Jimmy and I exchanged glances. In two decades, I'd never heard a detective describe a suspect that way before a raid. Yari's comment was not only irrelevant and inappropriate but disrespectful to the victim, in this case a fellow officer. In such briefings, we were routinely warned that a suspect might be armed or had pit bulls, things we needed to know for officer and bystander safety. But to tell us to go easy on a guy who'd assaulted a cop? I found that about as egregious as telling us to do the opposite—as Trump might say, to rough him up a little.

So I spoke up, and walked out of the briefing.

Now, four months later, the same guy I'd called out in front of other officers had been assigned to investigate my Capitol assault case. I didn't say anything at first. But about a week later, before the detective had even interviewed me, a friend on the force forwarded texts Yari had sent to a third officer.

The text string began when the officer sent Yari a link to the *Washington Post* story that included a nice posed picture of me and Jimmy.

Don't get me started on him, Yari responded.

Oh, which one? the officer said.

Both really, but mainly Fanone, Yari texted. He criticized my decision to speak publicly about my attack, even though he had to know that the interviews were initiated and authorized by the department's public affairs office. He was also upset that Jimmy and I told the media that we worked in plainclothes and that we posed for pictures out of uniform.

But hey, Yari texted of me, at least he got a new Tinder picture out of it.

Oh shit, really?

I'm heated, Yari wrote. I never liked the guy but I kind of respected him when I first watched [the body-worn camera footage]. Then he decided to go wild when talking to the media.

Oh man, is it really that bad?

Yari replied, All I know is: Don't talk to the media about active investigations. Don't admit to the media you are a plainclothes officer, when you damn well know that's unauthorized. Don't curse if you decide to talk to the media. Don't admit you've never put your uniform on.

I was floored. The detective investigating an assault was belittling the victim. Belittling me.

This is how we treat our own?

When I asked one of Yari's supervisors about it, I was told to relax. "C'mon," the supervisor said, "he's really a good detective. Do you really want to ruin his career over something like this?"

I made a few more calls, and eventually Yari was removed from my case. In fact, almost all of the January 6th cases, including mine, were later transferred from MPD to the FBI.

To be clear, the MPD approached me in mid-January to speak to the media. I did not seek the limelight. I was merely one of several injured officers the MPD asked to speak on behalf of our colleagues. I was very cognizant of that. After each media interview, I asked colleagues what they thought, and what else they wanted the public to know. I was just telling the truth, and it felt like the right thing to do. It *was* the right thing to do. I wasn't doing it for Mike Fanone. I wasn't trying to score political points. I was doing it for everyone on the force.

All of this—the *Post* article, the TV press conference, the GOP votes against Trump's impeachment, Yari's texts—happened in the tense days between the riot on January 6th and the inauguration on January 20th. During those two weeks, the media focused on Capitol security failures and preparation for a peaceful transfer of power from Trump to Biden. My body was still racked with neck pain and headaches from the brain injury. I was still slurring my speech.

Yari's text messages felt like an immense betrayal.

Talking about what happened had been cathartic. Now fellow cops were calling out my public remarks as egotistical. At the time, I couldn't quite grasp why. Looking back, I guess I was too naive to see the political narrative shift: Less than two weeks after the insurrection, Trump supporters and some Republicans were already trying to minimize the violence for political reasons. Apparently, that group included police officers and a union loyal to Trump.

Weird shit was happening on the left as well. Liberal commentators made grotesque remarks of their own on television and on social media. They suggested that if the rioters had been Black Lives Matter supporters, the police would have used *more* force against them. It would have been more of a bloodbath, they argued, because the police are racist and therefore would have opened fire if the rioters had been Black.

It was a stupid, insulting thing to say. For one thing, a Capitol Police officer on the House floor actually *did* use lethal force to stop Trump supporters from entering the chamber, killing rioter Ashli Babbitt, a white woman, in the process. For another, our Civil Disturbance Unit, led by Commander Glover, performed heroically and professionally. Though their lives were in jeopardy many times, not a single MPD officer panicked and used lethal force on January 6th. The officers exercised incredible discipline, even after being beaten about the head with metal pipes. The officers should have been celebrated—not abused to score political points on Twitter.

It was one thing to watch these new narratives develop on television. But it was another to experience them personally. Shortly after I saw the derogatory text messages from Yari, my mom attended a regular Wednesday night adoration at her Catholic church. Adoration is mostly a prayer and meditation session, a solitary affair. There were about five people spread out in the church, and at one point a deacon approached her and said he had heard about what happened to me. The deacon told her he hoped I was doing okay, then, referring to the riot, he said:

"You know, that had nothing to do with Trump. They were all people who dressed up like Trump supporters. They got all the Trump hats and paraphernalia, but they weren't actually Trump people."

My mom was too stunned to reply.

Unfortunately, this was only the beginning. There would be waves and waves of riot-denier bullshit to come.

For twenty years, my professional law enforcement career had been grounded in three principles: observation, action, and consequence. We followed logic and facts. There was a procedure for everything.

Suddenly, I was being attacked by people who didn't give two shits about reality, order, or procedure. It was disorienting. It was fucked up. It was as if I'd left the hospital and entered the Twilight Zone.

CHAPTER 16

Trauma Is Trauma

In the weeks that followed, Jimmy and I spent a lot of time together trying to make sense of what happened. At one point, Jimmy told my mom he was racked with guilt about what happened to me. In the Lower West Terrace Tunnel, one moment he had his hand on my back, the next someone called out "Knife!"

At the warning, Jimmy swiveled his head. When he looked back, I was gone. I'd have turned my head, too. In that situation, anyone would have. I didn't blame Jimmy, and I told him so. If anything, he saved my life by wading into the fucking melee to help haul my ass back inside. He got my vest off when I was struggling to breathe, and got me to snap back to consciousness. I doubt I would have made it to the hospital in time without my partner.

Over many, many beers, Jimmy and I talked about the hypocrisy emerging on both the right and the left, and the personal and professional betrayals. We could not believe elected officials and ordinary citizens alike were already trying to mute our sacrifice and suffering. I had obtained a copy of my body-worn camera footage, and Jimmy and I watched the video again and again, critiquing our moves.

Looking back, I held on to that video like a security blanket. It was proof that I wasn't crazy. Despite all the noise, the riot was real, and so were my injuries.

My scarred neck and back were still sore as fuck, and my head ached constantly. The doctors diagnosed me with post-traumatic stress disorder, or PTSD. They told me to expect unexplained mood changes, unexpected flashbacks to traumatic memories, and unusual physical and emotional reactions. They were right; in the first few weeks, I experienced all of those symptoms. Massages eventually helped heal my neck and back, but I struggled to find a psychologist who could really help heal my brain.

Everyone copes differently. Less than two weeks after the riot, two officers committed suicide. The first was Capitol Police Officer Howard "Howie" Liebengood, a fifteen-year veteran and son of a former Senate sergeant-at-arms. The second was MPD Officer Jeffrey Smith, who took a fucking crowbar to the head during the riot from a Trump supporter. By year's end, two other MPD officers who responded to the Capitol assault also would kill themselves: Kyle deFreytag and Gunther Hashida. Though I didn't know Kyle, I did know Gunther. In my first years on the force, we worked together targeting a crack house in the First District.

Another fallen warrior, Capitol Police Officer Brian Sicknick, died in the line of duty. On January 6th, Officer Sicknick engaged rioters and was badly injured around 2:30 p.m., when he was sprayed with chemicals by someone in the crowd. Later that evening, while still on duty guarding the Capitol, he suffered a series of strokes. He died the following morning.

Jimmy coped in his own way. In late January, he took off on a multi-week, cross-country trip, mostly camping solo at national parks. I grew more concerned the longer he remained off-grid. I also started to worry about my own mental health.

=====

I began to experience very dark thoughts. Like anyone, I'd been depressed at various moments in my life, but I'd always been able to think of my girls—a reason to live—and I'd snap out of it. This time, though, I couldn't shake the despair. I considered suicide. I never sat anywhere and put a gun in my mouth, but I'd be lying if I said I didn't think about it.

My mom saved me. I was insanely lucky to have a mother who happened to be a retired trauma therapist. She understood how angry I had to be that people were denying the riot ever happened. She understood the reason some people turned against the victims of the Capitol assault was because we stood as inconvenient and daily reminders that the attack did, in fact, happen.

By analogy, she told me the story of a teenage girl whose father got drunk one night and went after her with a hammer. The poor child needed stitches across the back of her head. The police arrested the father, convinced the daughter to testify against him, and he was sent to prison for many years. The mother, having lost her lover and the family breadwinner, took it out on the daughter. The girl started skipping school. That's when my mom, working as a therapist for the Alexandria juvenile court system, got involved. My mom told the girl that she'd done nothing wrong, and while the dad remained in prison, the girl continued to excel at school. But once the father was released, he moved back into the home, and the girl was re-traumatized. He never beat her again, but he refused to apologize and the rest of the family blamed the girl for her father's new criminal record, which made it hard for him to get a decent job. The family tried to sweep the whole thing under the rug, as if this terrible thing just never happened. Her parents told her to get over it and move on with her life, precisely the wrong thing to say to a trauma victim. This drove the girl insane; her grades plummeted and she dropped out of school.

"Michael," my mom said, "the same thing is happening to you and your other officers. Trauma is trauma."

I didn't disagree, but I wasn't really sure what to do about it. I felt overwhelmed.

In early February, I received a call from Washington Hospital Center that went to voice mail. The doctor who left a message said she was calling on behalf of Leslie Perkins because I was listed as the emergency contact. The number the doctor left went to a general line, which no one answered. I had not seen Leslie since January 5th, but after the Capitol riot she had called me to see how I was doing. I assured her we'd be working together again soon.

When I received the call from the hospital in February, I wasn't too concerned. It was not unusual for Leslie to check herself into a mental health ward from time to time, just to take a break from life and the drugs. "Three hots and a cot," she'd joke.

I dialed one of Leslie's friends, an eighty-year-old blind man I knew only as Pops, who let her live in his apartment. Over the phone, Pops gave me the bad news.

"Leslie died."

In shock, I dropped to one knee and took a breath. "What happened?"

"She got really sick and Kenny"—her boyfriend—"called 911, but she didn't want to go to the hospital."

I found out later that Leslie suffered a series of strokes, slipped into a coma, and then passed away. She lived for sixty-eight years, surviving more than a *half century* on the streets, enduring sexual abuse, AIDS, diabetes, hepatitis, poverty, and unrelenting hate based on her choice of gender.

My first reaction was guilt. When she needed me most, I wasn't there.

My second reaction was that this marked the end of an era. Without Leslie, I couldn't see myself returning to the same job at the MPD. With twenty years on the force, I still had five years left to earn my full pension. I didn't know what I would do, and honestly, in the weeks after Leslie died, I didn't really care. I could fucking ride a desk or direct traffic. At that point my only goal was to heal enough, physically and mentally, to be able to return from sick leave to full-time duty as an officer. I'd sort out the rest later.

A few weeks after Leslie passed, my mom decided to drive up to Baltimore to see my sister and her family. About a half hour after she left, I realized that it was among the first times I'd been left alone in the house. The dark thoughts returned, and so I called her. She was still on Interstate 95 when she picked up.

"Mom, I really don't like it when you're not here."

I did not explicitly say that I felt suicidal—and I'm not sure I was—but my comments rattled my mom enough that she turned around and drove straight back.

I made a lot of new, unexpected friends in 2021, but I owe a ton to Don Lemon, the CNN anchor. Less than a week after the riot, Don reached out to me and we began to have daily conversations and text exchanges. Other high-profile TV journalists contacted me in January 2021, but they used producers to call or text me. I understood that that's how they operate, and that's fine. But Don took the time to call personally, and that's why I took his initial call, which lasted two hours.

Sometimes you just click with people; that's what happened with Don. He got my sense of humor, and I got his. He seemed genuinely interested in my perspective on shit, and I found myself genuinely interested in what he had to say. All of that made the conversation easy. Once we hit it off, we naturally segued from talking about January 6th to the other big issue in America: race and policing.

Our early conservations were private and off-the-record, but the fact that we were talking was not a secret. Don mentioned it on air as early as January 18th, during the nightly "handoff" segment at 10 p.m., when the host of the 9 p.m. program signs off and Don signs on.

"You know that officer, Michael Fanone?" Don said on air to the 9 p.m. host, then Chris Cuomo. "Every day I talk with him. I think he wouldn't mind me sharing this: He said one of the good things that happened out of this horrible thing is that I get to have conversations with you. And in those conversations, we get to know each other and our awareness of each other and America, and the world expands because we are open to it."

Don, who is Black and openly gay, and largely supported the Black

Lives Matter movement, noted that he and I had little in common on the surface. "He's got kids, he's a straight white guy, law enforcement."

"So why do you talk every day?" Cuomo asked.

"Because it helps," Don replied. "It helps both of us understand this particular moment where we are. If you want to call it kismet, whatever. If we are really going to continue this grand experiment that we call America, then we're going to have to do it together, and we're going to have to have some grace with it. We're going to have to understand each other."

Apparently, Don said on air, too many of the people who attacked the Capitol grew up learning a flawed or false history of the United States.

"Yes, we are a great country," Don said. "We are the greatest democracy on Earth, but there is a lot of history that has been whitewashed, that people have not been taught in school. And so now they are angry because the truth is coming in many ways, and they don't believe it."

On that January evening, Don played a clip of U.S. senator Ron Johnson, a Republican from Wisconsin, who said that it would be incorrect to call the riot "an armed insurrection" because he didn't see any firearms. I suppose being armed with tasers, pepper spray, rocks, flagpoles, bike racks, knives, sticks, ladders, and stolen police riot shields doesn't count.

On air, Don was apoplectic. "What the hell is he talking about?" he said of Johnson.

One day in early February, when Don and I were talking privately on the phone, he asked how many members of Congress had reached out to me after January 6th.

"Zero," I said. "Not a single fucking solitary one."

"You gotta be kidding me," Don said.

Within the hour, Representative Eric Swalwell, a California Democrat, called, and then so did Senator Amy Klobuchar, Democrat from Minnesota. Swalwell arranged a meeting with House Speaker Nancy Pelosi, and I found her to be empathetic and genuine. To be clear, I don't endorse politicians. I'm too busy living my life to know where Speaker

Pelosi or any other politician stands on every issue. Speaker Pelosi is a leader of the Democratic Party and has to make compromises and decisions based on what's best for the party. I get that and I don't agree with every political decision she makes.

But I feel eternally grateful to Speaker Pelosi because when I was struggling, when my family was hurting, she was incredibly supportive. She took the time to meet with me and truly listen, and then followed up with random phone calls, throughout 2021, just to check in on my mental health. On a personal level, I think she was quick to grasp the trauma that January 6th brought to police officers and staff who worked in the Capitol. Her own aides were trapped for hours in an anteroom, hiding under desks while violent rioters roamed the Capitol, calling out frightening taunts, "Nannnnnncy! Nannnnnncy! Where are you?"

Over the next month, I took it as slowly as I could. My weeks were filled with doctors' appointments, and physical and mental therapy sessions. I never intended to make any more public appearances or perform advocacy of any kind. Then, in late March, Trump called into Fox News and on live TV praised his supporters for storming the Capitol. He whitewashed any violence.

"It was zero threat, right from the start," Trump said. "Look, they went in, they shouldn't have done it. Some of them went in, and they were hugging and kissing the police and the guards."

I saw the clip and reached for my new blood pressure monitor. *Zero threat? Hugging and kissing?*

I wanted to respond publicly, but the department refused to allow me to go on TV again. My mom was so angry that she wrote an essay she hoped would be published by a newspaper or a prominent website. I overheard her talking about it, and so I offered to send it to Don. He read it and asked her to appear on his show. She'd never been on TV before but was so pissed at Trump that she said yes instantly.

CNN brought a big satellite truck out to my mom's place in Alexandria and set up a live shot in the driveway. I stood just off camera, cold beverage in hand.

On air, Don introduced my mom, played a clip of Trump, then asked her, "So what goes through your mind when you hear the former president trying to rewrite history on January 6th, there was zero threat?"

"What goes through my mind is really outrage," she said, adding that thousands of officers from around the D.C. area responded to the riot. "It is diminishing. It is devaluing."

Where, she wanted to know, was the outrage from Republicans for such a preposterous and insulting claim?

"The silence to me implies indifference . . . or complicity," she said. "For our family, and for each and every police officer that I know that Michael is in touch with constantly, it's outrageous. It is so dehumanizing."

My mom spoke clearly and methodically. After the first few questions, her confidence grew. When Don asked her what she would say if she could speak directly to Trump, she smiled.

In a soft, strong voice she said simply, "Where's your courage?"

A few feet away, just off camera, I let out a silent laugh. On national television, my seventy-two-year-old mother had just called Donald Trump a coward.

My mom wasn't done. She offered a message for everyone else complicit in Trump's trashing of the truth and sliming of police officers who risked their lives. To Trump's supplicants, she said: "How dare you? How dare you take advantage of people who were defending and fighting for their lives that day to save others, preserve democracy, civility, and to restore the Capitol? All these officers stood with you, why don't you stand with them?"

Don closed the interview by asking my mom about some of the people arrested for assaulting me. The charges, she said, were a good start on the road to accountability.

I had questions of my own about the four men arrested so far.

Like: What sort of American tries to overthrow democracy?

And: What kind of man becomes so consumed by a false belief that he drives across the country, storms the Capitol, and assaults police officers?

Three months after the insurrection, I found out.

CHAPTER 17

An Army of Morons

As part of the largest manhunt in FBI history, the bureau posted pictures of seven men wanted in my assault. These were among the hundreds of other fuzzy images crowdsourced from video and still pictures posted by rioters and journalists. The FBI was inundated with suspects and with tips.

So Americans like Forrest Rogers stepped up to help.

Rogers is a Swiss-based, wiry, and white-haired journalist who studies online pictures and videos to investigate racist, criminal, and corrupt people. As a reporter at the Zurich-based *NZZ* newspaper, Rogers had the skills and tools to make sense of shaky cell phone Capitol riot videos and collate them in ways that made it easier to document crimes and identify suspects. After January 6th, he and friends started a Twitter account, Deep State Dogs, to do just that.

On January 26th, Deep State Dogs posted images and video from just outside the Lower West Terrace Tunnel entrance, at about the time I was tased. The pictures focused on a Latino man with a goatee and glasses in a heavy black coat. This man's face did not match any of the pictures of the seven men wanted by the FBI for their alleged role in my attack.

The man identified by Deep State Dogs looked about thirty-five years old, and he wore a red MAKE AMERICA GREAT AGAIN ball cap with a giant GOP elephant symbol on the brim. The red cap was distinguishable in the crowd because it was decorated with souvenir lapel pins.

In one close-up freeze-frame, the suspect wielded a small black object the size of a taser in his right hand and pressed it against my neck. The weapon didn't appear to be an actual name-brand "Taser," but a cheaper electroshock device, probably a stun gun. In slow motion, the video shows that after the man pressed the stun gun to the base of my skull, I collapsed.

Deep State Dogs tweeted a message with the photos. "Let's find this coward! This is Officer Michael Fanone being tased in the neck. Fanone suffered a heart attack as a result of this assault. I think 'TaserPrick' is an appropriate name."

The next day, someone who replied to the Twitter post identified TaserPrick as a familiar face from Trump rallies in Southern California, a man named Daniel J. Rodriguez.

On Twitter, Deep State Dogs did not confirm that the man was in fact Rodriguez, but wrote: "Can say with certainty that #TaserPrick has been identified & reported to the FBI. He is already on their radar."

A month passed.

I was unaware of the initial Deep State Dogs posts until February 26th, when two reporters from the *Huffington Post* published a long profile of Rodriguez. The headline said, "Revealed: Meet the Trump Fanatic Who Used a Stun Gun On a Cop at the Capitol Insurrection."

The *HuffPost* reporters used some clues from the Deep State Dogs video analysis, but also gathered a lot of new information. Their story said that Rodriguez's Facebook page included "pro-Trump, anti-Muslim, and right-wing memes" and "a 2017 YouTube video about how 'Pedophiles Rule the World.'" The reporters cited video from a prior Trump rally in which Rodriguez allegedly assaulted a wheelchair-bound Black Lives Matters demonstrator. The *HuffPost* story quoted three people who identified Rodriguez as the man who tased me. One of them said he first contacted the FBI in January, but hadn't heard back until agents learned that the reporters were on the man's trail.

Two weeks later, the FBI arrested Rodriguez. By April, the FBI had four men in custody in connection with my assault. Each of these fools had a criminal past. They were part of Trump's angry army of morons, misfits, and malcontents—independent losers who became emboldened within the mob, believing (or at least convincing themselves in the moment) that they were engaged in a historic effort sanctioned by the president of the United States. Once behind bars, two of these "patriots" wilted and renounced their membership in Trump's cult.

The four were among the more than 775 Americans arrested for breaching the Capitol on January 6th. Nine in ten were men. An astounding number—nearly four in five—were caught in part with evidence from social media posts. Still, by mid-2022, an estimated 300 unidentified suspects remained wanted by the FBI.

The feds involved in my case are top-shelf. I've been careful to let them do their jobs. After the arrests, I told one of them, "Hey listen, I've been a cop for twenty years, so I understand the rules. I'm the victim here and not the arresting officer, so I know you can't provide details about the investigation. But I do want to know one thing about each guy: Did the FBI have to resort to force during the arrest?" In other words, did the agents get to kick their asses a bit? The response I got: "Well, let's put it this way: They all cried. And Danny Rodriguez resisted."

I smiled when I heard that.

I'll get to Danny Rodriguez in a moment. But first, for history's sake, let me tell you about the other three gentlemen charged with assaulting me.*

Thomas F. Sibick of Buffalo, New York, was charged with ripping my badge from my vest and my radio from my belt.

---

*This footnote is for defense attorneys representing my assailants, and who someday may have the opportunity to question me on the witness stand: Relax. Details about your clients in this chapter can be found in public filings in the court record, except for how I feel about them.

After January 6th, Sibick spoke with agents four times, admitting more culpability each time, until he finally confessed and produced my badge, which he'd buried in his backyard. In court, his lawyer said Sibick struggled with his mental health and got most of his information from Fox News.

Sibick was no stranger to the criminal justice system. He had five prior convictions, including one for cocaine possession and one for fleeing police while driving a motorcycle at 120 miles per hour. In another case, he was convicted of disorderly conduct for calling the father of someone he was dating twenty-seven times in a twelve-hour period.

Sibick pleaded not guilty to assaulting me, but in fall 2021, he wrote a jailhouse letter to the judge, saying that after a little "self-reflection," he'd had a change of heart. I guess seven months in a D.C. jail will do that to you.

Sibick wrote, "The trauma suffered by Officer Michael Fanone, it is without question, unconscionable." He added, "While many praise Trump, I loathe him, his words and actions are nefarious, causing pain and harm to the world. What he honestly needs to do is go away!"

Kyle James Young of Redfield, Iowa, was charged with assaulting me and trying to take my service weapon. He's also the guy who yelled, "Kill him with his own gun!"

Young didn't come to D.C. on a whim. According to his Facebook posts, he began thinking about attending the January 6th event at least a full month beforehand. His wife later testified that the couple watched Fox News religiously and believed everything Trump said. Young even brought his sixteen-year-old son with him to the Capitol.

The elder Young had several previous felony convictions, mostly for drugs, and in 2007 was convicted of illegally possessing a firearm. Like most criminals, he wasn't very bright. By March 2021, Young knew he was wanted. He'd seen the FBI wanted posters with his picture. Yet when agents searched his home more than a month later, they discovered a smoking-gun piece of evidence that helped verify his identity:

the distinctive skull-and-swords T-shirt he wore during the January 6th riot. When the feds arrested him, they also discovered "a large amount of marijuana," a scale, and cash in small denominations.

In May 2022, Young pleaded guilty to assaulting me. Under his plea deal, he faces five to eight years in prison.

Albuquerque Cosper Head (yes, that's his real name) of Kingsport, Tennessee, is the idiot who pulled me into the mob, yelling "I got one!"

He didn't just pull me into the scrum. He held on tight for twenty-five excruciating seconds, rendering me helpless as I was kicked and clawed and stomped.

In reviewing videos from the Capitol, including from my body-worn camera, I instantly recognized his face. The FBI needed to put a name with that face, so they placed a screenshot from the video on a widely distributed wanted poster. Unfortunately for Head, his probation officer in Tennessee saw it and recognized him instantly. Apparently, Head had decided it was a good idea to partake in a riot at the U.S. Capitol *with just weeks remaining on his probation* from a 2015 case. By simply leaving the state of Tennessee to travel to Washington, he violated probation, and was subject to arrest.

Head is a frequent flier in the justice system. Since 1997, he's been convicted sixteen times, including for domestic assault, non-domestic assault, theft, evading arrest, vandalism, DUI, and unlawful possession of a weapon. Throw in his role on January 6th and I think a more appropriate first name for Mr. Head might be Dick.

Head pleaded guilty to assaulting me and faces six to eight years in prison.

Finally, there is the MAGA-hat-wearing loser who electrocuted me with a stun gun, Daniel Joseph Rodriguez of Fontana, California, aka "D.J." or "Danny."

Shortly before his arrest, someone called and asked if the FBI could borrow my handcuffs to take him into custody, a nice law enforcement tradition. I FedExed the cuffs to L.A. and Rodriguez was arrested in late March. A few weeks later, at a gathering near Capitol Hill, someone left a manilla envelope by my seat. It had my name on it. Inside, I found my handcuffs and a Polaroid picture of Rodriquez wearing them.

Later, I watched a video of Rodriguez's interrogation. The FBI's interview did not disappoint.

In fact, it offered a case study in the Cult of Trump. It revealed the feeble mind of a typical zealot. If we want to understand what we're up against, we need to grasp what drives people like Rodriguez, a failed drug dealer so desperate for a sense of belonging that he became an easy mark for a cult. After being bullied in high school and later by fellow drug dealers, Rodriguez fell in with Trump diehards who welcomed his support. He told the FBI agents that they made him feel proud and important. They gave him a sense of purpose.

Like most guilty people under arrest, Rodriguez dodged and evaded at the outset of his FBI interview, offering warped logic and pathetic excuses. He claimed to be brainwashed by years of listening to conspiracy peddler Alex Jones on *InfoWars*, but now, sitting in a tiny FBI interrogation room, Rodriguez realized he'd make a HUGE fucking mistake. In fact, before Special Agents Enrique Armenta and Nate Elias even started asking questions, Rodriguez began sobbing like a little bitch.

"You need some tissue or something, just let me know, okay?" Special Agent Armenta said.

"No sense in crying," Rodriguez mumbled through a Covid mask. "I don't know what's wrong with me."

"Take a breath," the FBI agent said. "I kind of feel like you want to get it off your chest."

"I'm so weak," Rodriguez said. "I'm crying."

"It's okay, man," the FBI agent said. "It's okay."

"Oh, God. I shouldn't be crying. I'm a grown man and I knew what I was doing."

In my career, I'd conducted or watched hundreds of interrogations, so I viewed this one mostly through an unemotional, professional lens. Still, I couldn't help thinking: *I can't believe I almost died at the hands of one of the dumbest fucking people on the planet.*

The dude was so full of shit politically—and so broke—that he funded his trip to Washington with the $600 monthly Covid stimulus check he received from the U.S. government. In other words, he used his check to attack the people who supplied it.

From the first minute of the interview, it was clear the agents would ultimately elicit a full confession. Special Agent Elias told Rodriguez that there was no shame in crying, no shame in processing what he'd done. The agents spoke every day to people who broke the law, they told him, and they never judged anyone for their crimes.

"This is an opportunity here for you to let us know and help us understand," Elias said, "because right now we don't frankly understand exactly what happened from your perspective."

When Rodriguez said he doubted his cooperation would lead to a reduced prison sentence, the agents played it perfectly.

"Well," Elias said, "let us read you some paperwork here and then we can talk about how you might be able to help yourself out of your situation, okay?"

The other agent began reading Rodriguez his *Miranda* rights. "You have the right to remain silent. Anything you say can be used against you in court . . ." Rodriguez hesitated, then signed the document. Then he cried again.

Armenta had done his homework. The FBI agent began the interrogation by describing video from a years-earlier California demonstration in which Rodriguez had stepped between protesters and police, preventing a confrontation.

"You had the guts to say something," the agent said. Armenta asked Rodriguez to help him reconcile that version of himself with the guy who tased a police officer at the Capitol.

"I don't know what happened either," Rodriguez said. He slumped into his chair and cried some more.

"Your story's an important story," the FBI agent said. "What happened in your life? Like, how did you start going to these rallies?"

"It was so fast," Rodriguez said. "I was a good guy and then, instantly, I became a bad guy."

"Tell me about that, Danny."

"There's people that have taken over this country from the inside, globalist and unelected officials, elitists, you know?" These people, he told the agents, are responsible for the growing gap between the rich and poor, the homeless and wealthy. "They lied all about Trump, saying that he's a bad guy, he's a racist and a horrible president and all this. So, no matter what they did to defeat him, it was justified. Cheat, lie, steal, whatever."

Rodriguez said he couldn't understand how Joe Biden won the election. "You don't have to be that bright to see that something wasn't right and it was rigged."

You don't have to be that bright . . .

I hit pause for a sec to grab a cold beer from the fridge. When I returned, Rodriguez told the agents he had been listening to *InfoWars* for years, instead of the mainstream media.

"I was trying to find the truth and answers," he said. He found a purpose in life, he said, by not only supporting Trump but by evangelizing on his behalf. For more than a decade, he'd been watching Trump on TV, including *The Apprentice*, and considered him so familiar and inspiring, he was "like, almost an old friend." Rodriguez started going to rallies and anti-Trump protests in Beverly Hills. At one such event, he claimed to have been among the small number of Trump supporters who faced off against protesters. He spoke with pride as he told the FBI agents about it.

"I argued with two hundred or three hundred people there for eight and a half hours, nine hours, without food or water, and I just annihilated every single one of them," he boasted. "I thought that that was like one of the greatest days of my life."

When Trump was elected, Rodriguez told the agents, he put on a Trump T-shirt, walked into a U.S. Army recruiting office, and tried to enlist.

"I got some weird looks," he told the FBI. "And I was like, man, you guys are not for Trump here? Like, I don't get it. But they just didn't follow politics."

Thankfully, the Army rejected him. Four years later, when Trump lost the 2020 election, Rodriguez said he knew—absolutely *knew*—it had been rigged for Biden. He told the agents he feared that Biden would round up all the Trump supporters. He said he prayed that God would direct him on the right path, and kept attending rallies in California. He would have done more, he said, but he didn't have any money.

The agents asked him why he traveled to Washington in January.

"Trump called us," he said. "Trump called us to D.C."

"Tell me about that."

"If he's the commander in chief and the leader of our country, and he's calling for help, I thought we were doing the right thing," he told the agents. "I had no plans of what was going to happen."

Plus, Rodriguez said, he'd never seen Trump actually speak in person at prior rallies and figured this might be his last opportunity. After Trump spoke near the White House on January 6th, he said he followed the crowd as it marched toward the Capitol. He said he wound up beneath the Capitol scaffolding near the Lower West Tunnel.

He acted like it was no big deal, and that he'd just been there, but hadn't done anything illegal. The agents pushed him. They told him this was his chance to tell his story, and maybe—just maybe—that cooperation might reduce his sentence. But, they warned him, you can't leave anything out.

"Uh, what am I leaving out?"

I snorted beer through my nose. *What am I leaving out?*

"Well," an FBI agent calmly deadpanned, "you're not telling us about how you ended up on the Capitol steps, in the tunnel, how Officer Fanone got pulled out."

Oh, yeah—that.

Over the next hour, Rodriguez dissembled in textbook fashion, slowly admitting pieces of his culpability, mixing truth, excuses, and lies, minimizing his violent acts, but eventually laying it all out, as the FBI agents pressed him. In law enforcement, we call this "progressive disclosure."

Rodriguez said he was on the tunnel steps when he saw me being pulled out. "I saw them pulling him out, and I tased him."

"How many times did you tase him?"

"Oh, just once."

Yeah, right.

The agents urged Rodriguez to be honest. They explained that they had been investigating him for more than a month, that they already knew the answers to virtually every question they asked. This was his chance, they said, to tell his version of events. Rodriguez told them that in the midst of the struggle to get inside the Capitol, he called out for a taser, and someone simply gave him one. The agents didn't believe him.

"Are you lying to us, Danny?" Armenta asked, reminding him that it was a crime to lie to the FBI.

"No," Rodriguez insisted.

The other FBI agent told him that they already knew that someone who had traveled with him by van from California to the Capitol also carried a taser, a knife, and pepper spray. Later, Rodriguez would admit to bringing walkie-talkies and smoke grenades, prepping for battle with anti-Trump forces. But for now, he stuck with his story about the taser, that some anonymous person in the crowd handed it to him.

Then he spun his biggest bullshit of all, that he tased me to "protect" me from the mob.

"Danny," one of the agents said, "you realize you assaulted that man, right?"

"Yes."

"And you realize right now whatever fabrication you're telling us is not helping your situation."

"I'm a hundred percent not fabricating anything."

I laughed and took another swig of beer.

One of the FBI agents pulled out his phone and started playing a video of one of my media interviews in which I described the attack. The agent then put his phone down and, for effect, mocked Rodriguez. "'Oh, I'm such a benevolent man, coming up to a poor officer who's struggling to survive, thinking he's going to die. Let me help him out. Let me taser him.'" The agent added, "Is that really the story you want to be written about you?"

"No, I wasn't trying to kill him."

"Then tell us what happened. Don't let the story be this crappy story you're telling us right now."

"What do you want me to tell you? That I tased him? Yes."

"Explain what you did."

"Am I a fucking piece of shit? Yes."

"Why did you tase him?"

"I don't know," he said through tears. "I'm a piece of shit. I'm sorry. He's a human being with children and he's not a bad guy. He sounds like he's just doing his job and I'm an asshole."

I agreed with that self-assessment.

The FBI agents showed Rodriguez video from the web in which he encourages protesters to enter the Capitol, moves furniture around inside, helps to bust a window, and tells people to put their goggles on. In other words, he was hardly a passive protester.

"It looks like a combat situation," Armenta said. "And so if you took the Capitol, then what?"

"Damn, dude. I don't know," Rodriguez said. "It's very stupid and ignorant and I see that it's a big joke, and we thought we were going to save this country."

Rodriguez offered a ridiculous rationalization: The Founding Fathers, he told the FBI, would have understood what he did on January 6th. "When we talk about 1776, we see there was a lot of violence. We had to go against the government and people died. Something good came out of that . . . I didn't think I was going to be the bad guy."

He started weeping again. "I'm so sorry," he sobbed. "I didn't know that we were doing the wrong thing. I thought we were doing the fucking right thing. I thought it was going to be awesome."

Rodriguez told the agents he got carried away by "the mob mentality." One of the agents called bullshit.

"In the moment you tased Officer Fanone and in the moments you went into the Capitol, you were aware you were there and you weren't having an out-of-body experience," the agent said. "You knew what was going on. You called for a taser. And not only did you take the taser, but then you put that taser on Officer Fanone's neck."

"Yes, I did."

Rodriguez asked the agents if they'd gone through taser training, in which trainees are often tased, so they know how it feels. The FBI agents said they had. If they knew that I hadn't—in the MPD only sergeants carry tasers—they didn't tell Rodriguez. They weren't going to stop him from digging a deeper hole with this lame logic.

"So," Rodriguez said, "he's been tased before, Officer Fanone. And he has a lot of neck tattoos. That's painful, too, right?"

"So you're saying he just had a little bit of pain?"

"I don't know how much pain he has. I've never been tased. I'm sorry I don't know what it's like. He can tase me."

Now there's an idea.

People have asked me if I forgive the morons and misfits who assaulted me on January 6th. Let me put it this way: The evidence against them is so strong, I certainly expect them to plead guilty. They would be nuts to go to trial, especially in a city where the jury pool isn't likely to be sympathetic to right-wing nut jobs. In an attempt to reduce their prison sentences, I expect each of them to apologize in court and take ownership of their actions. But I don't think an apology to me and society is sufficient. The terrorists who attacked me should be sentenced like anyone else who intentionally assaults a police officer. A judge should consider their mindset at the time, the severity of the crime, and prior criminal record. In my opinion, each of them deserves many, many years in prison.

But we shouldn't stop there. Anyone who engaged in sedition on January 6th should be arrested and charged.

Including Trump.

CHAPTER 18

Good Trouble

Lawyers live for loopholes. Mine found one while reviewing MPD's rules about officers speaking to the media.

The rules clearly forbade me from giving interviews in uniform without permission from the chief's spokesman. The rules also barred me from speaking publicly as a representative of MPD. But my pro bono lawyer, Chuck Tobin, discovered that nothing in the rules prevented me from speaking out as an individual. Chuck said that as long as I appeared in civilian clothes and spoke on behalf of myself, I would be okay.

At first, I was wary. I didn't want to risk getting fired or suspended—I was supporting a family with pay and benefits. I decided to play it cautiously, and had my lawyers draft a letter to the city outlining our interpretation of the rules. The letter asked for the city to respond with its view. More than a month passed without a response from the city.

By mid-April, about three weeks after my mom had appeared on Don's show, I decided that my lawyers had given the city enough time to object. I took the city's silence as confirmation that I could appear on TV in civilian attire. It was a no-brainer that I would give Don the exclusive. We were still talking or texting every few days. In the last week of April, I made a courtesy call to Chief Contee and let him know I was going to go on TV.

A camera crew returned to my mom's house about an hour before showtime.

"Mike, how are you doing?" Don said on air, choking up and then laughing at himself a bit. "I didn't know that I would get this emotional about just talking about your story, because when this happened we weren't friends. And now it feels personal to me because we're friends. What has this been like for you since that day?"

"It's been a roller coaster, man," I said. "Some days are better than others. Today's a good day. I'm happy that I've got the opportunity to speak out. It's been very difficult seeing elected officials and other individuals kind of whitewash the events of that day or downplay what happened—some of the terminology used, 'hugs and kisses,' 'very fine people'—is very different from what I experienced and what my co-workers experienced on the 6th."

Don asked me what I thought about Trump's comments that January 6th wasn't that big of a deal and that the protesters were patriots.

"I think it's dangerous," I said. "I experienced a group of individuals that were trying to kill me to accomplish their goal. And I think that—"

A fucked-up wave of emotion surged through my body, and I lost my train of thought. I dropped my eyes from the camera for a moment, and exhaled deeply.

"Sorry, Don," I said, looking back up and into the camera. "Man, I didn't think I'd get this emotional."

Don asked why I thought my experience had been so tough.

I said I wasn't political but I felt betrayed by the so-called party of "law and order." I stressed that I was speaking for myself, but that the view of first responders to the Capitol riot was getting lost, or buried, by politicians with their own agendas.

"It's not often that we get a perspective of just a rank-and-file police officer, and that's me, man. I am literally the lowest guy on the totem pole in my department. I want people to understand the significance of

January 6th. I want people to understand that thousands of rioters came to the Capitol hell-bent on violence and destruction and murder, and eight hundred and fifty MPD officers responded there and really saved the day. You know, those officers are moms and dads. They're sons and daughters. They have children and families. We're just regular people. I've got kids and baby mamas and I pay child support, and I got car payments. I stress about paying my taxes—you know, the same shit as everyone else."

Don asked about the tension between police and Black communities across the country. A week earlier, a Minneapolis jury had convicted Derek Chauvin of killing George Floyd.

I said that while I try not to second-guess officers in stressful situations, the footage of Floyd's death was horrifying. "I just watch it and I'm just like what the fuck are they doing? I can't make sense of that at all. I'm someone who's participated in thousands of arrests. I understand that most of those individuals didn't want to go to jail, and sometimes force has to be used, and force is never going to be optically pleasing. However, I mean there's some situations that are just cut and dry to me. And that was one of them. And it was wrong."

Don and I talked on air about our different backgrounds and the mind-opening private conversations we'd had by phone and FaceTime.

"I think we found that we agreed on more things than we disagreed," I said. "But the points that we didn't agree on or don't agree on, we don't have to kill each other over it."

Don asked me about my body-worn camera footage, which had yet to be released. Did I want it made public?

"Absolutely," I said. "I can't say it in stronger terms. I don't know how you can watch my body-worn camera footage and deny that January 6th was anything other than violent and brutal. January 6th was real. It didn't happen in a fucking movie studio in California."

"Thank you, brother," Don said. "I know this was tough for you. I know you've been wanting to do it for a long time. Thank you for your service. Thank you for your friendship."

"I appreciate that, Don. Thank you, buddy. I love you."

"Love you as well."

Yes, I said "I love you" to Don Lemon on live television. I didn't think about it before I said it, but what the fuck, I meant it.

I was thrilled that Don had asked about my body-worn camera footage. By that late April interview, I was beginning to wonder whether it might ever be made public.

I had good reason to worry. In February, the D.C. government had rejected a request by House impeachment managers to obtain the video for use during Trump's trial in the Senate. The MPD had delayed similar public-record requests from the media for my footage. The city's effort to keep Congress and the media at bay signaled that they didn't want it released for political reasons.

There was still a chance the footage might be made public if any of the four Trump supporters charged with assaulting me risked taking their case to trial. At trial, prosecutors surely would play the body-worn camera video as evidence in open court, at which point it would become a public record. But if the four pleaded guilty, hoping for shorter sentences, there would be no trial, and prosecutors might not get an opportunity to introduce the video into evidence. And even if the rioters went to trial, that probably wouldn't happen for at least a year, so the footage wouldn't see the light of day until 2022 or 2023. If I left it to the government, I'm not sure my body-worn camera footage would have ever been released.

Good thing I had a copy.

I decided it was time to spread the video around for safekeeping. I gave a copy to three people I trusted: my lawyer, my dad, and Don Lemon.

When I gave Don the footage, I told him I didn't know when I would give him the green light to air it. But I wanted him to have it, because I knew I could trust him to make it very public, if anything happened to me, or if anyone crossed a line of decency.

In mid-May, several Republicans crossed that line. This included Representative Andrew Clyde, a combat veteran from Georgia who on

January 6th had helped barricade the House floor from rioters. So it was mind-bendingly insane to hear him say on May 12th:

"It was not an insurrection. This is the truth . . . If you didn't know that TV footage was a video from January the sixth, you would actually think it was a normal tourist visit."

A normal tourist visit?

On the same day, Representative Paul Gosar of Arizona claimed that police officers were "harassing peaceful patriots."

Peaceful patriots?

Jody Hice, a Georgia congressman and former pastor, joined the denier choir: "It was Trump supporters who lost their lives that day, not Trump supporters who were taking the lives of others."

I wondered how Officer Sicknick's mother and widow felt about that.

I was livid. Livid at Clyde, Gosar, and Hice. Livid at other Republicans who refused to condemn their words. It felt like a coordinated, disrespectful attack on law enforcement. To add insult to injury, these insipid remarks came during National Police Week, when most members of Congress go out of their way to praise officers and participate in memorial services for fallen cops.

Until that moment, I had never even heard of Andrew Clyde, Paul Gosar, or Jody Hice. Now, I vowed to never forget them. As my friend and Capitol Police Officer Harry Dunn would say, quoting civil rights hero John Lewis, it was time to get into some "good trouble."

I reached out to Don and gave him the green light to air the body-worn camera footage. I explained that he couldn't reveal his source because I still worked for the MPD. Don was cool with that.

That evening, he aired the footage on his 10 p.m. program. I was out at a bar called Scarlet Oak with Ray, where we were regulars. When Don's show came on CNN, someone turned up the volume, and I watched from the bar, cradling a Modelo.

By now, I had watched the video more than one hundred times, but I'd only watched with friends, family, fellow cops, and a few Hill staffers.

I'd never experienced it with strangers. I'd never seen the footage on the news, and now in a way I'd never expected, seeing it on CNN somehow seemed to validate, at least in my mind, the significance of the event. On national television, in prime time. I broke down and sobbed, burying my head on the bar.

At that moment, I cried harder and longer than I have in my entire life.

I felt an enormous sense of release. I'd been talking about my experience for four months. Now people wouldn't have to hear it from my mouth, they could judge for themselves. They could see and hear everything from a cop's point of view. People could follow along as Jimmy and I responded and joined the officers already jammed in the chaotic tunnel. They could watch Ray in his overcoat, directing us like Patton. They could see how obnoxious and violent the rioters were, and how injured cops bravely held the line.

As important, I think the footage altered the narrative. On the body-worn camera, the officers in that tunnel look like warriors, not victims. Defending the Capitol, we look like the fucking Roman Tenth Legion, the legendary unit that protected Julius Caesar. (It's not lost on me that the Capitol's design was inspired by Roman architecture, or that the Statue of Freedom on top of the Capitol Dome was originally cast in Rome.)

The next evening, May 13th, I appeared on Don's show to talk about the body-worn camera footage. On air, I told Don that I was proud to work beside so many heroes.

"The courage, selflessness, bravery of all those officers is just incredible," I said. "There were injured officers there who, under normal circumstances, would have been on their way to a hospital in an ambulance. But they were picking themselves back up, getting back into the line, and fighting to protect the Capitol and their fellow officers—the most awe-inspiring scene of my life, and I'll never forget it."

Don asked about the crazy "tourist day" and "peaceful patriot" comments from some Republicans. I said I was trying hard to stay apolitical.

Then I added, "I don't expect anybody to give two shits about my opinions, but I will say this: Those are lies, and peddling that bullshit is an assault on every officer that fought to defend the Capitol."

Don asked how my experience had changed me.

"Oh, it's definitely changed my perspective on quite a few things. You know, I still am who I am. I'm a freeborn son of America. I make my own decisions about different issues. Nobody tells me what to think or how to think, but I recognize the dangerousness of political rhetoric, and how it resulted in the violence we saw on January 6th."

After my appearance on Don's show, I reached out to other networks to let them know I was available to talk about attempts to whitewash January 6th and dishonor the officers who defended the Capitol. CBS, MSNBC, and a few local affiliates took me up on my offer. I contacted Fox News repeatedly, but their bookers and producers told me I was not welcome on their network. One flat out told me that her bosses had banned anyone whose January 6th experience didn't conform with Fox's narrative.

"And unfortunately," she said, "that includes you, specifically, Mike."

CHAPTER 19

Hearts and Minds

A few days later, I got a call from Liz Cheney's office.

Congress was considering a bill to create an independent bipartisan commission to investigate the January 6th insurrection. While the bill was sure to pass the House, where Speaker Pelosi controlled a majority, Republicans had enough votes in the Senate to kill it with a filibuster. Representative Cheney's staff wanted to know if I'd be willing to join a small group lobbying Republican senators to change their minds and support the bipartisan commission.

There would be five of us: me; Capitol Police Officer Harry Dunn; former congresswoman Barbara Comstock, a Republican from Virginia; Gladys Sicknick, the mother of the slain officer; and Sandra Garza, Officer Sicknick's longtime partner.

I said yes immediately. Regardless of the politics, I thought it would be an honor to escort Mrs. Sicknick around the Capitol. It took a lot of courage for a mother to confront politicians who wanted to whitewash her son's death. I can't imagine how I would feel if someone tried to do that to one of my children.

Our goal was to change some hearts and minds. Unfortunately, it felt like a lot of the people we met with didn't have either.

We met with Mitt Romney of Utah first, but he already supported creating the January 6th commission. We met next with Ron Johnson of Wisconsin, and spent a lot of time listening to Ron Johnson talk about Ron Johnson and the ways in which Ron Johnson is misunderstood.

In several meetings, Mrs. Sicknick got emotional about her son, and I couldn't blame her. Some of the meetings were too short to have any real meaning, other than to insult us. As we were ushered in to see Ted Cruz of Texas, an aide whispered, "Okay, you're scheduled for eight minutes with the senator."

Aides to Senate Republican leader Mitch McConnell told us he was too busy to meet Mrs. Sicknick. Later, I learned that as Harry and I escorted the mother and partner of a dead Capitol policeman to advocate for an investigation into the circumstances behind his death, McConnell was working against us. The Republican leader allegedly told some senators that he would consider it "a personal favor" if they opposed a January 6th commission.

When I heard that, I remember wishing John McCain were still alive. I don't know much about the late senator's politics, but I knew he put country first over party. He had character and integrity. I'm certain he would have met with us and offered Mrs. Sicknick the respect she deserved.

We met with the two senators from South Carolina, Lindsey Graham and Tim Scott, together. At one point, as I was describing the assault in the tunnel, noting that we were vastly outnumbered, Graham interrupted.

"You guys should have shot them all in the head," Graham said. "We gave you guys guns, and you should have used them. I don't understand why that didn't happen."

Around the room, jaws dropped.

I said, "Well, Lindsey, I appreciate your enthusiasm, but there are rules that dictate what we can and cannot do when it comes to use of deadly force."

The senator grimaced and started tapping his fingers on a table, as if he had more important places to be. Mrs. Sicknick returned to the topic at hand—an independent January 6th commission. When she mentioned, offhandedly, that Trump incited the insurrection, Graham snapped harshly at the dead policeman's mother.

"If you're going to start talking about Donald Trump like that, we're going to end this meeting right now," Graham said.

Sandra Garza, the widow, gave Graham a tongue lashing. I can't recall what she said, specifically, but he shut the fuck up and slumped into his chair.

The next day, Graham joined nearly all Republican senators in a procedural move that killed the independent January 6th commission. In its place, Pelosi would create a special House committee to investigate the insurrection.

A few weeks later, the House considered a bill to award a Congressional Gold Medal to every officer who defended the Capitol on January 6th. It was a simple, apolitical gesture of recognition. The Congressional Gold Medal bill did not call for any kind of investigation or cast aspersions on anyone. It merely honored the officers who risked their lives to stop a violent insurrection.

Even so, twenty-one Republicans voted against it.

For the historical record, here are the names of those twenty-one spineless fucks: Andrew Clyde, Paul Gosar, Jody Hice, Lauren Boebert, Barry Moore, Ralph Norman, Matthew Rosendale, Chip Roy, Warren Davidson, Scott Perry, Mary Miller, Andy Biggs, Thomas Massie, Andy Harris, Matt Gaetz, Marjorie Taylor Greene, Louie Gohmert, Michael Cloud, Greg Steube, Bob Good, and John Rose.

The day after the vote, Harry Dunn and I decided to visit the twenty-one Republicans in their offices. We had a simple question: How could you do such a thing? None of them agreed to meet with us.

In a Capitol hallway, though, we spotted Clyde entering an elevator. We dashed over and slipped inside before the doors closed. I stuck out my hand. "How are you doing, Congressman?"

The coward froze. From his reaction, I could tell he recognized me. In my open-collared shirt, the neck tattoos were hard to miss.

I said, "I'm sorry, you're not going to shake my hand?"

"I don't know who you are."

"I apologize," I said and introduced myself. "I'm a D.C. Metropolitan Police officer who fought on January 6th to defend the Capitol, and as a result I was significantly injured." I briefly described my injuries.

Clyde fiddled with his phone and backed farther into a corner of the elevator. When the doors opened, he fled. I think he thought—wrongly—that I was going to punch him. At least, I hope that's what he thought.

I was amused by the encounter, sure, but I was also angry. I had risked my life for a man who wouldn't even shake my hand, let alone thank me. I told Representatives Eric Swalwell and Adam Kinzinger about my little encounter, and they tweeted it out. The tweets triggered a story in the *Washington Post*, and suddenly my elevator brush with Clyde was all over the news and social media.

By the way, to give you a sense of what kind of person Clyde is, the same day he refused to shake my hand, he was one of just fourteen congressmen to vote against making Juneteenth a national holiday to recognize and remember the horrors of slavery.

The other person we struggled to meet with was Kevin McCarthy, the Republican leader. McCarthy ducked me for months. Speaker Pelosi and Eric Swalwell pounded him publicly for being such a coward. In mid-May, during a National Police Week event, McCarthy publicly promised to meet us, but after a whole month passed without an actual invitation, Speaker Pelosi sent out another press release, "McCarthy Breaks Promise to Meet With Officer Injured on January 6th." A week later, McCarthy finally agreed to meet me, Harry, and Mrs. Sicknick.

That meeting—the one I recorded and in which the Republican leader said he couldn't control his own members—left me as disillusioned and depressed as ever. It occurred around the same time that I had a frustrating interview with a journalist who prodded me with political questions, instead of asking about honoring the officers. I felt wiped out, and my message and my mission seemed to be going nowhere. As part of the healing process, my therapists had encouraged me to talk about my January 6th experience as much as possible. But I began to feel that some Hill meetings were doing more harm than good. It was one thing to talk about my experience with people who were empathetic and believed in reality—that was cathartic. It was quite another to meet with people like Graham and McCarthy, who chose loyalty to Trump over reality and downplayed the insurrection—those encounters only increased my trauma. After the Graham and McCarthy meetings and the unsettling TV interview, I seriously considered giving up.

"What's the fucking point?" I said to a friend just after the McCarthy meeting. "No one is listening. I'm having zero effect. I'm making a fool of myself walking around Capitol Hill . . ."

My friend was sympathetic and gave me an out. She said, "You don't have to keep doing this. You've already done your job and you don't owe anybody anything."

I told her I had to keep going. I repeated what I had told McCarthy, "I feel like this is an extension of my service on January 6th."

"Okay," she replied. "But just make sure you're taking care of yourself, too." By way of analogy, she cited the familiar line from every flight attendant's preflight safety briefing: In case of trouble, place the oxygen mask over your nose and mouth first, before trying to help others.

Good advice.

During the period I spent lobbying on the Hill—May to June—Ray and I saw a lot of each other. We were both divorced with young kids, so on weekends when we could, we brought our kids to his apartment's rooftop pool or my dad's pool in Alexandria. While the kids swam, we sipped beers and shot the shit.

Inevitably, we talked about January 6th, the trauma and fallout. As an MPD commander, Ray couldn't speak publicly about how he felt, and he had to tread very carefully about his mental health inside the department. But he could tell me anything in confidence. I won't break that confidence here, but it's fair to say that Ray suffered the same trauma experienced by nearly everyone who fought in the tunnel. I can't imagine how hard it was for him to keep so much bottled inside.

I loved hanging out with my kids, and being an affectionate dad and role model. If there's a silver lining from January 6th, it's that the attack forced me to stop working as a street cop. No more unexpected overtime. No more working evenings or the weekend. Instead of executing pre-dawn search warrants on Sunday mornings, I took my girls to Dunkin' Donuts.

For the first time in my life, I controlled my own schedule. I met the girls at the bus stop after school. I caught Piper's and Mei-Mei's soccer games. I took the girls camping, canoeing, and rock climbing. The four of us visited my hunting property and friends in Highland County, Virginia. We went tubing at Shenandoah River Adventures and when the owner recognized me, he kindly comped us, and gave the girls free T-shirts. On another trip, we scaled Old Rag Mountain in Shenandoah National Park—three hours to the summit, and three hours back. When she could, my college-aged eldest daughter, Caitlin, joined us.

In June, I attended Hensley's graduation from kindergarten. For the first time since my divorce, I started going out to dinner with the kids and my ex, Hsin-Yi. We took a "family" vacation to the beach. It was nice.

Back in Washington, I was grateful that others reached out during the difficult months of April, May, and June. Liz Cheney took me out to dinner with her father in Old Town Alexandria, and I got to joke with the former VP about his shotgun skills. Speaker Pelosi continued to check in from time to time by phone.

Of all the politicians I met, I probably spent the most time with Adam Kinzinger, a Republican, and Eric Swalwell, a Democrat. They were instrumental behind the scenes, setting up meetings and offering advice. They also took the time to get to know me over coffee during the day and beers at night. Adam and Eric are both about my age so there was a natural connection. I admired Adam's bravery as one of the few Republicans willing to stand up to Trump and his nonsense. Eric is a former prosecutor and his dad was a cop, so we had plenty in common.

I had a lot less in common with someone else I met around this time,

Joan Baez. For starters, she's a hippie and I'm a narc. The Rock & Roll Hall of Famer is known for hanging out with civil rights icons Martin Luther King Jr., Cesar Chavez, and Nelson Mandela. I'm known for hanging out with anyone who will buy me drinks and listen to me yammer.

Joan is also a prolific painter, and her work sells for five-figure sums. On January 19th, she posted a haunting painting of me online based on the news photos, howling in pain, surrounded by a sea of red hate. I'm no art critic, but the oil-on-canvas captures my moment of horror. It's not easy to look at.

Joan tweeted a picture of her painting with the caption, "Thank you, but fuck you for being there." My cousins saw it on Facebook and reached out to the art gallery where it was up for sale. Word got to Joan, and she graciously shipped the painting to my mom as a gift. When Joan came to Washington in late May to be fêted at the Kennedy Center Honors, she asked me to join her as a guest, along with Dr. Anthony Fauci. During the event, honorees are celebrated by other artists on stage, but are not told in advance who will perform their music. In Joan's case, that artist was none other than Sturgill Simpson. I got to meet him afterward. That was cool. Really cool.

People in Hollywood reached out, too. Some, like Sean Penn, just wanted to thank me for doing my duty. At a time when I was feeling very low, the original Spicoli took me out for a night on the town, no strings attached. He warned me to be careful about people dangling opportunities, and I soon came to learn what he meant. It turns out that some of the other people I met on the Left Coast didn't truly give a shit about me or my fellow officers. It seemed like they just wanted to fucking cash in on my new fame, and make money off the memories of dead and injured police officers. In my mind, those people were no better than the twenty-one Republicans who voted against the Congressional Gold Medal bill.

It's possible that I misunderstood some of the overtures. I was struggling with PTSD, trying to heal, and I found it hard to concentrate. It was a tough dynamic. People I didn't know very well were urging me to become an activist or a politician, to join a lawsuit for their cause, or become the face of some product they wanted to sell. It became overwhelming. There were days when I powered down my phone and shut off my mind. Sometimes, I cut neighborhood lawns just to clear my head.

The other group of people I got to know a bit, of course, were the reporters who cover Capitol Hill. They trailed Harry and me and Mrs. Sicknick, waiting in the hallways as we visited congressional offices. Almost all of these reporters were working inside the Capitol on January 6th. Some were trapped in the House and Senate chambers, and then evacuated with everyone else to safe rooms. In many ways, they struggled with the same trauma afflicting so many Capitol Police officers. To do their jobs, they had to return to the scene of the crime every day. For some, that meant reliving a trauma on a daily basis.

I remember chatting with a network television reporter who shadowed me, Harry, and Mrs. Sicknick. While we were all waiting around for something to happen, just killing time, the reporter mentioned that her father was a retired police sergeant out West. Then she just burst into tears. I pulled her aside, away from the other journalists, and told her to tell me about her January 6th experience.

"I feel ridiculous talking to you about this—it's nothing compared to what happened to you," she said. "I was just locked in a room. I wasn't assaulted, just scared to death." She didn't need to state the obvious: With a face as recognizable as hers, she knew she'd be a prime target if the Trump mob reached her.

"Hey, trauma is trauma," I said. "Everyone has their own way of dealing with it. Some people turn to the bottle. Some people turn to drugs. Some people turn to mindfulness. Some people turn to yoga."

In 2021, I had similar conversations with dozens of other journalists, Hill staffers, and MPD and Capitol Police officers. I urged nearly all of them to seek therapy, and emphasized that overcoming emotional trauma can be as difficult as recovering from physical wounds.

I hope our conversations helped some of them. I know that speaking with them about January 6th certainly helped me. With so many people trying to whitewash the riot, it helped to talk with others who could give witness to the day's violence.

After the January 6th insurrection, the Capitol was closed to the public, and so I had to be escorted by a Capitol Police officer or a staffer wherever I went. Each time I visited the Capitol, I thought about retracing my steps to the Lower West Terrace Tunnel. But I guess I always became too preoccupied with the mission at hand to ask someone to take me down there. Then, in late May, at the end of a long day lobbying, someone who worked at the Capitol asked me if I'd been back to the tunnel. When I said no, she offered to escort me.

I wasn't sure what to expect. The Crypt and the route down the stairs certainly felt familiar, but once we entered the tunnel itself, I became a bit disoriented. The outer doors were closed—the space was no longer used as an official entrance—and so the tunnel was empty and silent. Without the smoke, yelling, and chaos, the tunnel felt longer and wider than I recalled. The whole place felt too sterile, too clean. I looked to the left and right and saw hallways I didn't remember. *Was this really the same place?*

I backed up to the beginning of the tunnel and took out my phone. I turned it horizontally and began playing my body-worn camera footage, retracing my steps as the video rolled. I walked and watched, my eyes darting from the screen to the tunnel and back again. I let the footage roll for a good five minutes. I cranked up the volume and the chaotic soundtrack from the body-worn camera footage echoed around the empty tunnel. When I reached the end, I stood at the double doors and stared out across the National Mall, and I began to cry.

CHAPTER 20

Betrayal

Of all the groups that resisted recognizing our response to the Capitol riot, one disappointed me the most: my fucking police union.

In twenty years as a dues-paying member, I'd never seen the local or national Fraternal Order of Police hesitate to back its officers. Of late, they'd been quite outspoken, raising alarms about the city's rising crime rate and pushing back against the "defund the police" movement. Whenever an officer was injured or killed in the line of duty, you could count on the FOP to make a strong statement of support and offer help behind the scenes. I didn't actively attend meetings but I always supported fellow officers in need. In two decades, I could scarcely remember a month that went by without a union-wide appeal to help a fallen officer or his or her family. Though I was usually broke, I'd almost always made a small contribution. Yet since January 6th, I'd received virtually no outreach or support from the union.

The reason sickened me: The union supported Trump.

In mid-July, I called Pat Yoes, president of the national FOP, and asked him why his response to January 6th had been so muted. I asked him why the FOP had declined to back the congressional bill to honor officers—FOP members, all—who had responded on January 6th.

"We're not a political organization," he told me.

I laughed into the phone. "Pat, that's exactly what you are! You're a lobbyist for law enforcement. You endorse candidates. You make contributions. You meet with legislators." Hell, on Election Days, I added, the FOP has cops make calls on behalf of candidates.

Yoes made a lame attempt to deflect and bond. He is a cop, too—a deputy sheriff in Louisiana—and so he began comparing our work. I declined to get into a dick-measuring contest with him. As veteran cops, we'd both experienced a lot of stress and violence on these streets. So what? What the fuck did that have to do with the Capitol riot? I asked him if he'd reached out to the dozens of other officers still reeling from physical and emotional trauma. I told him that the MPD staff psychiatrists were overwhelmed.

In response, Yoes offered to help me find some therapy.

"Listen," I said. "I've already been seeing shrinks for six months. If I'd sat around waiting for your fucking invitation, I'd be dead by now."

After the call I heard that Yoes planned to attend a regular local FOP meeting that very evening in Washington. He'd be there with Gregg Pemberton, the chairman of the local MPD union. I could confront them both there.

The FOP lodge is a squat two-story building near Chinatown, a brutalist eyesore in an otherwise up-and-coming neighborhood. The first floor of the lodge has administrative offices and a gift shop. The second floor has a bar and a ballroom, where they hold regular meetings. That evening, I showed up with Harry Dunn and, in my pocket, an audio recorder rolling.

Harry and I entered a union ballroom filled with a few dozen regulars and retirees. We arrived a few minutes late and Yoes was already speaking. The national president touted the FOP's efforts to lobby Congress to retain officers' rights in any proposed police reform legislation. Yoes then asked the members to support his candidacy for reelection. He and his leadership colleagues, he said, had worked hard to "change the current narrative" about the police in social and mainstream media.

I saw an opening and raised my hand. "So I understand the things that the national and local lodges have done to combat the narrative that we need to 'defund the police,'" I said. "What have we done at the local and national level to combat the narrative that January 6th, the defense of the Capitol, in which I participated, was not some love-fest between law enforcement and insurrectionists?"

Yoes jumped in, noting that we'd spoken earlier that day. "I appreciate your passion and I appreciate your frustration. I truly do. My heart goes out for you and everyone else who was affected by this. This was a tragedy." He claimed that the FOP had reached out to Trump during the riot and asked the president to tell his people to back down. "And he did. He did."

But in terms of supporting January 6th first responders, Yoes said he couldn't act without coordinating with his MPD and Capitol Police union unit chairs. "I'm looking for them to give me some direction."

Direction? Six months after the insurrection? I was speechless.

Harry spoke up. "I'm a United States Capitol Police officer. I was also there on January 6th . . . I don't know what narrative or whatever is being attempted. However, we have members of Congress and the former president, as late as this Sunday, calling the officer who shot Ashli Babbitt an executioner. The FOP has not defended him." Harry cited a Department of Justice review that cleared the officer and said, "That officer did his job correctly."

Harry grew angrier as he spoke.

"We are just officers. You are the voice," he said. "You need to stand up for our officers. We need to let them know that we all have each other's back." Then he added, "Forgive me for yelling. I am extremely passionate."

"And I appreciate your passion," Yoes responded, but repeated that he needed to coordinate with leaders in the Capitol Police's local union. "That's the way our organization works. I'm not going to circumvent the role of that lodge." The national president offered to set up a meeting, and moved on to the next member's question, a tangent about "strategic relationships."

I raised my hand again. When it was my turn, I tried a different tack, realizing that our initial attempt had been too abrupt. I'd assumed everyone in the room knew our story. Dialing it back a bit, I calmly laid out my background, my role on January 6th, and my injuries. Then I told the union members about the recent visits Harry and I had made at the Capitol on behalf of the thousands of officers who responded that day.

"I never thought in my wildest dreams that I would become responsible for convincing not only lawmakers but also the general public that not only was the day brutal but that it actually fucking happened," I said.

I said I didn't understand why the police union was allowing false narratives about January 6th to grow and fester.

"What I'm asking for today is a commitment on behalf of the national FOP and my local FOP to combat those narratives in the public," I said. "These are not political statements. These are lies. And their characterization of that day as being anything other than what it actually was: a brutal, violent assault on our Capitol against law enforcement officers who responded there with no political motivation whatsoever in mind, other than to fulfill their oath. And what I've heard from within these organizations, with which I'm a member and have been for twenty years, is silence. And to me, six months out, silence has become complacency."

"I will make that commitment," Yoes said, then quickly repeated his caveat. He'd commit to working through the local union committee—the same committee that hadn't done shit for six months.

Jody Shegan, the union rep for the First District and a cop I'd known for two decades, said he had a question for me. "Do you go on other networks? Or just CNN, when they talk bad about law enforcement?"

I studied Shegan's face before answering. I'd considered the guy a friend and colleague for decades. We'd been drinking buddies. We'd gone fishing together. The insinuation that I deliberately spoke only to "liberal" news outlets was bullshit, and felt like a total betrayal.

I responded that I had tried many times to appear on conservative networks, and that I was willing to speak to almost any reporter willing to spread my message. But, I added, I was shot down every time by Fox bookers.

Shegan switched tactics, and followed up with a snide and reckless smear aimed at Harry. Shegan implied that in his earlier remarks about the Ashli Babbitt investigation, Harry had improperly discussed confidential details.

"As for the shooting in the Capitol," Shegan said, "I'm not aware of that report being released to anybody to say the officer was justified or not just justified."

It was a dick move: In a semipublic setting like a union hall, you don't publicly accuse a fellow cop of leaking confidential information without absolute proof. And anyway, Shegan was wrong. The Justice Department had issued a press release months earlier, clearing the officer who shot Babbitt.

Harry lost it. "How dare you!"

Pemberton jumped in and scolded us for creating an embarrassing fracas before the national president. Yoes tried to placate us. He said that at the FOP national conference, the group was expected to approve a resolution declaring that the officers who responded on January 6th are national heroes.

Harry, having recovered his composure, apologized for his outburst. I tried to speak again, but got cut off and union leadership steered the meeting back to its regular agenda: mind-numbing talk about fundraising, the national conference, taxes, hotel banquet rooms, and the sorry state of the union's finances. This went on for about twenty-five minutes. One thing became clear: The union was so broke, many members believed the only way to rescue it was to sell the lodge building.

Somebody I didn't know raised a hand and brought the discussion back to January 6th. "These gentlemen," he said, motioning to Harry and me, "were officers doing their job and right now they feel like they've been abandoned."

I took my cue. I said that during the first two weeks after January 6th, injured officers received an outpouring of support, mostly from law enforcement colleagues. "After that, there was nothing from the city administration. I never heard from anyone. I never heard from a single member of the city council, after I reached out."

I corrected myself. Actually, I said, one council member did return my call. "'Michael,' she told me, 'I'm sorry for what you experienced but never underestimate how much people hate the police in Washington, D.C. It would be politically disastrous for any one of us on the city council to acknowledge the performance of MPD on January 6th.'" In fact, she told me that she brought up the idea in a community meeting and was shouted down.

My adrenaline was pumping now. "I reached out to the mayor— not a fucking word. Nothing. As an officer who received a traumatic brain injury and a heart attack, to not receive so much as a fucking handwritten note, text message, or phone call from the mayor? Fucking disgraceful."

On Capitol Hill, I said, I'd met similar rejection lobbying for the Gold Medal bill. I had initiated every contact with lawmakers on both sides. No one ever reached out to me. The only Democrats who wanted to be seen meeting with a cop were Speaker Pelosi and those who prosecuted Trump's second impeachment. The only Republicans who would meet with me were those who voted to impeach Trump.

"I am not here to say one political party supports or does not support law enforcement." Raising my voice, I said, "What I am here to say is that as law enforcement officers, make them earn our support!"

I said I didn't want to hear another political leader say he or she "backs the Blue" or pander to us by attending memorial services or bullshit publicity stunts.

"I'm sick and tired of my service and our collective service being used by people that don't give a fuck about police officers!"

That drew light applause, but also generated a lot of yelling back and forth. I was ruled out of order, and told I'd already had my chance to speak.

"This doesn't help," a union leader said. "It's not what we're here for."

Another cop spoke up. He said the "silent majority" of D.C. residents still support the police. He assured me, "There is somebody out there who cares."

"I appreciate that." I repeated that I was not alone in expressing my surprise by the lack of support post–January 6th from MPD management and union leadership. "I talk to guys all the time who say, 'Mike, where is everyone?' I'm simply trying to say to you that your public response was not enough."

The room fell silent and Harry said, plaintively, "Why do we have to beg for help? Why the fuck am I here just to beg for you to acknowledge us and ask for help? Why do I feel that way? I'm just asking for help."

A union official said, "We're here to give you help."

"It doesn't seem like it," Harry said, his voice cracking. "It doesn't seem like any of you care. I went to talk to Internal Affairs today and I did not want a union rep with me because I do not feel they have my back—"

"Sir!" someone yelled. "You're out of order."

"*You're* out of order!" Harry shot back.

"We will keep order and we will continue our business," the chair said.

We stood down.

But we didn't leave. Twenty minutes later, as the meeting broke up, Pemberton came up to me and we spoke for a bit. With my recorder still rolling in my pocket, I told the union official that I was already using my new relationships with both Democrats and Republicans on the Hill to informally lobby for issues critical to police officers. Pemberton said that was great but told me he had to walk a fine line on January 6th.

"These people run the gamut," the MPD rep said of his union membership. "I've got Trump supporters on one side. I've got others on the other side. When I start to engage in supporting or not supporting the work that you have done, I get pigeonholed that I'm either taking the membership all the way to the left or all the way to the right. You're appearing with Pelosi and Swalwell. I need to watch out for that."

I steamed. The dude was more interested in photos posted on Twitter than substance. I was glad the phone in my pocket was still recording.

I explained that I'd also met with Liz Cheney and Kevin McCarthy and had seized the opportunities in those meetings to advocate on behalf of police officers in general, on issues unrelated to January 6th. I told the union chief that in similar meetings I'd warned Democrats, including Pelosi, that if they tried to pass new laws restricting police powers and liability, I'd go on TV and bash them.

That's great, my union chief told me, but really, I needed to stop posing for pictures with Democrats who have criticized the police.

"This is my world," he said. "How am I supposed to react when I see that?"

I told him I preferred to work with the union, rather than allow such stupid misperceptions to fester. I'm not a Democrat, I insisted. I offered to help broker a meeting between the union and Pelosi.

"I would love to do that," Pemberton said. "The one thing I want to be very clear about is that I'm hesitant to start putting out information, one way or the other about January 6th. My job is to represent 3,500 people."

Well, I said, how about a simple statement condemning anyone who says that January 6th was "a love-fest" or a "normal tourist day"?

"Yeah," Pemberton replied. "But does anybody really believe that? Do you think if people believe that, is there anything we could say to change their mind?"

It couldn't hurt, I said. "Coming from a group like the union, people like Kevin McCarthy, who's looking to lead the future Republican Party, might see that it's no longer politically advantageous to embrace this bullshit because we're starting to lose support from entities that have always supported us."

I told him that Representative Paul Gosar of Arizona had sent a fucking fundraising message that called the officer who shot Ashli Babbitt a murderer. Why can't the union respond to that?

I said, "We defend police officers involved in disputed use of force all the time."

Pemberton said there was nothing he could do.

I came to the sorry realization that many fellow officers turned against me not only because they believed I'd crossed some blue line of solidarity but because I'd challenged their führer, Trump.

Outside, we found reporters waiting for us. Harry and I kept it civil. We told the press that the meeting had been productive and that we looked forward to the union's support. "We're just looking for the truth to get out about January 6th," I said.

A reporter pressed. "But the union is still supporting the former president. Did the union make any promises that they would help you in the future?"

I was uncharacteristically diplomatic. It didn't feel like the right moment to take a shot at the union or Trump. It was Harry's turn to tell the truth.

"It's been lonely," Harry said. "Six months in, it's been lonely."

CHAPTER 21

Testimony

A few days after the union meeting, I was asked to testify before the Select Committee to Investigate the January 6th Attack on the United States Capitol.

The committee planned to kick off a series of hearings with police officers as witnesses on July 27th. I'd never testified before Congress, of course, but I'd done it scores of times in court, and so I prepped the same way.

My strategy was simple: I would soberly lay out the facts, without injecting emotion or my political beliefs, just as I would as an officer testifying in a criminal trial. I'd keep my tone professional, offering a clear and concise accounting of what happened, what I witnessed, and what I experienced. My pro bono lawyer, Chuck Tobin, helped me outline what I wanted to say and I wrote it up. Like the other witnesses, I'd get five minutes to lay out my story, uninterrupted. But I knew the most important moments were likely to come during the unscripted Q&A that followed. And I fucking relished that. It meant that I'd have the chance to go toe-to-toe with Representative Jim Jordan of Ohio.

At that point, Jordan's appointment by McCarthy to the January 6th Committee felt like a near certainty. So I did some homework to prepare.

Jordan and another likely appointee, Representative Jim Banks of Indiana, were leading election deniers and Trump loyalists. I studied hours of film of Jordan at hearings, with his sleeves-rolled-up, tie-askew schtick, a former college wrestling coach badgering genuine heroes like Alexander Vindman and Fiona Hill with nonsense. Banks, the other Looney Tune, spent a lot of airtime trying to draw a false equivalency between the January 6th sedition and looting during the 2020 BLM protests.

Jordan and Banks thought they were theatrical and effective. I thought they were jokes. I planned to beat them over the head with the facts.

Representative Eric Swalwell and Liz Cheney's staff helped me prepare. They offered advice on how to combat Jordan's more aggressive tactics and warned me to prepare responses ahead of time. Jordan liked to make long-winded attacks, disguised as a question, then use a parliamentary maneuver to cut a witness off before he or she could answer. If that happened, I planned to just speak anyway, even if they cut my mic. I'd say, "If I were you, I wouldn't want to hear what I have to say either."

Jordan's likely personal role in the coup attempt also felt like fair game. It's a fact that the congressman spoke directly to Trump at least once on January 6th. It's also a fact that on January 5th, Jordan forwarded to the White House chief of staff a text that outlined a legal maneuver that would keep Trump in power. At a minimum, those two overt acts made Jordan a witness in a criminal inquiry, if not a coconspirator and suspect. If things got really heated with Jordan at the hearing, I planned to quip, "You know, this is a first for me. It's the first time a suspect in a criminal case has ever been allowed to question me."

Unfortunately, Pelosi rejected Jordan's and Banks's appointments because she believed they'd be too obstructionist, and were instrumental in pushing Trump's lies. (A year later, Pelosi's instincts would be confirmed; Jordan and five other Republicans, including McCarthy, would be subpoenaed after refusing to testify before the January 6th Committee.)

Only two Republicans would sit on the select committee, Liz

Cheney and Adam Kinzinger, and both believed in reality. I joked with Kinzinger that without an insurrection denier on the panel, the hearing figured to be pretty boring.

I never asked permission from MPD to testify. I agreed to do it because I saw it as an extension of my service on January 6th, and I felt I had a civic duty to do so. I was already appearing on TV and giving print interviews on my own. As long as I spoke in civilian clothes, the MPD didn't seem to care. At the very least, they ignored me. I did, however, presume that I would testify before Congress in uniform. I mean, other than a wedding or a funeral, what the hell could be more formal than congressional testimony? Then I spoke with Officer Daniel Hodges, the officer whose primeval howl for help as he was crushed in the Lower West Terrace Tunnel went viral. Dan, who is assigned to a Civil Disturbance Unit, also expected to testify. He told me that MPD wouldn't let us appear in our uniforms because we'd be testifying in our "personal capacities."

I did not take the news well.

The move reeked of cowardice by overcautious city bureaucrats. I hadn't self-deployed to defend the Capitol as Michael Fanone, private citizen. I'd self-deployed as Metropolitan Police Department Officer Michael Fanone—and I was going to fucking testify as Officer Fanone. I couldn't understand what the problem was. I called a couple of people inside the department to say what-the-fuck, and then I called a reporter. Word soon reached the top. Within a day, the department reversed its stance. But now, the MPD suits had to scurry to solve two practical problems: My badge remained locked in an FBI evidence vault and, as an officer on medical leave, I wasn't permitted to keep a uniform at home. I was issued new dress blues, and the city rushed to mint me a new badge. A few days later, in a nice touch, Chief Robert Contee III presented the new badge in person, and wished me luck.

As I entered the hearing room on July 27th, my biggest worry was what my fellow panelists would say. I had hoped to testify beside Jimmy, Jeff, and Ray, professionals I knew could command a room from the witness stand with confidence and facts. The evening before the hearing, I learned that I would be testifying alongside Dan Hodges and two Capitol Police officers, Harry Dunn and Aquilino Gonell. I carried immense respect for all three of them but I had no idea what they planned to say. Given their regular police assignments, I knew that none had much experience testifying in court. I worried that they might (understandably) let their emotions get the best of them and get too political, playing into the hands of Trump's defenders in the conservative media.

I'd come to criticize Donald Trump not because of his policies and his cruelty but because he'd incited a fucking insurrection. Cops got hurt. People died. It was the most disgusting fucking moment in American history. Period.

I hoped the hearing would stick to those facts.

At 9:31 a.m., Representative Bennie Thompson rapped his gavel, and the marathon hearing began. The seventy-three-year-old chairman may be less well-known than his January 6th Committee colleagues, in part because of his low-key, bipartisan, and gentlemanly style. But the thirteen-term congressman from Mississippi has been fighting for civil rights since he was a college student in the late 1960s, working with the Student Nonviolent Coordinating Committee (SNCC) to organize voting drives in the Delta. First elected to Congress in 1993, Thompson represents a district that surrounds Jackson, the state capital, and he is the lone Democrat in Congress from conservative Mississippi. Thompson was the senior Democrat on the House Homeland Security committee. When Pelosi appointed Thompson to chair the January 6th Select Committee, key Republicans from the Homeland Security committee praised him for his cool demeanor and bipartisan ethic.

Indeed, Thompson opened the hearing with a stern promise. "There's no place for politics or partisanship in this investigation," he said. "Our only charge is to follow the facts where they lead us. And while we have a lot to uncover, there are a few things we already know . . ."

In a calm, deliberate cadence the chairman said, "We know that the insurrection on January 6th was a violent attack that involved vicious assault on law enforcement. We know there is evidence of a coordinated, planned attack. We know that men and women who stormed the Capitol wanted to derail the peaceful transfer of power in this country. We know that seven people lost their lives, that more than one hundred and forty police officers suffered injuries. We know that efforts to subvert our democracy are ongoing, and a major part of the select committee's work will be to find ways to eliminate that threat. We also know that the rioters came dangerously close to succeeding. If not for the heroism of the United States Capitol Police and the Metropolitan Police Department, many more lives might have been lost and the rioters could have accomplished what they set out to do, upend American democracy."

The chairman looked up from his notes and nodded at us.

"It's an honor to have four of these heroes sitting before us today," he said. "We welcome them for appearing here, and more importantly for your heroism on January 6th. You have the gratitude of this committee and this country. You held the line that day. I can't overstate what was on the line, our democracy. You held the line."

Mere words, Thompson said, can't come close to describing what happened, and he instructed an aide to roll some video.

Familiar images filled large screens in the hearing room: Trump supporters breaking through barricades and windows, screaming "Take the building," "Fuck you, police!," followed by the desperate law enforcement radio broadcasts, and then, shaky video of hand-to-hand combat in the smoke-filled Lower West Terrace Tunnel.

"Heave, ho! Heave, ho!"

"Patriots to the front!"

Then Dan Hodges on video getting crushed, wailing in agony. I stole a glance to my left and saw Dan curl his lip as he watched himself on the monitors.

More familiar images and voices, this time from my body-worn camera. "Heave, ho! Heave, ho!" "Let's get some fresh guys up front!" "Pull them out! Pull them out!"

Thompson vowed the committee would investigate the roots of the insurrection.

"Some people are trying to deny what happened, to whitewash it, to turn the insurrectionists into martyrs," he said. "But the whole world saw the reality of what happened on January 6th, the hangman's gallows sitting out there on our nation's mall, the flag of that first failed and disgraced rebellion against our union being paraded through the Capitol, the hatred, the bigotry, the violence, and all of it for a vile, vile lie."

Liz Cheney, the committee vice chair, opened by thanking all officers who defended the Capitol. She said the videos "show the unbelievable violence and inexcusable and intolerable cruelty" the police faced on January 6th.

"People need to know the truth," she said. "If Congress does not act responsibly, this will remain a cancer on our Constitutional Republic, undermining the peaceful transfer of power at the heart of our democratic system. The question for every one of us who serves in Congress, for every elected official across this great nation, indeed for every American, is this: Will we adhere to the rule of law? Will we respect the rulings of our courts? Will we preserve the peaceful transition of power? Or will we be so blinded by partisanship that we throw away the miracle of America? Do we hate our political adversaries more than we love our country and revere our Constitution? I pray that that is not the case."

Amen, sister.

The chairman asked us to stand and raise our right hands for the oath. I did so, and it felt familiar and calming. I'd done this a hundred times in court. I felt well-prepared and in a good frame of mind. This far into the hearing, I barely noticed the photographers and klieg lights.

Aquilino Gonell testified first, and introduced himself as an immigrant and patriot, a man living the American Dream while also serving his country. As a child in the Dominican Republic, he said, he idolized

America as the land of opportunity. After legally entering the United States in 1992, he became the first person in his family to graduate from college. He joined the U.S. Capitol Police and Army Reserve in 1999. In Iraq, he spent a hellish 545 days dodging mortar and rocket attacks fired at his army base. To support comrades in the field, Aquilino volunteered for resupply missions he knew would take him on roads routinely targeted by insurgents with roadside bombs.

"But on January 6th for the first time, I was more afraid to work at the Capitol than my entire deployment to Iraq," Aquilino told the committee. "In Iraq, we expected armed violence because we were in a war zone, but nothing in my experience in the Army or as a law enforcement officer prepared me for what we confronted on January 6th."

During the riot, Aquilino said, he was kicked, pushed, shoved, spit on, and sprayed with chemical irritants. Someone targeted his eyes with a laser. He was attacked with hammers, rebars, batons, police shields, rods, and a metal pole flying an American flag. Aquilino said the rioters tried to pull him into the crowd, and one of them beat him with his own baton.

"I, too, was being crushed by the rioters," Aquilino said. "I could feel myself losing oxygen and thinking to myself, 'This is how I'm going to die, defending this entrance.'"

Aquilino suffered injuries to both hands, his left shoulder, right calf, and right foot. His foot and shoulder wounds—a labrum tear and rotator cuff damage—required painful surgery. Nevertheless, he told the committee he'd respond the same way, if called again. Indeed, despite his injuries, he returned to work on January 7th. He said he was proud to be an immigrant, proud to be a police officer, proud to be an American, proud to defend our seat of democracy.

I was up next. I flipped on the microphone and began to read my statement.

"Thank you, Mr. Chairman and members of the committee for inviting me to provide my eyewitness testimony on the assault on our nation's Capitol . . ." I explained that I joined the Capitol Police shortly after 9/11 and since 2004 had served the MPD, focused mostly on removing drug traffickers and violent criminals from city streets. I said I often worked undercover. Then I got to the point.

"In this line of work," I said, "it probably won't shock you to know that I've dealt with some dicey situations. I thought I'd seen it all, many times over."

I paused, glanced up at the dais, then kept reading.

"Yet what I witnessed and experienced on January 6th, 2021, was unlike anything I had ever seen, anything I had ever experienced or could have imagined in my country."

As I said the words out loud, I felt the first surges of an odd uneasiness. I gripped my written remarks firmly, curling the pages.

"On that day, I participated in the defense of the United States Capitol from an armed mob—an *armed* mob—of thousands determined to get inside. Because I was among the vastly outnumbered group of law enforcement officers protecting the Capitol and the people inside it, I was grabbed, beaten, tased, all while being called a traitor to my country. I was at risk of being stripped of and killed with my own firearm, as I heard chants of 'Kill him with his own gun.' I can still hear those words in my head today."

I tried to keep my focus on the words written on the page, but as I spoke my mind whirled. *What the fuck am I even doing here? Is this just a dog and pony show? Will anything I say convince those who refuse to believe the riot took place?*

I tried to push the doubts aside and read on. "Some have asked why we ran to help when we didn't have to. I did that because I simply could not ignore what was happening. Like many other officers, I could not ignore the numerous calls, numerous calls for help coming from the Capitol complex."

I briefly described how Jimmy and I made our way to the Lower West Terrace Tunnel. I conveyed my admiration for Ray's command presence on January 6th. The nation needed to know of his heroism.

"The bravery he and others showed that day are the best examples of

At an award ceremony early in my career with MPD Chief Charles Ramsey and Assistant Chief Michael Fitzgerald.

2.

Duck hunting with my partner
Jimmy Albright on the Patuxent
River in southern Maryland.

3.

Commander Ramey Kyle and I returned to the
Lower West Terrace Tunnel on January 6, 2022.

My three youngest girls: Mei-Mei, Hensley, and Piper.

5.

Under attack by the Trump mob on January 6, 2021.

6.

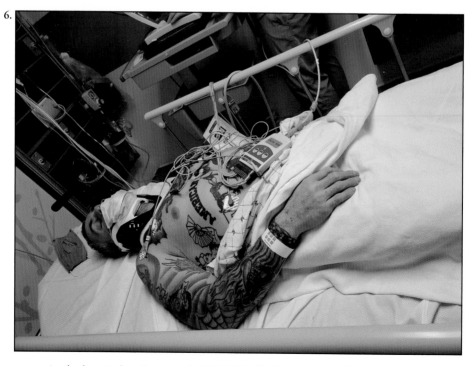

At the hospital on January 6, 2021. I drifted in and out of consciousness.

7.

On Don Lemon's show in March 2021, my mother, Terry Fanone, called Trump a coward.

8.

At the Capitol in December 2021, after turning in my MPD retirement paperwork.

9.

Reviewing my body-worn camera footage with Representatives Stacey Plaskett (*front left*) and Madeleine Dean (*front right*). Standing behind us are Representative Eric Swalwell and Montana Miller, an aide to Speaker Nancy Pelosi.

10.

With Lt. Col. Alexander Vindman at CNN's studios in summer 2021.

11.

At the Kennedy Center Honors with Paul Pelosi, Gabriel Harris, Joan Baez, Speaker Nancy Pelosi, and Sturgill Simpson.

The painting Joan Baez posted online after the insurrection
and later gave to my mom.

duty, honor, and service," I said. "Each of us who carries a badge should bring those core values to our work every day."

I stole a glance around the room. *Was any of this sinking in?*

I summarized the scene in the tunnel. "Many of these officers were injured, bleeding, and fatigued, but they continued to hold the line." Then I described how the rioters pulled me into the mob and attacked me, and how I feared I would be torn apart or shot to death with my own gun.

"I was electrocuted again, and again, and again, with a taser," I said. "I'm sure I was screaming, but I don't think I could even hear my own voice."

My own voice. I could hear my voice echo as I said the words. My mind drifted again, even as I kept reading, and I tried to suppress a growing sense of anger.

I urged those who had not yet viewed my body-worn camera to watch it. "The portions of the video I've seen remain *extremely* painful for me to watch at times, but it is essential that everyone understands what really happened that tragic day."

I described my physical injuries: a concussion, heart attack, and traumatic brain injury. Then I turned to the hardest part: the mental anguish.

"As my physical injuries gradually subsided and the adrenaline that had stayed with me for weeks waned, I've been left with the psychological trauma and the emotional anxiety of having survived such a horrific event, and my children continue to deal with the trauma of nearly losing their dad that day. What makes the struggle harder and more painful is to know so many of my fellow citizens, including so many of the people I put my life at risk to defend, are downplaying or outright denying what happened."

As I said the word "adrenaline" I could feel it building inside. I caught glimpses of politicians on the dais, the remote video cameras, the kneeling still photographers and thought, *Why am I on a TV stage instead of a grand jury room? Am I just a prop in a theater production? Will my testimony have meaning?*

My pulse quickened, and I grew angry—angry about the way officers who responded to the insurrection were treated by Trump's people. Angry at the way they were treated by the media. Angry at the way they were treated by police unions. Angry at pro-Trump cops who said we injured officers got what we deserved for picking the wrong team.

I looked up at the politicians and said, "I feel like I went to hell and back to protect them and the people in this room, but too many are now telling me that hell doesn't exist or that hell actually wasn't that bad."

I let that sink in.

Then I fucking lost it.

Raising my voice and slowing my speech, I said, "The indifference shown to my colleagues is disgraceful!" and slammed my right palm to the table, like an exclamation point.

The table shook and I worried it might keel over. I steadied myself by reading the next few sentences quickly. Then I said, "Being an officer, you know your life is at risk whenever you walk out the door, even if you don't expect otherwise law-abiding citizens to take up arms against you. But nothing—truly nothing—has prepared me to address those elected members of our government who continue to deny the events of that day, and in doing so betray their oath of office."

I closed my remarks with a reminder that I agreed to testify because I don't think the process should be politicized. A crime was committed on January 6th and it deserves a criminal, not a political, response.

"What my partner Jimmy and I suited up for on January 6th didn't have anything to do with political parties or politics," I said. We did not self-deploy as Democrats or Republicans. We responded as American police officers.

Dan Hodges followed me, and told his harrowing story in minute detail. Dan was assigned to the Civil Disturbance Unit. His brutal day began at dawn with a posting on Constitution Avenue and did not end until well after midnight, even after he became crushed between the doors inside the Lower West Terrace Tunnel. I knew his story—almost everyone knew his story—and yet, as he retold it, it felt as fresh and outrageous as the first time.

His voice cracking, Dan described the moment he realized he was trapped between doors, unable to move. "I knew I couldn't sustain much more damage and remain upright. At best, I would collapse and be a liability to my colleagues. At worst, I would be dragged out into the crowd and lynched. Unable to move or otherwise signal the officers behind me that I needed to fall back, I did the only thing that I could do, and screamed for help."

Dan looked up from his testimony and took a long, slow gulp from his water glass. "Thankfully," he continued, "my voice was heard over the cacophony of yells." Despite multiple injuries and exhaustion, Dan did not leave the Capitol until 1 a.m., when the all clear was given. As Dan spoke, I could sense the trauma in his eyes, a long-distance look of sadness.

Harry Dunn gave the final opening statement. He began by asking for a moment of silence for his fallen fellow officer, Brian Sicknick—a stand-up gesture.

Harry said that on the morning of January 6th he reported to roll call as usual and then to his post on the eastern front of the Capitol, the side facing the Library of Congress and the Supreme Court. He stood on the outdoor steps leading to the Senate. At 10:56 a.m., he said he received an alarming text from a friend. It was a screenshot from one of the protesters that said "the Capitol" was "the objective."

"Trump has given us marching orders," the text said. "Keep your guns hidden." The instructions urged people to "arm up" in "six to twelve man teams."

Harry said the text surprised him, because he hadn't been warned of any potential violence during roll call. During the noon hour, the Trump crowd began to grow and become more menacing. Around 1 p.m., he heard over the police radio reports of a bomb discovered at Republican National Headquarters. Harry also heard disturbing reports about clashes on the western side of the Capitol. He was already carrying an M-4 rifle, but now he put on his steel breastplate, and raced around to see what was happening.

"I was stunned by what I saw. In what seemed like a sea of people, Capitol Police and MPD were engaged in desperate hand-to-hand fighting with rioters. Until then, I had never seen *anyone* physically assault a Capitol Police officer or MPD officer, let alone witness *mass assaults.*"

Harry helped officers flush their eyes of chemical irritants. When he heard a radio report that rioters had breached the interior of the Capitol, he rushed inside. Harry fought insurrectionists in the Crypt and outside the Speaker's Lobby. He ordered them to leave, and one responded, "No, no, man, this is our house! President Trump invited us here! We're here to stop the steal. Nobody voted for Joe Biden!"

"Well, I voted for Joe Biden," Harry said he told the rioters. "Does my vote not count? Am I nobody?"

Harry blew out a long sigh before he continued.

A woman in a pink MAGA shirt yelled back, "You hear that, guys? This nigger voted for Joe Biden!" A crowd of about twenty people joined in, Harry said, screaming, "Boo! Fucking nigger!"

As he spoke the incendiary words, Harry looked up from his prepared remarks and around the room.

"No one had ever, ever, called me a nigger while wearing the uniform of a Capitol Police officer," Harry said. Later, he said other Black officers shared with him similar stories of racial abuse from January 6th.

Once the worst of the attacks concluded, Harry said he collapsed on a bench in the Rotunda and told a fellow Black officer about the racial abuse. Harry became emotional speaking with his colleague, and began yelling. "How the [fuck] could something like this happen? Is this America?"

Rage turned to tears. "I began sobbing," Harry told the committee.

Harry closed with a quote from a congressman who late that night took to the floor of the House to condemn the attacks:

"The violence, destruction, and chaos we saw earlier was unacceptable, undemocratic, and un-American. It was the saddest day I've ever had serving in this institution."

That congressman was Kevin McCarthy.

Next, the hearing shifted to questions from the committee. With so much scripted political theater, it's hard to call anything in Congress "spontaneous," but we truly didn't know what to expect next.

The chairman asked Harry to elaborate on the racial abuse. The officer said he couldn't process it fully at the time because he was too busy defending the Capitol and protecting himself.

"I was just trying to survive," he told the chairman. Later, at home, he said, it hit him, and it hurt. "My blood is red. I'm an American citizen. I'm a police officer. I'm a peace officer. I'm here to defend this country."

Cheney asked Aquilino how he felt when he heard Trump say, "It was a loving crowd. There was a lot of love in the crowd."

Aquilino called it upsetting and pathetic, given that Trump "himself helped to create this monstrosity." Aquilino added, "I'm still recovering from those hugs and kisses that day."

Zoe Lofgren, a thirteen-term Democrat from Northern California, used nearly all of her hearing time to play my body-worn camera footage, and then asked me to provide a minute-by-minute narration. By this point, I'd told my story many times on television, though with rare exception it had aired only in bits and pieces in short segments on different channels. Now, for the first time, I would narrate the entire trauma, from self-deployment to unconsciousness, to a national and international audience. I spoke uninterrupted for eight and a half minutes, an eternity in Congress.

It certainly didn't feel like eight and a half minutes to me. I felt at ease, like a policeman clinically explaining body-worn camera footage to a jury, step-by-step. It was cathartic.

Kinzinger, the only other Republican brave enough to sit on the committee, stated the obvious: Congress was not prepared for the riot because no one dreamed such a thing could happen in America. He rejected the comparison between the January 6th insurrection and the urban riots and looting of 2020. As an Air National Guardsman,

Kinzinger deployed for those riots, but, he noted, "Not once did I ever feel that the future of self-governance was threatened like I did on January 6th. There is a difference between breaking the law and rejecting the rule of law, between a crime, even grave crimes, and a coup."

Kinzinger turned to the four of us and acknowledged that he'd gotten to know us a bit, and that we represented hundreds of officers who responded on January 6th.

"I think it's important to tell you right now that though you guys may individually feel a little broken, and you guys all talk about the effects you have to deal with, and you talk about the impact of that day, but you guys won. You guys held."

Jamie Raskin, the brilliant and perpetually disheveled Maryland Democrat, asked me about internet conspiracies that alleged I was beaten by the mob because I was mistaken for an Antifa agitator.

I stifled a smile. "Well, I was in full uniform. I was wearing my uniform shirt adorned with the Metropolitan Police Department's patch. I had my badge on until somebody ripped it off my chest." I could have added that I also wore a jacket with the words "METROPOLITAN POLICE" stenciled across the back and a helmet emblazoned with the letters "MPDC." Keeping a straight face, I told Raskin, "I do not believe I was mistaken for a member of Antifa."

The congressman followed up. "You mentioned in your testimony that there's some people who would prefer that all of this go away, that we not have an investigation—let's let bygones be bygones," he said. "But you seem pretty determined to get the country to focus on this. Why is that so important to you?"

It's important not just to me, I told Raskin, but to every officer who responded on January 6th, especially those who were injured, physically and mentally.

"Downplaying the events of that day is also downplaying those officers' response." If we gloss over this, we gloss over the harm inflicted to the officers, your institution, the rule of law, and to democracy. "For some of the officers, part of the healing process from recovering from the traumatic events of that day is having the nation accept the fact that that day happened."

Representative Elaine Luria, from my home state of Virginia, spoke last. I didn't know her well, but the bio I read before the hearing impressed me. Before Luria won election to Congress in 2018, she spent two decades in the U.S. Navy, the longest military tenure of any Democrat in the House. She retired at the rank of commander and served on six ships as a nuclear-trained surface warfare officer. Luria was one of the first women in the navy's nuclear power program and among the first to serve her entire career on combat ships. She was a warrior. Of all the January 6th Committee members, I figured, Luria could best empathize with what we were going through.

"I know it's been difficult today as we've watched these images from the Capitol," Luria said, "but I did want to share one more video." This time, the congresswoman said, she asked people to close their eyes and focus on the spittle of hatred leveled at the police. "Just listen to what is being said as these brave men were being overrun."

"Die."

"You should be mad, too. Fuck you."

"You're on the wrong side of freedom."

"Fuck you guys. You can't even call yourself American. You broke your fucking oath today. 1776!"

"Traitors! Traitors! Traitors!"

The clip ended and Luria asked me how these epithets made me feel. At the time, I said, I kept it professional. I had people and property to protect, and fellow officers who needed assistance. I relied on twenty years of training and street sense to tune out the noise. "At no point that day did I ever think about the politics of that crowd. Even the things that were said did not resonate in the midst of that chaos, but what did resonate was the fact that thousands of Americans were attacking police officers who were simply there doing their job, and that they were there to disrupt members of Congress who were doing their job."

As the hearing wound up, three hours and twenty-nine minutes after it began, the chairman asked each of us what we hoped the committee would accomplish. I said that while I supported investigations to determine the serious security failures on January 6th at the Capitol—including preparation, planning, intelligence, and deployment—the committee should not stop there. It ought to find out who stoked the mob.

Clues abound, I said. This crime should be investigated like any other.

"In the academy, we learn about time, place, and circumstance in investigating potential crimes, and those who may have committed them," I said. "And so the time, the place, and the circumstances of that rally, rhetoric, and those events—to me, it leads in the direction of the president."

CHAPTER 22

Truth and Consequences

Leaving the hearing room that day, I felt pretty good. It seemed like the four of us had accomplished our goals. Outside the hearing room, I checked my phone and scrolled quickly through a few stories and texts from friends and supporters. I was elated as I could be, given the circumstances.

Then I checked my voice mail.

I had a message from an unknown number: "This is for Michael Fanone, Metropolitan Police officer. You're lying. You want an Emmy or an Oscar? What are you trying to go for? You are so full of shit, you little faggot fucker. You're a little pussy, man. I could slide you upside the head with a backhand and knock you out, you little faggot. You're a punk faggot, a lying fuck. How about all the scummy Black fucking scum for two years destroying our cities and burning them, and stealing all that shit out of the stores. How about that? Assaulting cops and killing people? How about that, you fucker? That wasn't shit in the goddamn Capitol. I wish they would have killed all you scumbags. You people are scum. They stole the election from Trump and you know that, you scumbag. Too bad they didn't beat the shit out of you more."

I didn't feel afraid. I felt sorrow. I felt sadness for our country and for everyone who wears a uniform to serve the public.

I thought of Lieutenant Colonel Alexander Vindman and his bravery. I thought of General James "Mad Dog" Mattis and General Mark Milley. I thought of Khizr Khan, the Gold Star father who dared to criticize Trump. I thought about the late John McCain.

And I realized: This is what happens to people who tell the truth in Trump's America.

I was already scheduled to appear on Don Lemon that night, so I called him and told him about the voice mail. He asked me what I wanted to do.

"Play it, motherfucker—put it on air, and don't censor it."

To Don's credit, he did so, uncensored, on his 10 p.m. program that evening. When he asked me for my reaction on air, I was ready.

"This is what happens to people who tell the truth in Trump's America."

Don played a clip of Laura Ingraham on Fox News, who said I deserved an Oscar for "best performance in an action role." On his show, the weasel Tucker Carlson snidely doubted the depth of my injuries and said my testimony politicized the police.

Don asked me what I thought about all the name-calling.

"I spent quite a bit of time in my career testifying in court, and I always felt most comfortable when defense attorneys resorted to theatrical tactics because I knew that they no longer had facts to support their argument, and so they had to insult me, insult my appearance," I said. "So if they want to disparage me or call me a member of Antifa or talk about my neck tattoos, I couldn't care less. What does concern me is that those entertainers have an audience and that audience takes their words and the rhetoric they use and that has real-life consequences. We saw the results of that on January 6th."

What happened next was both surprising and overwhelming.

I got letters. Thousands at first, then tens of thousands. The letters and cards of support came from across the country, almost all handwritten, and tons bearing American flag stamps. They began arriving shortly after my congressional testimony. People addressed the letters to me at MPD headquarters, and they arrived in giant tubs. It reminded me of the courtroom scene near the end of *Miracle on 34th Street*, when the bailiffs burst through the doors, hauling sacks and sacks of letters. The volume of cards, notes, and letters I received would take a whole book to reproduce, but here's a quick sample:

From Martha Domont of San Anselmo, California:

Just know that there are millions more of us who are grateful and honor your efforts then and now. Your testimony was chilling and powerful and cut right to the core of what happened then and continues today.

From Elizabeth Gelgud of Charlotte, North Carolina:

The brutality you endured was horrifying. When you said, "The indifference shown to my colleagues was disgraceful!" a chill went up my spine. Please do not give up hope. Thank you for testifying. You are a credit to the D.C. police and everyone who believes in the rule of law.

From Judith Blazek-Nobel of Vestal, New York:

We will forever be in your debt.

From Dr. Joan Hess-Homeier of Missoula, Montana:

As a clinical psychologist, I have spent many years treating victims of PTSD. I have learned that the important thing is to keep talking. Talk about what happened, your feelings, and experiences. Talk to your fellow officers, friends, family, and a therapist, if you so choose. Don't stay silent.

From Mary Ellen Navas of Salt Lake City, Utah:

I am one of the millions of Americans who watched the body cam footage . . . The restraint that you exercised by not using your weapon is a critical detail. I salute your strength, self-control, and passionate expression of anger at elected officials who have abandoned their responsibilities by misrepresenting the events of the day.

From Patricia Hull of Shoreline, Washington:

If that was a peaceful protest, I am a giraffe. It so happens I am not a giraffe.

My mom opened every letter, and I read as many as I could, and she filed them for safekeeping in boxes, along with other gifts people sent. One lady sent a dozen heart-shaped pillows, and my mom distributed them among her grandchildren. Another lady took the time to sew me a queen-sized quilt. At bars and restaurants, strangers sometimes bought me drinks and managers picked up my tab. While getting gas in Alexandria, an elderly woman filling her tank at an adjacent pump approached tentatively and asked, "Are you Michael Fanone?" When I said yes, she wrapped me in a big hug.

I was grateful for the letters, gifts, and gestures from so many strangers. But I found it hard to reconcile them with the opposite reaction I received from people I had known for most of my entire adult life. People whom I considered dear friends ghosted me because they thought I was too outspoken. It didn't make sense, and made my already fucked-up mind race, fueling doubt and depression. I would have traded those thousands of letters in a heartbeat to reclaim my old friends, and to return to the job I loved for twenty years.

About a week after my House testimony, the Senate passed the Gold Medal bill unanimously. The next day, August 4th, I received a call around 9 p.m. from a senior MPD official. He told me that President Biden planned to sign the bill during a Rose Garden ceremony late the following afternoon, and that I was invited, along with other officers, the mayor, the chief, and congressional leaders.

"Okay, great, thanks," I said. "Where are we meeting to caravan over?" I had never been to the White House, but for most external events, it was standard MPD procedure for officers to travel together.

"Oh, we'll just meet you there," the MPD official replied. "The White House will be in touch on the details."

The Gold Medal bill did not call for medals to be distributed to the officers it was designed to honor. Only four medals would be created. One would be displayed at MPD headquarters, one at Capitol Police headquarters, one inside the Capitol, and one at the Smithsonian Institution. That struck many officers, including me, as weird because in Washington elected and appointed officials make a big deal out of handing "challenge coins" to virtually every visitor as a memento. To some, challenge coins are a status symbol. Some people collect them the way others collect celebrity autographs, and prominently display them in their homes and offices. The challenge coins, sometimes called medallions, usually bear the crest or seal of the office holder on one side and a motto or signature on the other. In the 1990s, they were popular in the military—generals and specialized units presented them to guests—and that tradition later spread throughout the government, including across Congress. When Harry, Mrs. Sicknick, and I visited senators and representatives, many meetings ended with a photo op and the presentation of a challenge coin. They give them out like participation trophies—all it means is that you met someone "important." So I was surprised to learn that when Congress voted to honor the cops who defended the Capitol on January 6th, it neglected to authorize an actual medal for each officer.

It wouldn't have cost that much to create 2,000 medals the size of a challenge coin, maybe $20,000 at most. A challenge coin costs about two or three dollars to manufacture, if that. Put a ribbon on it and you have a medal. I couldn't fathom why Congress wouldn't pay for actual medals to honor those who defended them. For so little money, it would have meant so much to so many officers.

This was just one reason why I debated whether to attend the White House event. It didn't help that months earlier I had written Biden a letter, asking him to recognize the valor of those who defended the Capitol. I followed up, but never got a response from his people.

I'm not deeply schooled in the ways of Washington. I realize that the president of the United States is a busy guy who receives a lot of mail. Hell, I can be lousy at returning phone calls or emails myself. But when I was invited to the White House event, it struck me that Biden's aides might be trying to use me as a political prop, maybe not as nakedly opportunistically as Trump had used those officers in Long Island back in 2017, but still.

On the other hand, I didn't want to appear ungrateful or hypocritical. I had spent months lobbying for recognition for all of the officers, and if this was going to be the pinnacle of that recognition, so be it. We'd earned it.

I put on my dress blues and drove my truck into the city.

When I arrived, I noticed that other MPD officers had caravanned to the White House with the chief. Before the ceremony, we were steered to a holding room with the mayor. I chatted with Dan Hodges, Harry Dunn, Aquilino Gonell, and a few other officers. The mayor came over to Dan and shook his hand. She did not shake mine.

Though it was just before 5 p.m. when we entered the Rose Garden, the humid August sun was still sweltering. My wool dress uniform hung like a winter coat, and I instantly started to sweat. From across the garden, Speaker Pelosi caught my eye and came over. I think she recognized my wariness about participating in a political event and greeted me with kind words that briefly set me at ease.

The tone in the Rose Garden was not celebratory. How could it be? Among the guests were the families of the fallen officers—the widows and fatherless children. In some ways, it felt like a wake.

Biden took the podium around quarter past five.

"Folks," he said. "Not even during the Civil War did insurrectionists breach the Capitol of the United States of America, the citadel of our democracy—not even then. But on January 6th, 2021, they did. A mob of extremists and terrorists launched a violent and deadly assault on the People's House and the sacred ritual to certify a free and fair election. It wasn't dissent. It wasn't a debate. It wasn't democracy. It was an insurrection. It was a riot and mayhem. It was radical and chaotic. And it was unconstitutional. And maybe most important, it was fundamentally un-American."

Biden said he understood that the ceremony was bittersweet. "I offer you not only our condolences, but recognize your courage," he said. "And you have our most profound gratitude." He added, "My fellow Americans, the tragedy of that day deserves the truth above all else. We cannot allow history to be rewritten. We cannot allow the heroism of these officers to be forgotten."

Afterward, Biden asked the officers and the families to step forward and stand with him as he signed the bill. Some small children, presumably among those whose fathers had died as a result of the insurrection, gathered closest to the president. After signing the bill into law, Biden turned to the officers and thanked us all again for defending the Capitol, and he thanked the families of the dead for their service. In the presence of the president of the United States, most of them genuflected, replying with polite "thank yous" of their own.

That felt like an odd response, so I called out, "You're welcome!"

Biden laughed and jokingly shook his fist at me. "That one, he's tough."

I smiled back, politely. But inside, my pulse throbbed and my mind raced. I felt a familiar anxiety building.

When I woke that morning, I had believed this day would mark a milestone, and it did. Afterward, I was glad that I decided to attend the Rose Garden ceremony.

But during the ceremony, I began to realize that this day would also mark an unexpected turning point, one that triggered mixed emotions and mental whiplash. In retrospect, what happened next helped explain the cold reception from the mayor and instructions from MPD to drive to the White House on my own.

Once the Rose Garden ceremony ended, I came face-to-face with this new and unexpected shitstorm.

CHAPTER 23

Time to Go

On the same day as the White House ceremony, *Time* magazine posted a 6,600-word profile, putting my personal life out there for the first time. The piece had been in the works for weeks. It criticized the city's, the MPD's, and the White House's lack of response to my calls to honor the January 6th officers. The timing could not have been worse.

In the print edition, I appeared alone on the magazine's cover. In a gritty black-and-white photo, I posed outside the Capitol in my MPD dress uniform. The headline said, "THE AFTERMATH. Why Officer Mike Fanone Won't Let America Forget Jan. 6th."

Though I had told my January 6th story to many, many journalists, it gnawed at me that people I could not control were twisting my words to suit their agenda. A growing false narrative portrayed me as a darling of the Left. I worried that I was being used by both sides. So did some of my closest friends, including Jeff, Phil, and Ray. Online, people seemed to be turning me into a cartoon I didn't recognize.

I had a singular mission: respect for officers who responded to defend the Capitol on January 6th, and accountability for those responsible for and those involved in the insurrection. Period.

In June, Molly Ball, a *Time* journalist who had recently written a book about Pelosi, reached out to propose an in-depth profile, and I said okay.

Over the summer, Molly and I talked about a dozen times, in person and by phone. She was present in the small hearing room when I testified, and visited my mom's home. We talked about things I hadn't yet discussed publicly, including details about my personal and professional life before and after January 6th. I had no idea how long or detailed her story would be, or what shape it might take. But given her questions, I understood that the story would be deeply personal.

The *Time* article began with the emotional moment in May at the bar, when my body-worn camera footage first aired on CNN, and I cried.

In the introduction, Molly wrote that this would be "a story about what we agree to remember and what we choose to forget, about how history is not lived, but manufactured after the fact. In the aftermath of a national tragedy, we are supposed to come together and say 'never forget,' to agree on the heroes and the villains, on who was at fault and how their culpability must be avenged. But what happens if we can't agree? What if we're too busy arguing to face what really happened?"

The *Time* story summarized my progression as a police officer from "adrenaline junky" who "wanted to run and gun" to professional officer, "thinking things out and planning ahead and being meticulous." In general terms, the story described my physical and emotional recovery, as well as my struggles with the department, and Republicans who refused to describe the riot as anything other than what it was—a violent assault on democracy.

Near the end of the *Time* piece, the author wrote:

"What does Mike Fanone deserve? A parade? A key to the city? He's not asking for any of that. He's not asking to be called a hero—he just wants us to remember what his sacrifice was for. Fanone believes we can't keep trying to outrun this thing; we've got to turn around and face it, defeat it once and for all. That if all we do is turn away and hope it fades, it will just keep getting stronger until it comes back to kill us all."

Exactly.

We have to hold the line, somewhere, and say enough is enough.

I thought the article was well done and served its intended purpose. It used my experience on January 6th to force people to recall sacrifices hundreds of police officers made that day. Yes, I stood alone on the cover, but not because I was special. As the article made clear, I wasn't a "good" cop or a "bad" cop. I was "every" cop.

Unfortunately, people read into things whatever they want to read.

The article triggered another wave of strong reaction, pro and con, on social media and in real life. I really didn't give a shit about most people's reactions. *Time* magazine isn't intended to be an organ of the left or the right, or, for that matter, the MPD or BLM.

I was surprised, however, by the reaction from Ray and other officers. Hate from right-wing nut jobs was one thing, but the hostility from fellow cops and friends fucking stunned me.

Ray called me a few hours after the story was published. Ray believes cops should operate within certain parameters, and maybe that's why he was management material and I was not. He couldn't understand why I spoke so intimately about myself and my work as a police officer.

Apparently, cops aren't supposed to cry. If they do, they aren't supposed to talk about it publicly. Cops aren't supposed to admit that they sometimes get an adrenaline rush when they arrest criminals, or if they do, they aren't supposed to talk about that publicly. Cops aren't supposed to criticize the police union, or if they do, they aren't supposed to talk about it publicly. I guess cops aren't supposed to act like other human beings, or if they do, they aren't supposed to talk about it publicly.

"Why would you say these things?" Ray asked. "We don't say those things out loud. Those are things we keep to ourselves."

"Look," I said, "maybe *that's* part of the problem. Maybe you're missing the point. What I was trying to do was to show the progression of a police officer, how we need to stop viewing the people we encounter on the streets as the enemy. I realize that not everyone ends up enlightened. Some cops end up the same way they started, aggressive, running and gunning, doing things on the heavier side of recklessness."

We need to change that, I told him. If we want to improve relations between the police and the public we serve, we've got to drop the siege mentality and get real, even personal.

"We've got to tell people what cops really fucking experience throughout their careers. We've got to normalize police officers, humanize them." And, I added, "As officers, we've got to remember to see the people we meet on the streets as human."

The conversation didn't end well. Ray and I did not speak again, much less hang out with each other's kids, for a very long time.

I spoke to another officer with executive-level connections who warned me that the MPD brass and the mayor's office believed that I'd become a divisive figure within the department. Trump supporters inside the force—and there were hundreds of them—were growing louder and bolder in their objections to my public statements. Incredibly, some pro-Trump cops were opposed to prosecuting anyone arrested during the January 6th insurrection for assaulting police officers.

The personal animosity toward me had grown so strong, my friend told me, that some MPD leaders worried that if I returned to street patrol, I might end up like Frank Serpico. The NYPD whistleblower was shot under mysterious circumstances in 1971, and nearly died awaiting a suspiciously delayed response.

In other words, my friend warned me, I'd become inconvenient.

Things came to a head in September 2021, following eight months of physical and mental rehab. I was cleared for a return to limited duty. A doctor I'd been seeing asked me where I wanted to work. I'd given it a lot of thought.

I couldn't return as a regular patrolman and I certainly couldn't go undercover—I had become too visible. Plainclothes work posed risks, too, because if I was recognized as a cop it might put fellow officers in danger. I understood and agreed, but I wanted to be productive and couldn't wait to get back to work. I wanted to contribute.

I offered three suggestions:

First, I could work as an expert witness in court, testifying in complex crack, meth, and heroin cases. As an expert, I could explain the economics, culture, and language of the drug trade to juries. Behind the scenes, I could assist young prosecutors and help rookie cops prepare for trial.

Second, I could create a training program for special mission units, the kind of thing I'd done my whole career. The execution of search warrants, as we have seen in other cities, poses an enormous danger to both officers involved and the residents whose homes are being raided. The stakes are so high, each raid must be carefully planned and executed. I could offer years of experience and supervision.

Third, I could work at the MPD academy, training new recruits. I was already doing so with young officers in the First District. At the academy, I could not only train new recruits, I could help train the trainers.

The doc said the academy sounded like a great fit. "I'll make some phone calls and set it up."

Two weeks passed without a call about my new assignment. A few days before my return date, around Labor Day, I called Ralph Ennis, the academy commander and someone I knew pretty well. Ralph told me that he'd received a call asking if he'd be willing to take me, and he'd told them, "Yes, of course." But after that, he said, he hadn't heard another word.

On my first day back, I had a previously scheduled meeting with the department shrink who had been helping me find a new assignment. She asked me if I was excited about working at the academy. I told her it sounded good to me, except I hadn't been assigned there, or anywhere. The doc was confused.

"Yeah, me too," I said. "I don't know what to tell you." We got up and went to see her supervisor.

He immediately backpedaled. "I just make recommendations. I don't have anything to do with placement."

My shrink was pissed. "Well, the last time we were here, I was under the impression that Fanone was going to the academy, and Fanone was under the impression he was going there. Now what? Where is he supposed to go? He's back to limited duty today. He's got to work somewhere."

The supervisor turned to me and said, "Well, just go home and somebody will call you."

"Damn," I said, "I guess we've come a long way from 'We want you to come back and have significant input' to 'Just go home and wait for a call and we'll put you somewhere.'"

On my ride back to Alexandria that afternoon, I dialed Peter Hermann at the *Washington Post*.

"Hey, Mike, how's your first day back going?"

I told him.

"Wow," Hermann said. "Okay, let me do a little follow-up."

I arrived home, and as soon as I cracked a beer, my phone rang. It was Morgan Kane, my former First District commander. She was now assistant chief in charge of the Technical and Analytical Services Bureau.

"Hey Mike, long time," she said. "Why don't you swing by the office and come chat with me?"

"Well, maybe some other time," I said. "I'm at home."

"No, no, just come on by."

"I'm already back home. Maybe we could hang out some other time."

"Mike, don't make me order you to come back in."

I drained the beer, climbed into my truck, and drove to Morgan's office at headquarters. She explained that she'd been in the chief's office with other assistant chiefs when he got an urgent call that Peter Hermann was asking why the MPD had let my assignment fall through the cracks. The chief turned to his assistants and asked for volunteers to take me. Morgan had raised her hand.

I appreciated Morgan's loyalty and compassion, but after twenty years on the streets, I was ill-suited to transition to an administrative desk job. I was assigned to a soul-sucking cubicle in an otherwise empty room under construction. The other employees assigned to the area, crime analysts who studied stats and trends, worked from home almost every day of the week because Covid was still raging. Intentional or not, I was isolated.

The only saving grace was that my buddy Phil McHugh worked there, essentially as Morgan's chief of staff. In a shitty situation, I could not have been luckier to draw Phil as a boss. We'd been in touch regularly since the day I was released from the hospital, when he'd met me at the First District station.

After January 6th, Phil took to asking me, "How's your mission going?"

By "mission," he meant my effort to ensure that people never forgot the sacrifices made by MPD and Capitol officers during the insurrection. Phil knew me well enough that while I might be, as he liked to put it, "a little rough around the edges," that I was all about the mission.

On dark days, especially after a frustrating experience with the medical system or a nasty text from someone I had considered a friend, I would call Phil and he would let me vent and second-guess myself.

"Phil, am I right or wrong about this? Am I crazy for thinking this way? Why are people saying that I'm just doing what I'm doing just to get attention for myself? Am I being an asshole?"

"Dude," he would say, "you know me well enough that I will tell you when you're being an asshole." To his credit, a few times Phil *did* tell me to stop being an asshole and chill. And I appreciated it when he did so.

Phil took a risk backing me. At MPD, he was a rising star, and to put it politely, my outspoken manner created a potential liability to his career. By this point, I was critical of both management and the union. I have no doubt that there are officers who no longer speak with Phil because he was kind to me when I needed it most. I hope that writing about him in these pages will do no further harm, because Phil is exactly the prototype officer this nation needs. He is brave, educated, relentless, loyal, and compassionate.

Unfortunately, working at headquarters, where hundreds of cops pass each other as they go about their day, proved more stressful for me than working the streets. Whenever I left my cubicle, I was ostracized, treated like a leper. If I approached a group of other officers talking, they would walk away. Every visit to hit the bathroom risked a confrontation. It was not lost on me that most of the venom came from white cops. Black cops, for the most part, were supportive. From them, I got hand-shakes and hugs. Most white cops averted eye contact. A few literally turned their backs.

Clearly, too many MPD officers prioritized their allegiance to Donald Trump over their oath to the United States Constitution, including the Bill of Rights. That's a scary fucking thought, given the power each individual police officer can wield. I don't think the vast majority of officers support Trump over the Constitution, but a significant number do. And far too many officers are indifferent, and that includes the hundreds of cowards who failed to respond on January 6th.

My mere presence on the force bothered both groups. I'd become a walking billboard that confirmed one simple truth: January 6th actually happened and the response was disgraceful.

I gave the new assignment a couple of weeks, but it just wasn't working out. I faced a choice. If I remained with MPD for another five years, I'd receive my full pension. But that would mean five years in a cubicle, and five years dodging insults and watching my back. Fuck that.

I could have filed for a disability separation based on my injuries. But somehow, that felt like defeat. I didn't feel like giving up.

I could have sued MPD—more than a few people suggested that I do so. But lawsuits aren't my style.

Instead, I decided to leave on my own terms. I would wait until the department cleared me medically to return to duty full-time. Then I would retire. I aimed to leave MPD by year's end. Until then, I would keep my mouth shut and head down, and stay out of trouble.

In late October, I attended the department's annual award ceremony at the Walter E. Washington Convention Center. In addition to the usual Officer of the Year Awards and civilian honors, the chief bestowed a Ribbon of Valor on the 850 officers who responded on January 6th.

It was the city's first and only formal recognition for our service on January 6th. Given all that had transpired in the past ten months, and my efforts to win such recognition for my fellow officers, I struggled to process it. I didn't want to be rude or ungracious but it felt like too little too late. I was seated at a half-empty table in the back and didn't really get to engage with anyone I knew. Feeling awkward and anxious, I left early.

Walking out into the crisp October evening, I realized I'd made the right decision to leave the MPD. As I told a friend at a bar that evening, "I don't belong there anymore."

The next day, I called my pro bono lawyer to confirm the details of my exit. We aimed for a departure date of December 31st.

On a Friday in mid-November, I took Piper, age nine, and Hensley, age six, for a hike on the Virginia side of Great Falls Park, a small national park along the Potomac River, about fifteen miles northwest of D.C. It was a perfect fall day, breezy with temperatures in the forties. Hawks circled above, soaring toward patches of gray clouds on the Maryland side of the river. The Potomac forms a natural gorge at Great Falls and beyond the amazing view, it's a great place to climb on the jagged rocks that line the shore.

Late that afternoon, I drove the three of us into Washington for a ramen dinner near the Capitol. We ran into a friend who works on the Hill and she offered to take the girls on a quick tour. The Capitol was still closed to the public for security reasons, but my friend had a pass that allowed her to take us almost anywhere.

As we approached the Capitol, I recall that my six-year-old's colorful outfit kept cracking me up. Hensley wore a pink romper, teal hoodie, opaque white tights, and black combat boots splashed with silver glitter. Her getup lent a rambunctious burst of color and innocence to the Capitol's gray-and-white marble and stone.

Just before sunset, we entered the Capitol through the same entrance I used on January 6th, the one on the House side. This late on a Friday evening, we had virtually the whole place to ourselves. We walked past the Speaker's Lobby, where rioters trying to break into the House chamber were repelled by an officer's gunfire. We studied the statues in the Hall of Columns, toured the soaring Rotunda, and took the curved stairs down to the Crypt. As we walked, my friend gave the girls a CliffsNotes tour. Eventually, we made our way to the stairs that lead down to the Lower West Terrace Tunnel.

When we reached the bottom of the stairs, I kneeled to eye level with the girls, and I nodded toward the tunnel.

"This is where Daddy and Uncle Ray and Jeff and Jimmy, and thirty police officers fought to save the Capitol," I said.

Piper and Hensley shuffled forward into the tunnel, and my friend pulled back to give us a moment. At the end of the tunnel, the girls pressed their faces to the locked glass doors and looked out across the National Mall. In the growing darkness, we could see the blinking red lights of the Washington Monument in the distance.

We didn't say a word.

We just hugged.

EPILOGUE

"Legitimate Political Discourse"

On the last Friday in January 2022, I drove from my new apartment in Alexandria to Union Station. After crossing the Potomac, I took the 3rd Street Tunnel, which crosses the city underground near the Capitol. I emerged a few blocks south of Sursum Corda, and parked in a garage near a homeless encampment. Then I boarded a train for New York.

I found a seat, powered up my laptop, and took a long pull from a large cup of coffee, ready to work. I stared at a blank screen for about a minute, and as the train began to roll silently from Union Station, I closed my eyes and let my mind drift.

What a fuckin' year.

My last month at MPD had been quiet. My resignation took effect on December 31, 2021, and I had spent a day before Christmas taking care of the final paperwork, shuttling between clerical offices at MPD headquarters and the Marion S. Barry, Jr. Building. I took one last pass through First District headquarters and checked my locker, which was empty. I peeked into my old unit's tactical locker and found my body-worn camera still in its charging slot. The device still had my name on it, and it was ready to go. That made me smile.

No one threw a going away party and I didn't expect one. When I left MPD, I counted just two officers as friends.

Now, on the train headed north to New York City, I was on assignment for my new employer, CNN, which had hired me as a law enforcement analyst. As a former street cop, I could offer a boots-on-the-ground perspective that a retired police chief or FBI executive could not. Of course, CNN also hired me because of my connection to January 6th, and on the first anniversary of the insurrection, I provided commentary from dawn to midnight. It was an exhausting and emotional day. In between TV appearances, I was hit by rolling waves of anger. It all still felt raw.

On air, I was asked what it felt like to be back on Capitol Hill. I said that I felt sorry for the officers and staffers who had to walk the same halls as insurrectionist members of Congress. "I can't imagine what it's like sharing a workspace with those jackasses."

I was asked what I thought of President Biden's speech at the Capitol on the anniversary, one in which he said Trump "held a dagger to the throat of America" on January 6th. I said that while it was a strong speech, I couldn't understand why Biden had waited a whole fucking year to give it. I also wondered why I'd seen very few changes with the Capitol Police, both in terms of leadership and lessons learned designed to prevent future assaults.

For me, the highlight on January 6, 2022, was a segment I did for Don Lemon's show. In the piece, I revisited the Lower West Terrace Tunnel with Ray. In recounting the defense of the Capitol, Don asked Ray if he was ever scared. Ray's response: "No, there wasn't time to be scared."

After the insurrection anniversary, I had hoped to shift gears to talk about police reform, but in the weeks that followed, riot-deniers kept reopening the wounds.

At a rally, Trump declared that if reelected he would pardon January 6th insurrectionists. Anderson Cooper asked me on air what I thought about that, and I said that there's just no bottom for what Trump will say. "He's like America's crazy ex and he's just decided that if he can't have us, no one can, and he's going to tear apart our democracy and our country if he can't get reelected."

When Mike Pence made a rare statement about January 6th—he said that it would have been "un-American" for him to follow Trump's order to overturn the election—I said on air that Pence was just trying to salvage what might be left of his political career and reputation. "Because he knows inevitably history is going to take a big shit on his head."

I got in trouble for saying that last one on live TV.

But none of Trump's and Pence's drivel compared to what the Republican Party did a short while later. At its annual winter meeting, the GOP censured two of the people I admire most in Congress, Adam Kinzinger and Liz Cheney, for participating in the insurrection investigation. The only thing more asinine than the censure gesture was the actual text of the GOP resolution, which called the January 6th Committee inquiry "a Democrat-led persecution of ordinary citizens engaged in legitimate political discourse."

When I heard that, I reflexively reached for the scar tissue on the back of my neck, a souvenir from my encounter with "ordinary citizens engaged in legitimate political discourse."

I was nearly at a loss for words. It felt like we'd come full circle with the GOP on the insurrection: from condemning it to whitewashing it to legitimizing it. With this resolution, Ronna McDaniel and the Republican National Committee essentially became a political wing of the violent white supremacist groups that attacked the Capitol, including the Oath Keepers and the Proud Boys. Donald Trump, the ultimate carnival barker, had invited these people—most of whom were considered so extreme, they hadn't even been a part of the American political conversation—into the Republican Party. Equal blame goes to the cowards within the GOP who welcomed them.

Those enablers include the wife of a sitting Supreme Court justice and Fox News anchors who brazenly worked behind the scenes with the White House chief of staff to delegitimize Biden's election. They also include 230,000 Republicans in Pennsylvania, who in 2022 elected as their nominee for governor an election denier who used campaign funds to help bring busloads of insurrectionists to Washington.

In the summer of 2022, I would attend the January 6th Committee's second round of hearings in the front row, just a few steps from the witnesses. There, I would learn what many suspected all along but thought too outrageous to be true: Trump waited hours to respond to the violent attack on police officers at the Capitol because he embraced the insurrection and helped execute it.

Violence was always part of the plan.

That's the thing with the Trumps. The truth is always worse than you can even imagine—worse than the cruelty and selfishness exhibited by the most depraved drug dealers I encountered in twenty years on the streets. The Trumps are evil, and then some. They continue to shock the conscience.

The 2022 hearings proved that the Capitol assault was not the work of a few rowdy dickheads who got a little out of control. Long before January 6th, Trump and his henchmen conspired in illegal schemes. Trump personally pressured senior Republican state officeholders to illegally change the election results. He summoned followers to Washington on January 6th—"Be there, will be wild!" He filed baseless lawsuits, pushed a crazy conspiracy to create fake electors, and urged the Justice Department to pursue bogus election fraud claims. He kept at it, even after his attorney general told him he was full of shit. Trump ignored other government lawyers who warned him that his January 6th plot was illegal and that things might turn violent. "People are going to die and the blood's going to be on your fucking hands," the White House counsel reportedly told Trump's chief of staff. Trump didn't give a shit. As he told top Justice lawyers on the eve of the coup attempt, "Just say the election was corrupt and leave the rest to me and the Republican congressmen." It speaks volumes that afterward so many close associates and House Republicans sought pardons.

We now know what the president knew and when he knew it. He knew nearly everything, and he knew it from the start.

He was certainly told that he lost the election. Nearly all of his saner aides say they told him so. And we know that on January 6th, Trump knew that hundreds, if not thousands, of his diehard followers brought weapons, including knives, pistols, AR-15s and tasers, to Washington. We know Trump knew this because he threw a tantrum about crowd size when his armed supporters refused to pass through metal detectors to attend his Ellipse rally. Yet he still incited the crowd to march on the Capitol and became irate when the Secret Service refused to allow him to join his supporters.

At the hearings, I struggled to keep my shit together. I felt helpless and angry. At home, you can scream at the TV, let loose with your emotions, but in a hearing room surrounded by cameras, you have to mask your feelings. Though I remained stone-faced, it's hard to describe the level of rage I felt.

I felt enraged that so many White House staffers knew Trump's stolen election claims were batshit crazy yet said nothing publicly at the time. I felt enraged that these same people feared violence on January 6th but chose not to warn law enforcement. Perhaps most of all, I was enraged by the way so many of the Republicans who testified were portrayed by the media. They were held up as heroes, as if they had bravely appeared before the committee to help defend the republic and democracy itself.

Horseshit.

Let's be honest. Most testified to try to restore their reputations. I found much of their testimony self-serving and smug. Too many Republicans clung to the hollow position that while Trump may be "an imperfect messenger," they love his policies. Shortly after the Arizona House Speaker testified with pride that he resisted Trump's illegal pressure to overturn the election, he told reporters that if Trump became the GOP nominee in 2024, he'd support him. *What the fuck?*

I left the summer hearings struck by how fragile our democracy is, and how much we rely on an honor system to keep it operating.

Americans should demand full accountability for January 6th. Many Democrats and Republicans have been too soft on Trump. They need to ditch their belief that modeling decency is somehow going to direct Trump and his supporters to behave ethically. It doesn't work with people who are shooting up our streets and it certainly doesn't work with people like Trump.

The rule of law should mean something. If there is probable cause to believe Trump committed crimes—and by now there's little doubt—he should be charged, arrested, and tried. If convicted, Trump should go to prison for the rest of his life. He directed and unleashed an attack on American democracy and destroyed countless police officers' lives. People may say I'm bitter, but I don't give a fuck. I'm angry, I love my country, and I want justice.

Attorney General Merrick Garland, who is said to be reluctant to indict a former president, needs to grow a pair and do his job.

====

Back on the train, my thoughts shifted to the mission at hand, grappling with another divisive issue in America, one I knew a lot more about: policing.

I was headed to the funeral for NYPD officer Jason Rivera, who was slain with his partner, Wilbert Mora, while responding to a domestic disturbance call in Harlem. I didn't know either officer, but I wanted to honor their sacrifice and grieve alongside my peers. There is something awe-inspiring and bonding about the massive turnout at police funerals. They remind us that police officers risk their lives every day to serve the public.

After the funeral, I was scheduled to speak at CNN's New York studios to try to put the NYPD tragedy in context. I also asked to pen an essay for CNN's website, which is why I had the laptop open. In twenty years, I'd been to scores of funerals for the fallen, and so I had some sense of what I wanted to say. I started to organize my thoughts.

First some facts: We're in the midst of a surge in violent crime that

215 Epilogue | 215

includes a spike in homicides. In 2020, the last year for which FBI crime stats are available, 21,570 people were murdered in the United States. That's nearly 5,000 more than the previous year, a 27 percent increase and the largest year-to-year jump since 1968. Preliminary figures from cities the size of D.C. and New York show that the murder rate climbed again in 2021.

The rise in crime followed five years of calls to reform, if not defund, the police. Plainclothes officers were removed from the streets, training budgets were slashed, and proactive police measures, such as targeting the most violent criminals, curtailed. As more morally bankrupt cops like Derek Chauvin were revealed, distrust and outrage grew, and politicians, reporters, activists, and unions seized the moment to politicize the police.

Across the nation, officers are fed up. Morale is circling the drain. Officers are tired of watching the political pendulum swing back and forth, between heavy-handed and light-touch approaches to policing. By now, it ought to be clear that neither fucking works.

So what do we do about all this?

How can we as Americans honor the sacrifice of the two fallen NYPD officers, and the rest of the nation's 750,000 professional police officers?

How can we humanely combat a surge in violent crime, and also reduce the epidemic of officer-involved shootings?

The first step is to commit to an honest, civil, and inclusive dialogue.

If we truly want police reform, we need to have sincere conversations that include everyone affected. I look at it like a Rubik's cube. All stakeholders—residents, police officers, police leadership, shopkeepers, community activists, prosecutors, defense lawyers, unions, politicians, and the media—need to engage honestly. If we can't get the colors to line up on each side of the Rubik's cube, if everybody isn't all in, we're just verbally masturbating.

Next, we've got to stop the political pandering that uses police officers as weapons in our culture wars. People on the right need to stop saying,

"We back the Blue, except for those who defended the Capitol on January 6th." People on the left need to stop saying, "Cops in riot gear are evil, except for those officers who defended democracy on January 6th."

Most police officers don't care about politics. They just want the resources they need to keep communities safe. I know residents of crime-plagued neighborhoods are fed up, too. They just want to live in safe communities.

An honest discussion includes a frank look at racism. There's a long history of racism in this country and unfortunately law enforcement has played a significant part in that. I don't believe that police officers are above reproach, but I also don't believe that all white police officers are racist.

Are there racists in police departments across the country? Absolutely. But this should come as no surprise. The police are a microcosm of society. During my two decades on the force, I encountered anti-Black, anti-Muslim, anti-Asian, and anti-gay officers. I met MPD officers and supervisors who were white supremacists, or who were at least sympathetic to white supremacists and shared Trump's views on race. The racists don't dominate, but one is too many. To completely eliminate racism within the police ranks, we've got to work to remove it from society at large.

During the last seven years, MPD placed an emphasis on educating officers to understand and respect cultural differences—a smart thing to do. Police officers are deployed to protect and serve their communities, and that should include learning about cultural differences so that we can connect with our constituents.

But it's almost as if Americans can't walk and chew gum at the same time anymore. We've become so focused on cultural training that we've lost the ability to train our officers how to simultaneously safely and humanely arrest someone who resists arrest. No one wants to go to jail, ever. It sucks. So we have to do a much better job of helping cops make better arrests and better decisions when confronted with life-or-death situations.

We also need to address the fact that the American justice system is systematically classist. Intentional or not, major aspects of the system disproportionately hurt poor people, regardless of race. I don't think most Americans appreciate the ways in which a single traffic ticket or simple arrest can quickly spiral into economic hardship, based largely on administrative fees imposed by the court system. I'm not sure most Americans know what it's like to grow up in a neighborhood where drugs, addiction, and violence have been a way of life for generations. Money and education matter. Marc Gersen, the law student who sold meth wholesale, had the means and money to face justice in ways that someone like Leslie, or a person living in Sursum Corda, could not.

So what can be done? It all begins with training.

The first thing we should do is nationalize standards and training for law enforcement at every level. Right now, we have a patchwork of policies across the country, based mostly on size and funding, but also on local politics and tradition. We should create federal protocols for the way local police officers interact, both physically and verbally, with members of the community. These police procedures should be the same, whether an officer encounters someone on an inner-city street or a rural county highway.

Since it's unreasonable to expect almost any police department, large or small, to have enough skills and money to properly train their officers, Congress should create a program to do so. To some extent, this could be modeled on the training used by most federal law enforcement agencies at their academies. Congress should also draft universal standards that must be met in order to serve as a police officer in the United States, similar to the standards required to become a federal agent. That kind of national screening would go a long way toward preventing people who are either mentally, philosophically, or physically incapable of performing the jobs required of professional police officers.

If Congress is serious about this, the fed ought to pay for it all. Federal funds and standards would eliminate any excuse—whether practical or political—for shoddy standards and training at the local level. A national training initiative would quickly alleviate a lot of the problems we've seen recently, especially cases in which officers make poor decisions that result in people dying.

If we believe we have an epidemic of police wrongfully killing citizens, we need to be willing to pay to retrain our officers.

I cannot overstate this point enough: The current firearms protocol—static, semi-annual target practice—is nearly worthless, and counterproductive. Officers should be trained in simulated stress situations that create realistic scenarios for use of deadly force. Some departments use computer simulators but the technology is so dated, it reminds me of the days of DOS and floppy disks. We need virtual-reality-era solutions, or better yet, real-world stress training, the kind favored by the military. By that, I don't mean that every officer should train for military-style operations, like an FBI Hostage Rescue Team member or an MPD SWAT officer. What I mean is that officers should train as soldiers do—by repeatedly rehearsing their most stressful tasks, so that when confronted in real life with a life-or-death situation, they reflexively make the correct decision.

In some ways, it's harder to be a police officer than a member of Seal Team Six because a cop's objective is to safely and legally detain a target—a potentially violent American citizen who needs to be removed from the streets, at least temporarily, against his will. It can be done, if you have the proper resources and training. Unfortunately, we've removed so much of that training because people complained it was "too aggressive." For officer safety, the first time a cop takes a punch should be at the academy, not on the streets.

In addition to training, we must change our current policing mindset. We must eliminate formal and informal quotas for cops on the beat, and start grading them on the quality of arrests, rather than the quantity. We should focus on surgical strikes against the most violent criminals.

To be successful, police leaders, politicians, and neighborhood residents must learn to exercise patience, and avoid knee-jerk reactions. Too often, police leaders seeking to appease politicians and the loudest voices in their precincts make quick and hollow shows of force, flooding violent neighborhoods with uniformed cops, like some kind of occupying army. We start arresting people and get into brawls with residents pissed off that we've kicked in their door. We make some petty arrests, humiliate people in front of their families, and turn the neighborhood against us. This makes it that much harder the next time we need help with a murder or major drug investigation. We end up doing more harm than good.

One quick way to reengage is to restore plainclothes officers to the streets. During my trip to New York, I was pleased to hear that Mayor Eric Adams, a former NYPD officer himself, planned to do just that. The mayor also called for increased training and funding for mental health and social programs to help officers alleviate the violence.

But we need to do even more.

To earn the trust of the communities we serve, we need to become more transparent. Action Item No. 1: Publicly release body-worn camera footage following the use of deadly force and let the chips fall where they may. If the cops on video screw up, hold them accountable. If they follow procedure in high-stress situations and act like heroes, let the world know, immediately. I don't understand why so many departments wait so fucking long to release their body-worn camera video. Delays only fuel suspicion in the minds of reasonable people, and provide an opportunity for unreasonable people to fill the void with their own narrative. Why wait? Why allow the kettle to continue to boil? No more excuses. If a state law prevents footage from release, let's change that law.

To be successful, the police must engage the whole community. We need the people we serve to come to see officers as fellow humans, not monolithic tools of the security state. Engagement requires patience. It means hanging out with residents in non-adversarial situations. It means attending boring as shit civic meetings. It means getting to know and understand folks like Leslie and others who don't look or act like us. I can tell you from personal experience that while this takes courage and patience, the payoff can be immeasurable.

That's why "reforming" the police will only get us so far. We need a holistic approach to repair the entire criminal justice system and address inequities across the board. We must improve training and resources with respect to mental health, incarceration, recidivism, legal representation, and the crushing administrative court fees for defendants. We also need more elected leaders who understand what it means to serve something other than themselves.

Finally, to my fellow officers I say this: You are the backbone of our public safety infrastructure. Act like it. Don't lose sight of the humanity in those you serve no matter how much the job shits on you. This is the burden we bear, and it is an honor few will ever know.

Acknowledgments

First and foremost, my coauthor, John Shiffman, and I would like to thank every officer who responded to the U.S. Capitol on January 6th. Thanks also to the federal investigators, journalists, and citizen-sleuths who continue to seek to hold the rioters and *all of their conspirators* accountable for the insurrection.

At MPD, thanks to Chief Robert Contee III, Assistant Chief Morgan Kane, Commander Ramey Kyle, Sergeant Phil McHugh, and Officers Jeff Leslie, Jimmy Albright, Anthony Boone, Patrick Nugent, and Mike Perez. And to officers who prefer anonymity.

At the U.S. Capitol, thanks to Officer Harry Dunn, his colleagues, and the behind-the-scenes, reality-based staffers who really run Congress. With deep admiration for the courage displayed by Officer Brian Sicknick's mother, Gladys Sicknick, and his widow, Sandra Garza. A shout-out to the ten Republicans who had the guts to vote to impeach Trump for triggering the insurrection: Adam Kinzinger, Liz Cheney, Jaime Herrera Beutler, Dan Newhouse, Peter Meijer, Tom Rice, David Valadao, Fred Upton, John Katko, and Anthony Gonzalez. And thanks to Representative Eric Swalwell.

Thanks to Dr. Greg Vitale, who taught me how to breathe again, and his colleagues at Washington Hospital Center.

At CNN, thanks to Don Lemon, Jeff Zucker, Rachel Burstein, and Elizabeth Grodd.

For guidance in creating this project, special thanks to Joan Baez and Sean Penn. Thanks to Chuck Tobin for the outstanding legal advice. For help along the way, we're grateful to the United States Capitol Historical Society, Shannon Stapleton, Deb Bodner, Joe Tanfani, Mimi Hall, Peter Eisler, Ann Caspari, Abigail Gorman, Patrick Gorman, Kate Ebner, Dave Ebner, Greta Toodot, Sarah Salem, Jim Oliphant, Blake Morrison, Ronnie Greene, Mike Williams, Alix Freedman, Heather Carpenter, Andy Hill, Corinne Perkins, Nick Shiffman, Sam Shiffman, and the masterminds who created SeaQuench Ale.

Huge thanks to the team that helped publish *Hold the Line*, especially Larry Weissman and Sascha Alper at Larry Weissman Literary. The duo connected us with Amar Deol at Atria Books, whose passion for the project and skill at cutting the boring parts is much appreciated. Thanks also to his colleagues Elizabeth Hitti, Lisa Nicholas, Tamara Arellano, Jaime Wolf, Kyoko Watanabe, David Brown, Jimmy Iacobelli, Iris Chen, Paige Lytle, Milena Brown, and Nicole Bond.

With gratitude to our kin: Terry Fanone, Joe Fanone, Peter Fanone, Caitlin Fanone, Piper Fanone, Mei-Mei Fanone, Hensley Fanone, Hsin-Yi Wang, Paul Shiffman, and Cathy Shiffman.

And to Buddy and Lucy.

Appendix I:
Wanted by the FBI

During the insurrection, 140 law enforcement officers were seriously injured—about 80 from the U.S. Capitol Police and about 60 from the MPD. Some 14 officers were hospitalized.

The coup attempt caused $1.5 million in property damage to the Capitol, and live pipe bombs were planted near the Democratic and Republican national committee headquarters. The U.S. government is offering a $100,000 reward for information leading to the arrest of the person or persons involved.

Since January 6, 2021, the FBI has arrested at least 800 people for crimes related to the Capitol insurrection. At least 225 were charged with assaulting, resisting, or impeding officers. Of those, more than 75 were charged with using a deadly or dangerous weapon or causing serious bodily injury to an officer.

Too many suspects, though, remain at large.

The FBI is still seeking help identifying 350 people believed to have committed violent acts on January 6th. This includes more than 250 individuals who assaulted officers.

The FBI has posted their photos here: https://www.fbi.gov/wanted /capitol-violence.

Let's help identify and catch them.

Appendix II:
Ribbon of Valor Honorees

The following is a list of fellow MPD officers who were awarded the Ribbon of Valor by Chief of Police Robert J. Contee III, for responding to the attack on the United States Capitol on January 6, 2021.

The commendation reads: "On that day, the violent mob's sustained assault precipitated an unprecedented need for first responders, including an urgent request for the Metropolitan Police Department to aid in the defense of the Capitol. Without hesitation, hundreds of MPD officers responded to restore order and defend our country's democratic process. They were confronted by a mob intent on destruction, containing many who sought to harm law enforcement officers. MPD members did not retreat, and though outnumbered, exhausted, and injured, they remained determined and spent hours fending off the attackers without reluctance. These officers upheld their oath to protect and serve in the face of adverse circumstances. Their bravery is a testament to their commitment to our community and our nation, and their courage is a reflection of their heart. The Ribbon of Valor reflects this unwavering spirit and serves as a reminder of the actions each member took on that day."

Christopher Abbey

Carlos Abreu
Armstrong

Adams Brian Adams

Marcus Adams

Reginald Adams

Roberto Adams

Marcus Adams-
Delancey

Jerry Afari

Ruben Agosto

Kwaku Agyeman

Nizam Ahmed

David Aikin

Mustafa Ak

Owais Akhtar

Robert Akuoko

Araz Alali

Nelson Alas

Tabitha Alberti

Gregory Alemian

Abdo Ali

Anthony Alioto

Donte' Allen

Johnnetta Allen

Sean Allen

Yenli Almanzar

Wilson Almonte
De la Rosa

David Almy

Sarah Alobo

Asia Alston

Stephen Alston

John Alter

Kevin Alvarenga

Alexander Alvarez

Ty Amarant-West

Kevin Amaya

Roberto Amengual

Molly Ames

Jonathan Amigo

Stephen Amodeo

Joshua Anderson

Robert Anderson

Rodney Anderson

Seth Anderson

Sherman Anderson

Lance Andriani

Toni-Ann Annunziata

Ryan Anselmo

Markquat Anu
Amen-Ra

Joshua Arana-Jimenez

Ronny Arce

Ashley Archer

Gregory Archer

Olubunmi Aremu

George Arhin

Nicole Arnone

Robert Arroyo

Armand Artinian

Rana Ashfaq

Devon Atcheson

Brenton Atkins

Davonya Atwater

Derek Augburn

David Augustine

Michael Auls

Joseph Austin

Mikal Ba'th

Yaroslav Babich

Ellen Bader

Jason Bagshaw

Devon Bailey

Julie Bailly

Kelly Baker

William Baker

Carlos Baldera

James Ball

Bai Bangura

Daxzaneous Banks

George Banks

Troy Bannon

Michael Barbieri

Zeb Barcus

Robert Barillaro

Justin Barkley

Johnnie Barnes

Mikal Barnes

Clint Barnett

Orson Barnett

Jeffrey Barr

Mark Barrows

Robert Barusefski

Maurice Bateman

Darrin Bates

Matthew Batko

Scott Baum

Jonathan Beatty

Sarah Beaver
Leebra Bedney
Michael Beel
Timothy Beirne
Iris Beistline
Erion Bektashaj
Leonardo Bell
Darenn Bemiller
Manuel Benites
Carimaxy Benitez-
  Garcia
Bradley Bennett
Dallas Bennett
Stephen Benson
Kevin Bergeron
Jovan Bethel
John Bewley
Sardar Bhullar
Sean Billies
Allison Bingner
Vincent Biscoe
Kevin Bittner
James Black
Scott Blackwood
Christopher Blake
Cleveland Blake
Keith Blakely
Timothy Bland
Joseph Blasting
Zachary Blier
David Boarman
Joseph Boehler
William Bogner

Irving Bolton
Corey Bonds
Istmania Bonilla
Anthony Boone
Kenneth Boone
Tushar Botlero
Alfred Boyd
Clarence Boyd
Ebony Boyd
Monique Boyd
Christopher Boyle
Derek-James Braggs
John Branch
Victor Braschnewitz
Antoine Brathwaite
John Brennan
Charles Brevard
Brandon Brewster-
  McCarthy
Ronald Bridges
Kevin Brittingham
Matthew Bromeland
Marina Bronstein
Clarence Brooks
Shyanti Brooks
Ryan Brooksbank
Theodore Brosey
Anthony Brown
Arthur Brown
Brian Brown
Christopher Brown
David Brown
James Brown

Michelle Brown
Robert Brown
Scott Brown
Tashon Brown
Tyquan Brown
Kenneth Brown II
Edward Brownlee
Jeffrey Bruce
Taniqua Brumfield
Joseph Bruno
Brandon Bryan
Robert Bryant
Robert Buck
David Buerster
Ren Burke
Suzanne Burkholder
Kyle Burt
Donald Butler
Cory Buynak
Enrique Caballero
Julianna Calcagno
Shawn Caldwell
Edward Cameron
Anthony Campanale
Jawaun Campbell
Joseph Campbell
Guillermo Canales
Tracie Cannon
Matthew Cano
Christopher Cappello
Brian Carbonelli
Quenterra Carey
Angelique Carpenter

Quentin Carr

Ricardo Carrion

Jeffery Carroll

John Carruthers

Luis Cartagena

David Carter

Richard Carter

Christopher Cartwright

Tanya Cartwright

Bennett Casciano

Michael Cashman

Ana Casiano

Jose Casiano

LuisAngel Castillo

Raeniel Castillo

Raul Castro

Matthew Cek

Benjamin Celano

Taariq Cephas

Erica Cephus

David Chagnon

Matthew Chamberlain

Christina Chambers

Jennifer Chambers

Andrew Chan

Johniqua Chance

Katherine Changes

Adrian Channer

Justice Chaplin

Damian Chapman

Parker Chapman

Joel Charles

James Chastanet

Rickie Chasten

William Chatman

James Chatmon

Jimmy Checo

Dong Chen

Jonathan Chen

Michael Chen

Jonathan Cheng

Robert Chester

Timothy Chew

Stephen Chih

Brendan Chillemi

Travis Chinery

Eddie Choi

Lauren Chrismer

Bryan Christian

Christopher Christian

Stephanie Chukwurah

David Chumbley

Conor Church

Gary Ciapa

Christopher Clark

Leslie Clark

Clint Clarke

Felix Claxton

Christopher Clemens

Anedrea Cluff

Eric Coates

Steven Cobb

Michael Cohoon

Michael Colato

Brittany Cole

Collin Cole

Ernest Cole

Antony Coleman

Curtis Coleman

Jordan Coleman

Jake Coletti

Travis Coley

Michael Coligan

Jeffrey Colleli

James Collier

Bryant Collins

David Collins

Gregory Collins

Sean Conboy

Sean Connors

Robert Contee

Thomas Conteh

Stephen Cooke-Barnes

Derron Copeland

Nicole Copeland

Dwayne Corbett

James Corcoran

Sean Corcoran

Angelique Core

Antonio Cosey

Ivan Cosio Medina

Dalentina Costello

Christopher Costner

Brandon Cote

Thomas Cox

Cortney Craft

Terrence Craig

Terrence Crawford

Jacobi Crawley

Christopher Creech

Wade Cress

Kaila Crews

Kalia Crews

Benjamin Crimmins

James Crisman

Angel Cruz

Jason Cruz

Melvin Cruz

Pamela Cruz

Paulino Joshua Cucci

Jaime Cullen-Dega

Charles Culver

Tiffany Cunningham

Rodger Currie

Chad Curtice

Keith Cyphers

Brandon Cyrus

Salah Czapary

Michael Czerwinski

Michel DaCruz

Nicholas Damron

John D'Angelo

Elias Danho

Brian Daniel

Rarnesha Daniels

Kevin Danko

Ebony Darling-Costley

Wayne David

Casey Davies

Robert Davies

Marc D'Avignon

Andre Davis

Arthur Davis

Ashley Davis

Darrell Davis

Diamond Davis

Domonick Davis

Ernie Davis

Gregory Davis

Kenneth Davis

Levon Davis

Michael Davis

Ralph Davis

Leslie Davis-Kennie

Russell Dawes

Fawaz Dawodu

Christopher De La Cruz

Paul Dean

Arnold Decastro

Kyle deFreytag

Michael Dejager

Kirk Del Po

Anthony DelBorrell

Christopher Delisi

Joseph Della Camera

Kenneth Deloach

Kevin Delozier

Johndy Demosthene

Norbert Dengler

Ferney Dennis

Christopher Denton

Victor DePeralta

Aleksander De'Plour

Dorian Desantis

Isreal Deschaine

Rony Desir

Kenneth Deutschkron

Joseph Devlin

Abdul Dieng

Liam Dinchong

Stephan DiTullio

Marius Djoko

Joseph Dolan

Randy Done

George Donigian

Patrick Donlon

Ahmed Dorghoud

Jonathan Dorrough

Arthur Douglas

Evan Douglas

Wade Douglas

Christopher Dove

Daniel Dowd

Michael Dowling

Scott Dowling

Christopher Downs

Julito Drake

Bartlomiej Drozdz

Charles Duckett

Noah Duckett

Derek Dude

Timothy Dumantt

Thomas Duncan

Tonia Dunn

Manuelle Duvall

Brayden Dyer

Christopher Dyke

Daniel Dyn

Terrance Eberhardt

Patrick Ecelberger

Brad Eckert

Christopher Eckert

John Edelen

David Edelstein

Christopher
  Edmondson

Darren Edwards

Frank Edwards

Kelan Edwards

Richard Ehrlich

David Eley

Oliver Eligado

Rochelle Elliott

James Ellis

Ramond Ellis

Shea Ellis

Tia Ellis

Stuart Emerman

Scott Emmons

Marquita Ennals

Ralph Ennis

April Epps

Steven Epps

Melvin Evans

Timothy Evans

Mark Eveland

Ryan Exum

Alexander Farley

Eric Farris

Ronald Faunteroy

Ernie Faustino

Anthony Faverio

Terrence Felder

John Felenchak

John Fellin

Eric Fenton

Corey Fenwick

Derrick Ferguson

Jesse Fernandez

Isaac Fernando

Fabian Ferrera

Michael Ferris

Steven Ferris

Benjamin Fetting

Lauren Fevola

Heidi Fieselmann

Raul Figueras

Ana Figuereo

Benjamin Finck

Matthew Finn

Matthew Fitzgerald

Kaseem Fitzpatrick

Jonathan Fleming

Matthew Fleming

Walter Fleming

Christian Fletcher

Stephen Fletcher

Adam Floyd

Darren Floyd

Marcus Floyd

Patrick Flynn

Algernon Fogle

Aaron Follman

Jonathan Foote

Omar Forrester

Luke Foskett

Shantaley Foster-Bey

Henry Foulds

Jurithia Foust

Sheri Fox

Pierre Francois

Christopher Frank

Peter Franz

James Freeman

Ian French

Peter Frenzel

Dallas Frison

Norman Frost

Jabdiel Fuentes

Frantz Fulcher

Raymon Fuller

Setor Fummey

Richard Gabster

Christopher Gaglione

Malcolm Gaines

Samuel Gaines

Keenan Gallagher

Angela Galli

Rene Gallo

Willie Galtney

Pamela Garay

Marvin Garber

Oscar Garcia

Erick Garcia Burgos

LaCarsha Garrett

Niger Garrett

Aaron Garrison

Martin Garrison

Oliver Garvey

Grant Gates

Kyle Gatewood

Joseph Gatling

Scott Gaumond

Jean Gautreaux

Tonia Gay

Alphonso Gbatu

Richard Geiger

Taylor Geiger

Maurice George

Ralp George

Jacqueline Gerrish

Wayne Gerrish

Alaina Gertz

Tony Giles

William Gill

Caleb Gillett

Aiden Giuffre

Christopher Glascock

Michael Glean

Kevin Glenn

Robert Glover

Daniel Godin

Tivey Goldring

Andrew Gong

Christopher Gonzalez

Jonathan Gonzalez

Juan Gonzalez

Maynor Gonzalez

Harolin Gonzalez
Polanco

Jose Gonzalez Tirado

Rebecca Good

Haley Goodfellow

Jonathan Goodman

Melanie Gordon

Jake Goss

Adam Gottesmann

Antonio Gould

Tommie Grable

Elizabeth Grannis

Benedict Graumann

Dymone Graves

Brandon Gravesmill

Travis Gray

John Graziano

Brian Green

Donald Green

Jamal Green

Keith Green

Lauren Green

Toby Green

Amina Greene

Anthony Greene

James Greene

Kamau Greene

Arthur Gregory

Regenna Grier

Dalton Griffin

Randy Griffin

Richard Griffin

Christopher Griffith

Bernard Grimsley

Tyrone Gross

Adam Groves

Harrison Grubbs

Steven Grysko

Jake Gschwind

Anthony Guice

Matthew Guo

Gabriel Gutierrez

Wilfredo Guzman

Durriyyah Habeebullah

William Hackerman

April Hagans

Samuel Hahn

Darrin Haile

Marvin Haiman

John Haines

Tyler Haines

Eric Hairston

Lydia Hairston

Larry Hale

Christopher Hall

Colin Hall

Robert Hall

Kevin Halpin

Michael Hamelin

John Hamer

Bryan Hannah

John Hansohn

Raymond Hardaway

Kevin Harding

Timothy Hargrove

Justin Harkins

Marcus Harmon

Mosette Harmon

Gavin Harrell

Daniel Harrington

Brian Harris

Donald Harris

James Harris

Kevin Harris

Kullen Harris

Sharde Harris

Tyrone Harris

Joshua Harry

Jonathan Hart

Laschon Harvell

Daniel Harvey

Gunther Hashida

Jessica Hawkins

Kendall Hawkins

Raymond Hawkins

Dallan Haynes

Stephen Haynes

Steven Hebron

John Hendrick

Albert Henley

Karim Henry

Susan Henson

Carlos Heraud

Charlie Hernandez

Euri Hernandez

Josue Hernandez
  Martinez

Alan Herring

Jaron Hickman

Sean Hickman

Emma Hicks

Thomas Higdon

Reginald Hildebrandt

Bijon Hiligh

Kourtney Hill

Matthew Hiller

Ravi Hiller

Lorelei Hillgren

Kevin Hines

Harvy Hinostroza

Troy Hinton

Perry Hoak

David Hobbs

Daniel Hodges

James Hoever

Paul Hofmann

Patrick Hogan

Sheraton Hogan

John Holder

Brian Hollan

Kevin Holland

Nadiya Holley

Grady Holmes

Sabrina Holmes

Trevor Holson

Riley Hong

Colin Hopkins

Norma Horne

Andrew Horos

Daniel Houng

Nichole Howard

Michael Howden

Ivan Howell

Paul Hrebenak

Dena Hubbard

Isaac Huff

Dustyn Hugee

Lamont Hull

Maggie-May Humphrey

Stacie Hunt

Aaron Hunter

Syed Hussain

Mohamed Ibrahim

Sang Im

Nicholas Imbrenda

Afam Ishakwue

Olateju Ishola

Daryl Isom

Brian Israel

Anthony Jackson

Claude Jackson

Gregory Jackson

Keith Jackson

Eyonne Jacob

James Jacobs

Aminata Jallow

Davon James

Lorenzo James

Jennifer Jamieson

Josephine Jamison

Jeffrey Janczyk

Curran Michal
  Jankowski

Jose Jaquez

Tamar Jean Baptiste

Audrea Jefferson

LeMar Jefferson

Matthew Jefferson

Thomas Jefferson

Timothy Jefferson

Delante Jenifer

Byron Jenkins

Ivory Jenkins

Lenard Jenkins

Micheal Jenkins

Ryan Jensrud

John Jeskie

Enis Jevric

Analee Jimenez

Jose Jimenez

Christopher John

Blake Johnson

Brittany Johnson

Calvin Johnson

Charles Johnson

Dwight Johnson

Eric Johnson

Heinz Johnson

Jeremiah Johnson

Kierra Johnson

Randolph Johnson

Robert Johnson

Travis Johnson

Trina Johnson

Jeevon Jones

Lisa Jones

Markell Jones

Thomas Jones

Tiffany Jones

Lashon Jones Warren

Justin Jordan

Kristina Jordan

Myra Jordan

Ryan Jordan

Brandon Joseph

Joubert Joseph

Maxary Joseph

Thomas Joyce

Patrick Juster

Mohammed Kakay

Morgan Kane

Hakan Karaali

Gus Karanikolis

Bryan Kasul

Ashley Keels

Stephen Keirn

Cornel Kelemen

Daniel Kelly

Erin Kelly

Herman Kelly

Kiriaki Kelly

William Kelly

Eric Kennedy

Tracy Kennie

Norman Kenny

Essonani Kerim

Carlin Kern

Michael Kersey

Aqif Khalid

Faraz Khan

Sadiqul Khan

Richard Khoury

Tony Kibic

Robyel Kidane

Michael Kim

Kyle Kimball

Kristian Kimble

Endalkachew
Kinfemichael

Eric King

Michael King

Jayme Kingsley

Kimberly Kniffen

Jeremy Kniseley

John Knutsen

James Koenig

Oscar Kolts

Matthew Konkol

Brian Koonce

Jeffrey Kopp

Alimamy Koroma

Nicholas Koven

Paul Koyejo

James Krawczyk

Angelica Krumnow

Angelica Krupa

Jacob Krycia

Christopher Kurland

Gregory Kurtz

Alec Kurz

Myo Kyaw

Ramey Kyle

Dorothy Labun

Joseph Labun

Joseph Lafrance

Max Laielli

Mark Lakomec

Shane Lamond

Joshua Lancaster

Necka Lancaster

Ernest Landers

Renia Lane

Joenika Laney

James Langenbach

Giovan Langumas

Nicholas LaPier

Matthew Lapitsky

Daler Latif-Zade

Michael Lattimore

Jonathan Lauderdale

Louis Laurore

Christina Laury

Ivan Lawit

Nacal Lawrence

John Lay

Lawrence Lazewski

Martha Lazo

Evelin Lazo-Zelaya

David Le

Ho Le

Xavier Leake

Jesse Leasure

David Leaty

Adrian Ledesma

Jake Lee

Mark Lee

William Lee

Janine Leftwich

Kevin Leitzel

Diana Leo

Lee Lepe

Jeffrey Leslie

David Lessard

David Lester

Mason Letourneau

Thomas Lewis

Jessica Lewis-Hinds

Katherine Lieto

Daewoong Lim

Jesse Lin

Daniel Lingham

Jacob Lipscomb

Christopher Lisko

Serena Liss

Olivier Lissouck

James Little

Chadd Livezey

Pedro Lizama

Bryan Lligui

Antonio Lloyd

Glenn Lombardini

Frank Longarello

James Love

Stephen Love

Roger Lowery

Tyrone Lowery

Christopher Lucas

Mark Lucas

Roderick Lucas

Shannon Luckenbill

James Luckett

Lloyd Lumpkin

Osbaldo Luna

Michael Lybarger

William Lyke

Heather Lynn

Alexander MacBean

Craig Mack

Kenneth Mack

Bryan Madera

Brian Madison

Erika Magnuson

Candace Major

Lashay Makal

Matthew Malacaria

Bryan Maldonado

Ashley Mancuso

Wilfredo Manlapaz

Ernest Manley

Christopher Mann

Loius Manzan

Korey Marable

Isaac Mardy

Andrew Margiotta

Robert Marsh

Angela Marshall

Nicholas Marshall

Robert Marshall

Anntoinette Martin

Charlee Martin

Dexter Martin

Meghan Martin

Randall Martin

Miguel Martinez

Joseph Masci

Jeffrey Maslona	Iris Mendoza	Leonore Molina
Antoinette Mason	Jose Mendoza	Peter Molina
Jason Mastony	Roylanda Merricks	Kathleen Monahan
Alex Mateo	Jonathan Merrill	Demory Monroe
Marshond Matory	Daniel Merritt	Jonathan Monroe
Monique Maxwell	Eboni Merritt	Carolyn Montagna
Reginald Maxwell	Jacquelon Mertus	Alexander Montague
Amber Mays	John Merzig	Francisco Montano
Steven Mazanec	Kristen Metzger	Adam Moore
Neil Mcallister	Christopher Meyer	Alexa Moore
John McArdle	Larry Miles	Carter Moore
Andrew McCallum	Josemaria Militar	Duane Moore
Brian McCarthy	Blake Miller	Elisa Moore
Hanif McClinton	Caroline Miller	Jarrin Moore
Sean Mccloskey	Christopher Miller	Lawrence Mopkins
Antilecia McCoy	Cyrus Miller	Yezid Morales
Michael McCreary	Michael Miller	Michael Morawski
Danny Mccumbers	Thomas Miller	Patrick Moreland
John McDonald	Reginald Milliam	Erik Moreno
Stephen McDonald	Jerrita Millington	Perry Morgan
Taylor McDonald	Carrie Mills	Charles Morris
John McElhenny	Michael Milochik	Lila Morris
Matthew Mcfadyen	Fabien Milord	Anthony Morton
Dwight Mckinnon	Zar Min	Michael Moshier
Michael McLean	Thai Minh Nguyen	Thomas Mosier
James McNeill	Ricardo Minier	Brandon Motley
Eliseo Medina	Mark Minzak	Samuel Mott
Jason Medina	Willis Mitchell	Patrick Muamba
Thomas Meekins	Michael Mocca	Leroy Mucci
Carlos Mejia	Jovan Mock	Jake Mudrezow
Brianna Melendez	Carline Modl	Ahsan Mufti
Roy Melvin	Kareem Mohsin	William Mulkeen
Jeramiah Mendez	Andres Molina	Mark Mullen

Megan Mulrooney	Simeon Norfleet	Christopher Paige
Anam Mumtaz	Vincent Norris	Emily Painten
Winfred Mundle	Ryan Nosner	Keith Pakeman
George Mundy	Patrick Nugent	Jacob Palmiscno
Robert Munn	Apolinar Nunez	Gabrielle Panara
Clifton Murphy	Gabriel Nunez	Peter Pannoh
McHauley Murphy	Genesis Nunez	Jin Park
Robert Murphy	Stephen Nyakaana	Anil Parker
George Murray	Blair Colleen O'Brien	Jeffrey Parker
Steven Murrell	Malik O'Brien	Marvin Parker
Michael Muzzey	Kevin O'Bryant	Robert Parker
Astasia Myler	Brett O'Connell	Gage Parks
Joseph Myles	Charles Oconnor	Sally Parks
David Naples	Thomas O'Donnell	Leslie Parsons
Stephen Naticchione	Olugbenga Oduola	Nicholas Pastore
Kevin Naus	Justin Oehmke	Karisma Patel
Michael Nava	Trevor Officer	Valerie Patete
Jessica Navarro	Chinedu Offomata	Charles Patrick
Reinard Naves	Emmanuel Oladipupo	Dan Patrick
Gavin Nelson	Nicholas Oliver	Leano Sidney Paul
Jonathan Nelson	Matthew Oliveto	James Payne
Terrace Nesmith	Ryan Orgel	Tiffany Payne
Bernhard Neuhaus	Daniel O'Rourke	Brian Peake
Dustin Nevel	Angel Ortiz	Deborah Pearce
Jason Newman	Brian O'Shea	Michael Pearson
Khanh Nguyen	Santiago Osorio	Tametress Peden
Phuson Nguyen	Janai Ottey	Zachary Peiffer
Matthew Nickerson	Robert Owen	Pedro Pena
Narcisa Nicolau	Christopher Owens	James Penland
Joseph Nieves	Stephen Owens	Derek Pennington
Jose Nieves Campos	William Pack	Kevin Peralta
Robert Niewenhous	Anthony Padilla	Elmer Perez
Nicholas Nikitakis	Michael Page	Giancarlos Perez

Jesus Perez

Michael Perez

Ricardo Perez

Ricky Perez

Zurisadai Perez

Arnette Perkins

Sakeena Pernell

Darnell Peterson

Johnathan Peterson-
   Johnson

James Petty

Michael Petty

Andy Pham

Michael Phan

Paul Philistin

Karina Phillip

Justin Phillips

Keith Pierce

Cedrick Pierre

Scott Pinto

David Pitt

Lynn Pittmon

Millard Pitts

Sharlynn Plows

Caden Polk

Andrew Pollard

Curtis Pope

Epshane Porter

Nathaniel Porter

Scott Possinger

Divonnie Powell

Isaiah Powell

Reginald Powell

William Powell

Joy Preston

Kathryn Priebe

Sherry Pringle

Straneika Proctor

Topaz Proctor

Brandon Pryce

Mark Pugh

Michael Pulliam

Rachel Pulliam

Louise Pyant

Gregory Quaresma

Steven Quarles

David Quasie

Ivan Quiles

Marquis Quinones

Seema Qureshi

Raphael Radon

Bikram Rajbanshi

Tina Ramadhan

David Randolph

William Rapp

Noah Rathbun

Aaron Rauch

Nicholas Readmond

Daniel Reagan

Matthew Reddy

Sade Reed

Travis Reed

Michael Reese

Christopher Reisinger

Anton Rekounov

Kamil Rembiszewski

Abanoub Rezkalla

Richard Rice

Justin Rice-Moore

Aaron Richardson

Derek Ricks

Matthew Rider

Robert Rikard

Benjamin Rikhoff

Paul Riley

Stephen Riley

Cynthia Rios

Brandon Ripes

Dany Rivera-Euceda

Jacky Roach

Kerron Roberts

Michael Roberts

Cody Robinson

John Robinson

Mark Robinson

Philip Robinson

Christina Roccato

Gregory Rock

Ludovick Rock

Michael Rodd

Aida Rodriguez

Brian Rodriguez

Carmelo Rodriguez

Edward Rodriguez

Enmanuel Rodriguez

Kevin Rodriguez

Miguel Rodriguezgil

Ryan Roe

Enoch Rogers

James Rogers

Tahiyya Rohan

Jeanine Rollines

Leroy Rollins

Kevin Romero

Shawn Rooney

Sean Rosa

Stephen Rose

Ashley Rosenthal

Marcus Rosenthal

Alicia Ross

Dwayne Ross

Isaiah Ross

Kevin Ross

Justin Roth

Anthony Rotimi

Anthony Rowley

Johann Ruano

Benjamin Rubin

Roy Ruiz

Desiree Russ

Jerin Rutherford

Matula Saint Pierre

Steven Sajumon

Alexis Sakulich

John Salamone

Wilfred Salas

Scott Salcetti

Sammy Salha

Imar Samaraay

Johel Sanchez

Steve Sanchez

Justin Sand

Allorie Sanders

Darnell Sanders

Britnee Sangalan

Marc Sansone

Hokly Sarin

Kristina Saunders

Mark Saunders

Roderick Saunders

Dillon Savage

Michael Savage

Bridgette Sawyer

Jeffrey Scharf

Patrick Schaut

Alex Schmidt

Scott Schmoeller

Emily Schneeberg

Steven Schwalm

William Schwarzer

Lindsey Scott

Nico Scott

Robert Scott

Troy Scott

Wayne Seaward

Shellyann Seegobin

Charandip Sekhon

Mark Selbach

Michael Selgas

Vimary Serrano-
  Fernandez

Sirena Serratos

Aminatta Sesay

Riza Sever

Adam Shaatal

Andrew Shaheen

Omar Shareef

Ajay Sharma

Vijay Sharma

Stephen Sharp

Justin Shazier

Robert Sheaffer

Peter Sheldon

Lamal Sheppard

Qasim Sheroz

Gregory Shiffer

Ryan Shifflett

Jocelyn Shim

Rodgers Shipmon

Jessica Shoemaker

Patrick Shoemaker

Eric Sibley

Manuel Sibrian

Duarte Scott Siegel

Andres Silva

Nathaniel Silver

Filip Simic

Enrique Simmons

Thomas Simmons

Daniel Simms

Romayo Simon

Derron Simpson

Kimberly Sims

Amanpreet Singh

Ramandeep Singh

George Singletary

Harry Singleton

John Singleton

Daniel Sinotte

Jeffrey Sipes

Kathryn Skaluba

Brendan Slemenda

Curtis Sloan

Ryan Small

Andre Smallwood

Morgan Smiley

Joshua Smilow

Aaron Smith

Amina Smith

Anthony Smith

Austin Smith

Clayton Smith

Dion Smith

Edward Smith

Erik Smith

Jeffrey Smith

Kristopher Smith

Marcus Smith

Michael Smith

Nicholas Smith

Pria Smith

Joseph Solem

Craig Solgat

Linwood Solomon

Ameer Sorrell

Adam Sotelo

Marta Spajic

Lamond Sparrow

Ryan Spears

Corinne Spencer-Jones

Joshua Spicer

Bronson Spooner

Virginia Spooner

John Sprague

Jannique Spriggs

Brian Stacks

John Stadnik

Brandon Stagon

Stephen Stanford

Raymond Stargel

Joshua Starnes

Joseph Staten

James Steinbach

Wayne Steinhilber

Dorothy Stellabotta

Jason Sterling

Dustin Sternbeck

Dennis Stewart

Christopher Stokes

Jasma Stoutamire

John Streets

Andre Sturgis

Daniel Styles

Eddy Suarez

Philip Suggs

Brian Sullivan

Ryan Sullivan

Tyler Swatchick

Bobby Tabron

Andre Taggart

Mohamed Taher

Marcus Talley

Mark Tate

Nathan Tate

Tierra Tate

Azriel Taylor

Brian Taylor

Jacoby Taylor

Justin Taylor

Kenneth Taylor

Scott Taylor

Sean Taylor

Patricia Tchinda

Joseph Tedrow

Orlando Teel

David Terestre

John Terry

Daniel Thau

Franklyn Then

Ivens Thermidor

Arabia Thomas

Aretha Thomas

Assante Thomas

Augustus Thomas

David Thomas

Grant Thomas

Jashawn Thomas

Joel Thomas

Joseph Thomas

Kirkland Thomas

Natali Thomas

Stefeni Thomas

Kenan Thomas-Bartley

Jimmie Thompson

Kyia Thompson

Roy Thompson

Terry Thorne

Linwood Thornton

John Thurman

Yvonne Tidline

Megan Tiemann

Brandon Tiernan

Christopher Tilley

Tara Tindall

Daniel Tipps

Christian Tobe

Davon Todd

Jeffrey Todd

Alexis Toe

Nicholas Tomasula

Michael Tong

Tyrone Toran

Roderick Torrence

Elthson Torres

Tyler Toth

Claudy Toussaint

Anthony Tracey

Joseph Trainor

Bryant Tran

Aaron Treadwell

Adrian Treadwell

Philip Tridico

Peter Trifu

Justin Truby

Ormimi Tsenzuul

Alexander Tso

David Tucker

Michael Tucker

Alimamy Turay

Anthony Turner

Carole Turner

Carrie Turner

Gregory Turner

Leeann Turner

Michelle Turner

Nefetia Turner

James Tyler

Lindsay Tyler

Marvin Tyler

Rudolph Tyson

Onasis Ulloa

Donna Ulrich

Michael Vaillancourt

Patrick Vaillancourt

Keton Valcin

Timothy Valentin

Karen Valentin-Aponte

Kevin Valentine

Robert Valentine

Amanda Vamos

Christopher Vanacore

Dora Vandayburg

James VanderMeer

Michael VanDuyse

Margodane Vanriel

Clifford Vanterpool

Robert Varga

Brandon Varone

Alexandros Varvounis

Robert Vasquez
Gutierrez

Angela Vaughn

Shakira Vazquez

Kevin Veizaj

William Verna

Kevin Vidal

Charles Viggiani

Javon Voglezon

Ricardo Volcin

Kevin Wagner

Desiree Walker

Kevin Walker

Darrick Wallace

Shayne Wallace

Tyrone Wallace

Anthony Walsh

Joshua Wang

Daijuan Wardrick

Roshonda Ware

Alexander Warren

Mark Wascavage

Derek Washington

Melvin Washington

Terrance Watford

Matthew Watkins

Robert Watlington

Eric Watson

Makhetha Watson

Andrew Wayte

James Weaver

Thomas Webb

Michael Webber

Kyle Weber

Charles Weeks

Savyon Weinfeld

Harry Weiss

Michael Weiss

Paul Weiss

Terrence Welsh Jr.

Haley Wershbale

Alexander Wertz

Ryan Whelan

Darrin White

Ebony White

Quintin White

Tevan White

Jerry Whitfield

Winston Whitfield

Carlton Wicker

Christopher Wickham

Tashina Wilhelm

Carlton Wilhoit

Lacey Wilkins

Ronald Wilkins

David Wilks

Trevor Wilks

Adrenee Williams

Andre Williams

Asley Williams

Bredet Williams

Chase Williams

Damien Williams

Darius Williams

Davon Williams

John Williams

Karane Williams-
Thomas

Anthony Willis

Caleb Willis

Cloyd Willis

Richard Willis

Boniesha Wilson

Clifford Wilson

John Wilson

Joshua Wilson

Maia Wilson

Robert Wingate-
Robinson

Miriam Wishnick

Anne Wissa

Spencer Wolff

Annette Wong

Kuo Wong

Charles Woodard

Maurice Woods

Christopher Woody

Demaris Wooten

Bryon Words

Jerome Worthington

Chad Wyble

Umit Yakub

Kwamena Yarney

Nicholas Yarosis

Jamal Yates

Brian Yi

Audrey Yondji

George Young

Joseph Young

Kandice Young

Esmeralda Zamora

Kenneth Zaw

Matthew Zechman

Jairo Zelaya

Andi Zogo

Thomas Zurowski

Photo Credits

1. MPD
2. Michael Fanone
3. Don Lemon
4. Terry Fanone
5. Shannon Stapleton/Reuters
6. Jimmy Albright
7. CNN
8. John Shiffman
9. Speaker Pelosi's Office
10. CNN
11. Andrew McInnes
12. John Shiffman

About the Authors

Michael Fanone served as a Metropolitan Police Department officer assigned to the First District for twenty years. Working briefly as a patrol officer and then spending the majority of his career as a vice investigator in various small-mission units, Fanone participated in more than two thousand arrests for violent crimes and narcotics trafficking; served as a special task force officer for the FBI, ATF, and DEA; and earned more than three dozen commendations for his work. Fanone currently serves as an analyst for CNN, a security consultant, and a firearms instructor. He lives in Alexandria, Virginia.

John Shiffman is an investigative reporter for Reuters and a two-time finalist for the Pulitzer Prize. His previous books are *Operation Shakespeare: The True Story of an Elite International Sting* and *Priceless: How I Went Undercover to Rescue the World's Stolen Treasures*. *Priceless*, coauthored with FBI Art Crime Team founder Robert K. Wittman, was published in eleven languages and was a *New York Times* bestseller. Contact him at johnshiffman.com.